Movies and the Mind

Movies and the Mind

*Theories of the Great
Psychoanalysts Applied to Film*

WILLIAM INDICK

McFarland & Company, Inc., Publishers
Jefferson, North Carolina, and London

LIBRARY OF CONGRESS CATALOGUING-IN-PUBLICATION DATA

Indick, William, 1971–
    Movies and the mind : theories of the great psychoanalysts applied
to film / William Indick.
       p.   cm.
    Includes bibliographical references and index.

    ISBN-13: 978-0-7864-1953-1
    (softcover : 50# alkaline paper) ∞

    1. Motion pictures—Psychological aspects.   I. Title.
PN1995.I5655   2004
791.43'653 — dc22   2004017968

British Library cataloguing data are available

On the cover—(inset) Colin Clive, left, and Boris Karloff in *Frankenstein*
(Universal, 1931); background imagery ©2004 Photospin.

Manufactured in the United States of America

*McFarland & Company, Inc., Publishers
  Box 611, Jefferson, North Carolina 28640
    www.mcfarlandpub.com*

For Michelle Kennedy

Table of Contents

Acknowledgments

I owe many thanks to Mustafa Lokmaci, a graduate assistant in the Psychology Department at Dowling College, for compiling the filmography, subject index and film index. Much of the information in the filmography was retrieved from the Internet Movie Database (IMDB.com).

Much appreciation goes to Jim Garbarino at Cornell University, Suzanne Johnson at Dowling College and Frank Madden at SUNY Westchester Community College for their mentorship, guidance and advice.

I owe a debt of gratitude to the faculty and administration of Dowling College in Oakdale, New York, for their support of my research and writing projects.

Preface

In this book, the psychoanalytic theories of Sigmund Freud, Erik Erickson, Carl Jung, Alfred Adler, Joseph Campbell, Otto Rank and Rollo May are applied to film analysis. The psychoanalytic approach to film analysis provides an in-depth process for unearthing the latent symbolism in film imagery. An appreciation of these elemental issue and symbols provides a fundamental understanding of film structure that is invaluable to filmmakers, screenwriters, psychologists or anyone with an interest in psychology or film. The distinct analytic approaches provided in this book offer an integrative and eclectic perspective that will help all readers — not just psychologists — to gain a deeper and more personal understanding of the films they view.

The idea for this book emerged from my needs as an assistant professor of psychology at Dowling College in Oakdale, New York (a small liberal arts college). My two lifelong interests have been psychology and film, so it seemed only natural that I should integrate my dual passions into an interdisciplinary course, "Psychology in Film." A colleague in the psychology department expressed a mutual interest, so we created the course and proposed it to the college. The course would introduce undergraduate students to the major psychoanalytic theories by using films as the subject for analysis. It was designed to increase the students' knowledge of psychology while offering a unique way to gain a deeper understanding and appreciation of film. The course was approved and scheduled, but there was only one problem: We couldn't find an appropriate textbook.

I searched and searched, but could not find any book that applied the major psychoanalytic theories to film analysis in an integrated, coherent and eclectic manner. For example, *Jung and Film: Post-Jungian Takes on the Moving Image* by Hauke and Alister (2001) focuses on film representations of Carl Jung's theories of archetypes and the collective unconscious. *Psychiatry and the Cinema* by Gabbard (1999) focuses on the role of the psychiatrist in the movies. Similarly, *Psychoanalytic Approaches to Literature and Film* by Charney and Reppen (1987), *The Imaginary Signifier: Psycho-analytic and the Cinema* by Mertz (1986), *Screen Memories: Hollywood Cinema on the Psychoanalytic Couch*, by Greenberg (1993) and *The Analysis of Film* by Bellour and Penley (2002) all provide traditionally Freudian takes on movies. However, I have not encountered a book that offers a comprehensive and eclectic approach to film analysis using a broad variety of theories and a plethora of examples from both classic and contemporary movies. My solution to the problem was an expedient one. I decided to write the book that I needed myself.

The theories, approaches and analyses in this book are inspired and drawn from the lectures and discussions from my "Psychology in Film" class. For the most part, each chapter represents the topics and ideas that would arise from single lectures or course sections. The first two chapters demonstrate how both Freudian and Jungian methods of dream analysis can be applied to film analysis. Drawing out the parallels between film imagery and dream imagery is a perfect introduction to the subject of film psychoanalysis, as the film viewing experience and dream experience are similar on many levels. In subsequent chapters, the focus turns to the psychoanalysis and deconstruction of the primary figure in most movies: the hero character. A Freudian interpretation of the hero is provided in chapter 3. The hero character is analyzed according to Otto Rank's theories in chapter 4, while chapter 6 provides Joseph Campbell's model, and chapter 8 introduces an Adlerian perspective.

Chapter 11 applies Sigmund Freud's psychosexual stages to the horror film genre. Similarly, chapter 12 applies Anna Freud's configuration of the ego defense mechanisms to the family melodrama genre. And chapter 13 applies Erik Erikson's stages of identity crisis to eight different film analyses.

The other chapters in this book provide original theories and perspectives on psychological themes in film. Chapter 5 explores religious symbolism in films, chapter 7 traces the evolution of modern heroine characters in film history, and chapter 10 focuses on a handful of preeminent filmmakers whose monumental works warrant their ranking as "modern mythmakers."

A leitmotif running throughout all the chapters is the concept that film constitutes an ongoing modern mythology for contemporary society. This concept is explained in depth in the introduction to this book, and readdressed on different levels in every chapter. The conclusion is an integrated, eclectic film analysis of one film, applying all of the different approaches and paradigms described in the previous chapters. The final analysis demonstrates that film psychoanalysis, just like clinical psychoanalysis and psychotherapy, is most meaningful when the process is flexible, open and inclusive of all approaches.

Introduction: Film as Myth

Our fundamental notions of a good story and character come from the elemental building blocks of our culture — our myths. Just as letters and words constitute the bases of our language, myths and legends constitute the bases of our modern characters, literature and art. Film is only the latest mode of storytelling in a long line of literary heritage. In a sense, there are no new stories, merely new ways of retelling the ancient themes and characters that have been told and retold for thousands of years. So, if we wish to analyze the movies that influence our minds and lives, we must break them down to the most basic elemental level — the level of myth.

Myths and stories originate from the imagination, a part of the psyche that is mainly unconscious. Hence, myths and stories can be understood and analyzed as unconscious expressions. Sigmund Freud's greatest contribution to psychology was his ability to relate his ideas about the unconscious to the themes found in ancient myth. By relating neurotic conflict to the myth of Oedipus and the basic drives to mythological figures such as Eros and Thanatos, Freud revealed the link between the universal issues disclosed in myth and the personal issues repressed in the unconscious. In doing so, Freud uncovered the "Lapis Philosophorum" of psychoanalysis — the philosopher's stone that converts latent unconscious material into manifest psychological issues.

Carl Jung's departure from Freud was a bold venture into the area that Freud himself broached, the area in which myth and psychoanalysis intersect. Jung explained how the mythological archetypes that are personally meaningful in dreams become collectively meaningful through myth. Jungian and Freudian methods of dream analysis, though quite different, offer complementary techniques for the analysis of dreams. In turn, the same techniques can be used to analyze film, which — like myth — is a form of "communal dream." Film's visceral appeal as a larger-than-life medium makes it an extremely powerful psychological force. Viewers identify so readily with movie characters and become so emotionally connected with the films they see that the illusion on the screen becomes intertwined with their own fantasies. Film, fantasy, and dreams are the realm of the unconscious. We project our unconscious desires inwardly through fantasy and dreams, and we project them outwardly through the experience of film. In this sense, films can be psychoanalyzed in the same way as people's dreams.

Otto Rank applied the structure of mythological symbolism to psychoanalysis through his study of the "myth of the birth of the hero." Rank revealed that the primary symbolic figure in mythology — the hero — has a story that is ubiquitous in structure and universally resonant on a psychological level. Joseph Campbell wove Freudian, Jungian and Rankian theory together with his encyclopedic knowledge of world myth to create his structure of the "stages of the hero's journey." By applying Rank and Campbell's complementary models to film analysis, the film hero's character and screen story can be deconstructed in a way that is exceptionally appropriate for the study of the prototypical Hollywood action movie, which usually casts a classical hero figure in the leading role.

Alfred Adler, Erik Erikson and Rollo May each conceived of their own unique models of personality development and the unconscious mind. Their views on inferiority, identity and existential integrity broadened the field of psychoanalysis, which in turn broadens the palette for the film analyst, providing alternative models for the deconstruction of film characters, symbolism and plot. Like myth, film is a delivery system for the timeless archetypes, collective symbols and elemental images that communicate to audiences because they represent the universal psychological issues of personal growth and existential meaning. As the medium for modern mythology in contemporary society, film plays a crucial role in the recreation and expression of these issues. And in the hands of the modern mythmakers, the technical wizards and artistic geniuses at Disney, DreamWorks, Lucas films and other studios, these ancient archetypes are reborn into even greater visions through the most powerful and psychologically pervasive storytelling medium ever created — the motion picture.

Fairy tales and myths have persisted as central figures in the collective unconscious for thousands of years, with only human voices and picture books to illustrate them. Imagine how much more vibrant and alive these ancient archetypes become through the modern sorcery of graphic computer animation, philharmonic orchestrated scores and digitally enhanced sound. If a picture tells a thousand words, than a thousand, thousand pictures tell a whole universe of ideas.

1

Analyzing the Movie Dream

Sigmund Freud was born in Freiberg, Moravia, in 1856. He was educated at Vienna University and remained in Vienna for most of his life. After receiving his medical degree in 1881, he spent three years at the General Hospital of Vienna, then received an appointment as lecturer in neuropathology at Vienna University. Freud was influenced by French neurologist Jean Charcot's use of hypnotic suggestion in his treatment of psychological hysteria, inspiring him to focus his studies on psychiatry and psychopathology. Specializing in nervous diseases, he went into private practice in 1886.

Early on in his work, Freud abandoned the use of hypnosis as a method of uncovering the root of neurotic conflicts, and developed new techniques such as free association and dream analysis. In 1900 Freud published his seminal work *The Interpretation of Dreams,* which would become the first manifesto of psychoanalysis. In this book, Freud revealed his incredibly controversial and provocative theory of the Oedipal complex, in which infantile sexuality, aggressive impulses, sexual drives and unconscious repression play key roles in the mind of the neurotic. Freud was appointed full professor at Vienna University in 1902, which gave him the time and financial freedom to focus most of his time and energy on developing his revolutionary theory of the unconscious.

Freud's theories were publicly derided by most of the medical establishment during his lifetime. Nevertheless, his intriguing ideas spurred a psychoanalytic movement that grew steadily throughout Europe and America. At his peak, Freud was the central figure in a circle of psychoanalytic theorists that included Alfred Adler, Abraham Brill, Eugen Bleuler, Sándor Ferenczi, Ernest Jones, Carl Jung, Otto Rank and William Stekel. However, Freud's domineering personality and his insistence on a strict interpretation of his theory caused dissension among his disciples. Much to his chagrin, Adler, Rank and Jung defected and went on to develop their own psychoanalytic models. Nevertheless, all psychoanalytic theories owe a tremendous debt to Freud's conception of the unconscious mind. In his later years, Freud abandoned clinical work in favor of analyzing literature, religion, culture and mythology. The Nazi occupation of 1938 forced Freud and his family to flee Austria and move to London, where he died a year later.

In his first major book, *The Interpretation of Dreams* (1900), Sigmund Freud developed a sophisticated theory of dreams, which included a distinct method of *dream analysis*. In Freud's view, the primary function of dreams is wish fulfillment — the unreal, but nevertheless satisfying release of a repressed id impulse. The sexual fantasy dream resulting in a nocturnal emission (the "wet dream") represents the closest functional example of libidinal wish fulfillment in dreams. Laboratory research performed decades after Freud's death validated many of his ideas. Sleep researchers found that males almost always experience penile erection during REM sleep cycles. When males dream, whether or not they're dreaming of sex, their bodies are experiencing a state of sexual arousal. Libidinal release while dreaming is definitely physiological, if not always psychological.

But even Freud admitted that not every desire or wish is exclusively sexual in nature. Sometimes we need to release the impulses that are merely inspired by the sexual drive — the broader Eros needs for love and affection. Other times we need to release the impulses that originate from the aggressive drive — the Thanatos urges towards conquest, revenge and destruction. But however the wish is fulfilled, the unconscious fantasy of the dream is still the fanciful product of the imagination. Impulses and desires within the "dream-play" are transformed and switched around in a panoply of psychological distortions, so that many dreams make absolutely no sense to the dreamers in their conscious state. In order to understand the dream, it must be interpreted by referring back to its place of origin, the unconscious. Freud's "dreamwork" consists of various analytic techniques that guide the interpreter through the maze of unconscious images of the manifest content, in order to reveal the latent unconscious desire that gave birth to the dream.

Condensation

The first step to revealing the hidden meaning of the dream is understanding that the dream is created in an unconscious code that only the dreamer can understand. The code *condenses* the psychological material in the dream into images and events that all have specific and significant meanings for the dreamer. For instance, a patient in analysis may have a dream in which she is following a black cat through an empty movie theater while a Bugs Bunny cartoon is playing on the screen. Given this information alone, the dream does not seem to have any particular meaning.

However, an analyst would assume that the dream does have a meaning, and that this meaning can be revealed by exploring the patient's personal *associations* with the images in the manifest content. The analyst would begin by asking the patient to explore her associations with black cats, movie theaters and Bugs Bunny. The analyst may even use certain analytic techniques such as *free association*, which help the patient disengage her conscious resistance and allow unconscious associations to flow freely.

Through the process of uncovering her associations, the patient reveals that she had a black cat as a child, but the cat ran away. This association may suggest that the dream is referring to an issue originating from the patient's childhood. The patient, in exploring this association, goes on to reveal that she was very upset when her cat ran away, but she was even more upset by the unsympathetic reaction of her father, who did not comfort her and did not help her search for the cat. So the dream may be dealing specifically with a childhood issue involving the patient's father. In exploring her association with the movie theater, the patient reveals that she loves the movies, and goes to the movie theater often. In further exploration, she reveals that she once had an ambition to become a movie actor, but she gave up this goal shortly after her marriage. This association may suggest a link between the patient's regret for giving up her goal of becoming an actor and her childhood relationship with her father. And, finally, in exploring her association with Bugs Bunny, the patient reveals that she herself never cared for cartoons, but her five-year-old son loves them, especially Bugs Bunny.

Once all of the associations are drawn out, the interpretation can begin. The black cat is leading the patient back into her childhood. Condensed within the single image of the cat are the patient's memories of her relationship with her father, and within these memories are long repressed feelings that her father was unsympathetic, uncaring and unsupportive of his daughter's wishes and desires. All of these issues are linked with the movie theater. Condensed within the movie theater image are the patient's childhood dreams of a career in the movies, and her repressed feelings of regret for giving up these dreams. The movie theater in her dream is empty (*unfilled*), a link to her deep wish to be in the movies, a wish that has been repressed (*unfulfilled*). In analysis, the patient may explore her issues with her husband, who—like her father—is unsympathetic and unsupportive of her wishes, and ultimately played a decisive role in her decision to forego a film career. And finally, condensed in the image of Bugs Bunny is an association with her son. Like the cartoon on the screen, her son is now the focal center of her life, and the one issue that demands all of her attention. The patient's wish to be on the screen is now figuratively replaced by her son, whose presence fills the screen in her dreams.

The process described above demonstrates how a simple dream that seems meaningless may, through analysis, be interpreted as an extremely significant dream about major life issues. In keeping with Freud's theory, at the center of the dream lies a repressed desire — in this case, the patient's unfulfilled wish to become a movie star. A host of personal associations are condensed into each image in the dream. Every aspect of the dream is fodder for interpretation, and good analysts will leave no stone unturned in their dreamwork with their patients.

Just as dreams are analyzed on the psychiatric couch, they can also be analyzed on the movie screen. Films are subjective expressions of imagination and fantasy, just like dreams, and they can often be analyzed in the same way that dreams are analyzed. Film itself is a visual experience much like a dream, and the parallels between movie viewing in the theater and dream viewing in our sleep are robust. The theater experience itself, a dark, quiet room filled with psychologically resonant images and sounds, is reminiscent of the unconscious mind. The dream is the personal film that our unconscious, as directors and producer, projects to us as captive audiences within our sleeping minds. Certain films, such as *The Wizard of Oz* (1939), are actual depictions of dreams, and are therefore ideal examples for the application of dream interpretation to film analysis. *The Wizard of Oz* has the added benefit of being a universally adored movie, seen by virtually every film enthusiast.

Symbolization

The wish or impulse at the center of the dream is typically disguised as something else. Since dreams are not conscious, they are also not rational. They are not depictions of reality, they are products of fantasy and imagination. So, as in a poem or work of art, each figure within a dream stands as a *symbol* for many things. Dreams use psychological symbols to purvey a plethora of meaningful information in relatively short visual sequences. Film, as a medium, is the closest reproduction of the dream state because it creates similar visual sequences using similar techniques.

The Wizard of Oz

Kansas

Dorothy Gale (Judy Garland) in *The Wizard of Oz* enters her dream after being hit on the head by a window during a twister. The traumatic experiences Dorothy endured just prior to the dream provide the neurotic conflict that is played out in her dream. Dorothy is a young girl living on a drab, colorless, boring farm in Kansas with her elderly aunt and uncle. No mention of Dorothy's absent parents is made anywhere in the film. We don't know if she is an orphan or if she has one or both parents living somewhere else. Nevertheless, it must be assumed that the issue of Dorothy's parents, though never explicitly dealt with in the film, is a significant underlying issue for a young girl who wishes she were living somewhere else. Dorothy expresses this wish in her signature song, "Somewhere Over the Rainbow." The song is a fantasy about living in an idealized fantasy world. Again, though it is never explicitly referred to, the viewer may wonder if this ideal place over the rainbow would include a loving mother and father.

Dorothy's wish to leave home is exacerbated when her mean neighbor, Miss Gulch (Margaret Hamilton), takes away her beloved dog, Toto. Dorothy feels an incredible amount of rage towards Miss Gulch for cruelly taking away Toto, but she cannot express this rage directly. Her desire to hurt Miss Gulch is expressed in a statement of regret: "I wish I could bite you myself!" The primary wish in Dorothy's unconscious is her repressed desire to attack Miss Gulch.

Toto escapes from Miss Gulch and returns to the farm. Dorothy's connection to Toto is so strong that she decides to run away from home rather than give him up again. The viewer may wonder if Toto represents a precious link to a former life for Dorothy, a life with her parents. But even without the absent-parent issue, Dorothy's decision to run away is easily supported by her love for Toto, her feelings of unhappiness and discontent on the farm, and her tremendous frustration and disappointment with her aunt (Clara Blandick) and uncle (Charley Grapewin), who simply allowed Miss Gulch to take away Toto without even putting up a fight. Dorothy runs away to see "beautiful cities" and "the crowned heads of Europe." Her wish is to escape from her drab existence in Kansas and embark on the road of adventure (and possibly find her curiously absent parents, who may or may not live in the big city).

Just before being struck on the head and floating off to dream land, Dorothy was desperately trying to get home in the treacherous winds of the twister. The conscious wish to return home is transfigured into Dorothy's dream wish to return to Kansas. Since this wish is conscious and unrepressed, there is no need for it to be disguised or "displaced" through symbolism. The goal of returning to Kansas is explicitly expressed throughout the dream. The implicit or latent goal of Dorothy's dream stems from her desire to hurt Miss Gulch and her need to reconnect with her absent parental figures.

Day Residue

The unconscious has no eyes. All of our objective experience of the real world occurs during our conscious, waking state. Therefore, in order for the unconscious to put on its picture show at night, the unconscious must borrow all of its visual material from the images and experiences perceived during the conscious state. The people and places we see during the day seep down into the unconscious and become the material for symbolism in our dream world. Like the paint and canvas for an artist, or the actors and sets for a director, "day residue" provides the visible substance used by the unconscious to compose the dream. As Dorothy enters her dream, each figure in her conscious life, through the process of day residue, is cast as a figure in her dream.

Day Residue. Dorothy's supportive farmhands in her conscious life are recast as supporting characters in her dream world. *The Wizard of Oz* (1939), Metro-Goldwyn-Mayer. Dorothy (Judy Garland) in the foreground and, from left, the Scarecrow (Ray Bolger), Lion (Bert Lahr) and Tin Man (Jack Haley) in the background.

Over the Rainbow

As Dorothy slips into her dream, the image of Miss Gulch riding on her bicycle is transfigured into the Wicked Witch on her broom. Dorothy's real world has become a symbolic world. The casting of the dreadful Miss Gulch into the Wicked Witch character is parallel symbolism. Dorothy is projecting her feelings about Miss Gulch onto the Witch, so her rage, hostility and desire to hurt Miss Gulch are also projected onto the Witch. Similarly, the men who help Dorothy in her real life, the three farmhands, become the figures who help Dorothy in her dream life: Scarecrow (Ray Bolger), Tin Man (Jack Haley) and Lion (Bert Lahr). And the crafty character who redirected her home in Kansas, Professor Marvel (Frank Morgan), is cast as the cagey Wizard who is supposed to help Dorothy get back to Kansas from Oz.

When Dorothy enters the dreamland of Oz, her first primary desire is partially fulfilled. She remarks, "I don't think we're in Kansas anymore." The extreme contrast between the dreary colorlessness of Kansas and the bright colors of Oz makes it clear that Dorothy's wish has come true, she is "over the rainbow." Dorothy even meets a "crowned head"—Glinda the Good Witch (Billie Burke)—who is apparently the matron queen of Munchkin Land. Dorothy's wish to see palaces and royalty will be completely fulfilled when she gets to the big city, Emerald City, and meets the "crowned head" of Oz, the Wizard.

The appearance of Glinda at the beginning of the dream is a bit perplexing, as this woman is not day residue — she doesn't appear in Dorothy's conscious life. But Glinda's role as mother figure to young Dorothy is clearly the symbolic function of her character. Glinda is a very maternal figure, providing love, nurturance, aid and advice to Dorothy and to the childlike Munchkins. The Munchkins may even be interpreted as a symbol of Dorothy's childhood, a dreamlike memory in which she lived under the watchful eye of her loving mother. As a projection of Dorothy's wish for a mother, Glinda is everything a young girl would dream of. Glinda is beautiful, loving and kind. There is even a resemblance between Dorothy and Glinda — they both have fair skin with rosy cheeks, blue eyes and auburn hair. And to complete her maternal role, Glinda is Dorothy's guide and link to her lost father figure.

The Wizard

Dorothy encounters an enigmatic father figure, but he is merely an illusion. The Wizard tells Dorothy that he will only help her return to Kansas (her conscious state) if she brings him the Wicked Witch's broom.

The message behind the Wizard's charge is that Dorothy must purge herself of her feelings of hostility towards Miss Gulch, by killing the symbolic figure of the Wicked Witch. In the end, all of Dorothy's wishes are fulfilled in her dream. Dorothy experiences the big city (Emerald City). She encounters royalty (Glinda and the Wizard), who also serve as symbolic parental figures for Dorothy. And she also releases all of her pent-up hostility against Miss Gulch by killing the Witch. Dorothy wakes up, liberated of her earlier neuroses and conflicts, and perfectly content with her boring home and oldfangled aunt and uncle.

Vanilla Sky

The Wizard of Oz is a classic, timeless film about a young girl's dream. Not surprisingly, the film has been psychoanalyzed more times than Woody Allen. Recently, another popular film has been made about a dream. *Vanilla Sky* (2001), Cameron Crowe's remake of the Spanish film *Abre los Ojos* ["Open Your Eyes"] (1997), is a movie that takes place completely within a dream. The bits of conscious reality that arise are seen through the memories and reflections of the main character. He recounts them in his dream to an imaginary psychiatrist. In many ways, *Vanilla Sky* is much more complex and sophisticated than *The Wizard of Oz*. But at the core of the film, the main character David Aames (Tom Cruise) is dealing with the same issues as Dorothy Gale.

First, David and Dorothy share the dubious honor of having literary allusions for last names. Dorothy *Gale* is swept into her dream world by a twister — a powerful gale of wind. David *Aames* is in a dream world, but he is coming into awareness of the fact that his life is not real. David's *aim* is to discover the basic truth of his existence and to escape the dream of his life. *Vanilla Sky* is an elaborate tapestry of scenes representing disjointed pieces in the puzzle of David's life. With the help of his psychiatrist (Kurt Russell), David must interpret his dream and put all of these pieces together in order to figure out the truth about his existence.

Backstory

David's father was a billionaire media magnate who was always too busy to spend any time with his only son. David's mother was a beautiful artist with a particular penchant for Monet landscapes featuring surreal, cloud-covered "vanilla skies." David loses his parents as a child in a tragic plane crash, inheriting his father's multi-billion dollar media empire. In the First Act, Julie (Cameron Diaz), David's jilted lover, intentionally crashes her car in a fit of jealous rage with David in the passenger seat. David's gorgeous face is horribly mutilated. Unable to adjust to life after his disfigurement, David alienates himself from his best friend (Jason Lee), and he is rejected by Sophia (Penélope Cruz), the girl he loves. In a pit of despair, he commits suicide — but only after he arranges for his body to be cryogenically frozen in a state of "lucid dreaming." While David's body lies frozen, his brain is free to dream without ever waking into consciousness.

The Lucid Dream

The Life Extension company that monitors David's frozen dream state was kind enough to erase his memory of the suicide. In his lucid dream, David is free to fulfill all of his wishes. He reconnects with Sophia and they share a life together. David's desire for Sophia represents his deep longing for maternal love. The link between David's mother and Sophia is made through the "vanilla sky" symbolism, the Monet imagery that David associated with his mother, and which appears in the background behind Sophia's loving, nurturing face. Like Dorothy's dream in *The Wizard of Oz*, David's dream fulfills a deep wish to reconnect with his long-lost parents. David's lucid dream fulfills some other wishes as well. Doctors perform a miracle surgery that reconstructs his face, and David restores his relationships with his best friend and colleagues. But the dream begins to go awry when David indulges his darkest impulse.

Just as Dorothy wants to hurt Miss Gulch for taking away Toto, David wants to hurt Julie for ruining his life. The tremendous rage and hostility that David harbors for Julie, despite the fact that she is dead, lives on in David's unconscious and returns to haunt him. But, since his life is a dream, Julie's return is a surreal apparition in which she gradually replaces his lover, Sophia.

At this point, the dream becomes a nightmare. All of David's well-crafted illusions fall apart. At the climax of this psychotic sequence, everything David sees transforms into something else. Vivid images from the past flash indiscriminately before his eyes. His associations flow freely as a long repressed memory of his father hitting him as a child rises from the depths of his unconscious. As David makes love with Sophia, she is transfigured into Julie. Since David is now in the deepest, darkest part of the unconscious, logic and reason do not exist. His desire for Sophia is meshed with his desire for Julie. His hatred and rage towards Julie for destroying his face is meshed with his anger towards Sophia for rejecting him. Sex and aggression, love and hate, reality and fantasy — all become intertwined in the moment of homicidal madness, when David kills

Julie/Sophia as he is making love to her. David fulfills his wish to kill Julie, but in actuality, David never killed anyone but himself.

Open Your Eyes

The plot of the film is told through the recollections of David, who is in a prison cell speaking to his psychiatrist, Dr. McCabe. In this part of his dream, David is in prison for murdering Sophia. The psychiatrist is trying to determine if David is legally insane. The theme of being in prison for a crime is clever in its irony. Though David never killed Sophia, he is guilty. David is guilty of killing himself, and it is this tremendous sense of guilt that snaps the thread of David's dream fabric. Now he is in a prison of his own mind, speaking to an imaginary psychiatrist and trying to differentiate between reality and fantasy. Of course, everything in David's life is fantasy—a fact that every figure in his dream keeps telling him in obscured appeals to his rational side. At every turn, a different character tells David: "Wake up," "Be real," "Take control of your life" and "Open your eyes!"

Most of these appeals come from McCabe, who also plays the role of father figure. McCabe is merely David's projection of a good father, a wish fulfillment of the father he never knew. McCabe plays the part well. He is warm, protective, wise, caring, insightful and always talking about his kids. At one point, McCabe says, "I care about you, David ... you've become like family to me." McCabe completes his role as a mentoring father figure, guiding David to a realization that his perception of reality is distorted. But since McCabe is just a part of David's psyche, he cannot give him the outside information he needs to get an objective perspective on his situation. This information comes from Tech Support (Noah Taylor), an official representative of the Life Extension company, which has been monitoring David's malfunctioning dream.

Tech Support explains to David that every figure in his dream was day residue. The figure of Sophia, the girl on whom he projected his wishes for motherly love, is associated through the symbolism of the Monet-inspired "vanilla skies." The warm and protective psychiatrist, inspired by Gregory Peck's character from *To Kill a Mockingbird* (1962), is associated with David's wish for a father. There is even day residue of the Life Extension company—he repeatedly sees the infomercial for the company on television. In the end, Tech Support tells David how to wake up from his dream state. David has always had a fear of heights, a link to his parents' death in a plane crash. David must overcome his fear of heights by jumping off a tall building. In doing so, David experiences a final wish fulfillment. Flying through the air symbolically satisfies his desire to be free of his dream life. And overcoming his fear of heights symbolizes the fact that David has finally purged himself of his old neuroses and anxieties. Like Dorothy waking up in her bedroom in Kansas, David is ready to open his eyes and enter a new life.

2

Archetypes of Oz

Carl Gustav Jung was born in 1875 in Kesswil, Switzerland. Because he was the son of a Protestant clergyman, religion was an extremely significant theme in Jung's development, though from an early age his interests began to diverge from his father's strict parochial view of faith. In his university years, Jung became fascinated with eastern religions, mysticism and spirituality — subjects that remained lifelong passions. After completing his medical degree in psychiatry, Jung began practicing psychoanalysis and writing, a path that led him into a close collaboration with Sigmund Freud. Jung and Freud's lengthy correspondences focused on their mutual fascination with dreams and the use of psychological symbolism in the unconscious mind. Freud soon considered his brilliant young disciple to be his heir apparent to the royal seat of the psychoanalytic world. Unfortunately, their collaboration, correspondence and intimate friendship ended when Freud could not accept Jung's divergent theories of the unconscious.

The principal disputes between Freud and Jung centered on the basis for neurotic conflict. Jung believed that many symptoms of neurosis were caused by a feeling of spiritual disconnection with the world and with oneself. He placed less emphasis on libido and infantile sexuality, and focused more on the individual's innate need to synthesize all the different parts of the self into an integrated whole. Freud, however, remained rigid in his view that all neuroses spring from blocked or frustrated libido drives. Just as straying from his father's parochial view of religion freed Jung to explore new dimensions of spirituality, straying from Freud's inflexible view of neurotic conflict freed Jung to explore new dimensions of the psyche.

Jung's new dimension was "the collective unconscious," a part of the psyche made up of what he called "archetypes," or primordial images. The collective unconscious differs from Freud's view of the unconscious, labeled by Jung as "the personal unconscious," which consists of all of the ego's repressed memories and individual-specific complexes. The collective unconscious, on the other hand, is "transpersonal." The collective unconscious consists of those images, figures and experiences that are shared by all humanity. These shared associations are expressed as universal themes in myth, art, literature, fairy tales, legends and religion. The archetypes are the psychological patterns that symbolize the human experience. Archetypal figures such as the goddess, the wise old man, the monster and the trickster are psychological representations of the self. By expressing these archetypes as cultural symbols in myths and encountering them personally in dreams, the psyche is attempting to integrate these various components of the individual into the self.

Jung wrote extensively on his theories of the collective unconscious, and he also developed a model of the different functions of the personal unconscious, creating a model of personality types based on the opposing dispositions of introversion and extroversion. Jung's model of personality types has been extremely influential in the fields of psychoanalysis, personality psychology and personality assessment. Jung also wrote many volumes on analytical methods, focusing especially on dream analysis. His later writings addressed the relationship between psychoanalytic theory and the challenges of religious faith. Carl Jung died after a brief illness on June 6, 1961, at his home in Küsnacht, Switzerland.

Archetypal Dreams

By applying his concept of the collective unconscious to thousands of dream analyses, Jung was able to discern that there were universal themes, images and symbols in the dreams of his patients. This discovery led him to a process of dream analysis that disagreed sharply with Freud's "reductionist" view of dreams as libido-fueled expressions of wish fulfillment. To the contrary, Jung's interpretations "amplified" the dreams, analyzing the symbolism as expressions of universal, transcendental human issues. These "archetypal dreams" contain symbols that have shared associations among all people. They do not stem from the patient's "personal unconscious"—rather, they are "transpersonal" expressions of the collective unconscious.

Jungian and Freudian dream analysis also differ in their fundamental understanding of the function of unconscious symbolism. Freud believed that symbols disguise the unconscious meaning of the issues they represent, because these issues are essentially repugnant to the conscious mind. Contrarily, Jung believed that symbols express their meaning as best they can, considering that the message they convey is esoteric, metaphysical and essentially unknown to the conscious mind. Jung argued that the basic issues behind the symbol are not necessarily sexual or aggressive. The basic issues could be drawn from the individual's desire to simply become a better person. Furthermore, Jung argued that since archetypal figures and symbols transcend time and place, the psychological message they deliver through dreams are best interpreted within the frame of reference of the collective unconscious, rather than the personal unconscious. Hence, archetypal dreams could be analyzed and understood in reference to the myths and fairy tales that inspired them, rather than the strictly personal associations within the individual.

Jung objected to those who characterized his ideas as "mystical." He saw the collective unconscious as a process of "inherited thought patterns," in which the "instinct" to respond to archetypes becomes a universal human ability. Though human brains all contain different specific information, the processes of mental functioning are collective and universal. The universal instinct to process archetypal figures and themes in similar ways is the collective unconscious. The process of expressing archetypal themes exists collectively on a wide variety of levels. As a *cultural process*, everyone in the same culture hears the same stories and songs and sees the same images in books and on television and on movie screens. As a *developmental process*, all human beings go through similar experiences of growth and change as they go through the stages of life. And as an *evolutionary process*, the human mind has evolved over many thousands of generations, retaining elements of previous forms and instinctual responses to specific images and ideas. In Jung's words: "It is not a question of inherited ideas, but of a functional disposition to produce the same or very similar ideas in all people. This position I called 'archetype.'"

Individuation

Archetypal dreams serve a "transcendent function" that alerts the conscious mind of a problem or unbalance in the individual's unconscious. Archetypal symbols are part of a "self regulating psychic system" that connects the conscious mind to the ancient wisdom of the collective unconscious. The purpose of the transcendent function is to foster "individuation"—the goal of becoming one's true self. Analyzing one's own dreams and exploring the collective unconscious by experiencing archetypes in art, music, literature, theater and film are all attempts to achieve "self-realization"—the process of bringing unconscious wisdom into conscious awareness, which is the principal method of individuation. The end process of all this soul searching is a sense of "wholeness" and balance. When all of the disparate elements of the psyche are integrated and balanced, the individual is psychologically healthy. We do this by getting in touch with our archetypes.

Archetypes of the Self

In Jung's model, the *shadow* archetype is the embodiment of the individual's repressed impulses. The shadow is "the 'negative' side of the personality, the sum of all those unpleasant qualities we like to hide." Jungian psychology is directly influenced by the Eastern concept of *enantiodromia*— the psychology of opposites. Any extreme force, by the nature of its own power, begets an equally powerful opposing force — just as every physical action in physics is countered by an equally powerful reaction. The need for an opposing force is crucial in both Jungian psychology and Eastern philosophy because the metaphysical ideal in these models is always a sense of "balance," a state of equilibrium in which each part of the self is complemented by an opposing or conjoining part.

Just as the Yin has its Yang to complete the symmetry, the shadow has its opposing archetype in the form of the *persona*. While the shadow hides itself from the world, its opposing force — the persona — is the part of our self that we display. The term "persona" is a direct reference to the theatrical masks worn by the ancient Greeks. The persona is the side of ourselves that we show to others. And the persona is also the physical mask that hides the shadow — the side of ourselves that we need to hide. In our dreams, we typically play the role of our own persona. In films, the *hero* usually plays the role of the persona. As the protagonist of the story, the hero must encounter archetypes in his environment that he must integrate or overcome in order to develop. Just like the persona in the dream, the hero in the myth or film is unaware that these figures are symbolic of psychological elements within his own psyche. However, like the persona in the dream, the hero in the film gains strength and wisdom through his encounters with these archetypes. Though the symbols are depicted through external figures, the significant development in both the dream-persona and the myth-hero is always internal — development is within the character himself.

Like Freud, Jung also believed that the psyche will typically incorporate the same-sex parental figure as an internal role model. Hence, for males, the internal representation of the father is symbolized by the *wise old man* archetype. In females, the internal representation of the mother is symbolized by the *earth goddess* archetype. Though both of these archetypes may exist in both male and female dreams, the wise old man typically symbolizes the role model or *mentor figure* in the male psyche, while the earth goddess typically symbolizes the role model or mentor in the female psyche.

Finally, since humans are not sexually balanced (we are either male or female), the psyche must balance itself by incorporating the essence of the opposite sex via the opposing sex archetypes. The balancing or opposing female archetype in the male psyche is the *anima*. In Jung's words: "Every man carries with him the eternal image of woman, not the image of this or that particular woman, but a definitive feminine image." The anima archetype holds all of the stereotypically female personality traits, such as love, emotional wisdom, sensitivity, empathy, etc. The opposing male archetype in the female psyche is the *animus*, the male archetype that embodies all of the stereotypically male personality traits such as strength, courage, independence, etc.

Within these six figures—*persona, shadow, wise old man, earth goddess, anima and animus*— are the primary archetypes of the self that reveal to the individual, through myth and dream, both the hidden issues in the personal unconscious and the ancient wisdom of the collective unconscious.

The Wizard of Oz (revisited)

The themes, figures and images from *The Wizard of Oz* have become engrained in the memories of generations of film fans. The film is a shared fairy tale — a collective myth — a transpersonal dream. Consequently, *The Wizard of Oz* is not only a vivid example of archetypal images and symbolism, it has become an integral part of the American collective unconscious as well, creating the visual form of the archetypes even as it symbolizes them.

Dorothy

Dorothy Gale (Judy Garland) plays the role of the persona archetype in her dream. She is the hero of the story/film/myth, and her physical form is the outer presence of her character. In dreams, the persona represents the individual self. In myth and film, (the terms are now synonymous), the persona becomes the hero, who represents the collective self— the cultural ideal of the individual. As the audience watches the film, they identify with the hero and experience her story as if they were seeing their own personas in their own personal dreams. In Dorothy's dream, the persona must encounter the different archetypes of the self in order to "integrate" the parts of her personality that are unbalanced. For Dorothy, a parentless child who feels powerless in her isolated environment, every part of her psyche other than her persona lacks expression and balance. However, the central archetype in the film, the Wizard, holds the most symbolic significance for Dorothy.

Father Archetype

The Wizard is clearly a representation of the wise old man archetype, the worldly, strong and powerful father figure that is so clearly absent in Dorothy's life. The Wizard is the father figure that Dorothy so desperately needs. When mean old Miss Gulch takes away Toto, the first person Dorothy runs to is her uncle. Instinctually, she feels that this surrogate father figure will defend her, fight for her, take care of her and make everything all right. But Dorothy's uncle is a weak and ineffectual old man. He does nothing. On one level, the Wizard represents Dorothy's wish for a big strong Daddy who will be there for her and solve all of her problems. On a deeper level, the Wizard represents the strong and courageous parts of her Self that Dorothy needs to get in touch with. Dorothy integrates her own inner strength by projecting it into the external archetype of the wise old man, and making her encounter with this archetype the central theme of her dream.

Mother Archetype

Glinda represents a caring and nurturing mother figure for Dorothy, and she also fulfills the function of mentor required by the same-sex parental archetype. In their first encounter, Glinda guides Dorothy onto the yellow brick road. In their second encounter, Glinda aids Dorothy by waking her from her poppy-induced slumber and clearing her path to Emerald City. And in their final meeting, Glinda guides Dorothy back home by showing her how to use the ruby slippers. At each encounter, the mother archetype is loving and caring, but she is also a good mentor in that she doesn't overcome Dorothy's obstacles for her. As mentor, Glinda merely guides and instructs, while Dorothy herself must take the proactive steps to proceed on her own journey of self discovery.

The Wicked Witch

Dorothy's shadow is the Wicked Witch — the symbol of the unexpressed violence, hatred and rage that she feels towards Miss Gulch, the evil woman who took away her beloved dog. When Dorothy enters her

Archetypes. Dorothy is protected by her Goddess figure as she confronts her Shadow figure. *The Wizard of Oz* (1939), Metro-Goldwyn-Mayer. The Wicked Witch (Margaret Hamilton), Dorothy (Judy Garland) and Glinda the Good Witch (Billie Burke) from left to right.

dream world in the twister sequence, the physical presence of Miss Gulch on her bicycle is transfigured into the symbolic presence of the Wicked Witch on her broomstick. The transfiguration from actual to archetypal is doubly symbolic for Dorothy because the Witch represents not only her repressed negative feelings for Miss Gulch, but also her repressed negative feelings about her actual mother, who—like her father—is also conspicuously absent from Dorothy's life. While the central archetype in Dorothy's dream is her search for a father figure (the Wizard), her encounters with both positive and negative mother figures are the axes upon which the story and Dorothy's character revolve.

Scarecrow, Tin Man and Lion

The opposing-sex archetype in Dorothy's psyche, her animus, is represented by the three farmhands at her homestead. Like Miss Gulch, the farmhands are also transfigured into Dorothy's dream world, cast as the Scarecrow, Tin Man and Lion characters. The animus archetypes tell Dorothy to integrate three stereotypically male personality traits into her personality. She must get in touch with her inner masculine powers of intellect, heart (emotional strength) and courage in order to develop a more balanced sense of self. Dorothy's lack of balance, her need to integrate her animus, is evident in the scene where she first encounters the apparition of her father figure. The Wizard introduces himself as "Oz ... the great and powerful." In reply, Dorothy introduces herself as "Dorothy ... the small and meek." Clearly, Dorothy needs to balance her feminine side with some masculine qualities. Until she can identify the qualities of being "great and powerful" within herself, she will remain undeveloped and unbalanced.

Trickster

The last card in the Tarot cycle is the fool — the "Trickster" — the archetype that has gone through all the stages before it, and now can wander through the world with humor and carelessness rather than fear. Behind the trickster's laughter and jokes is wisdom of the world that is deeper than the hero's or even the wise old man's. Professor Marvel is a trickster, a charlatan who despite his con-man tactics has some deep insights into Dorothy's psyche. When Professor Marvel is transfigured into the Wizard at the end, we see the same wisdom masqueraded under the same veil of trickery and chicanery. The parallel function of the trickster and wise old man archetypes reflects their parallel symbolism as representations of the father figure. The gods and deities of myth and religion are often tricksters who play jokes on mere mortals and enjoy their ability to both confound and astound the dull humans as if they were rubes at a carnival sideshow.

The mentor archetype is often double-billed as a trickster as well. The trickster mentor guides his hero by acting as a mirror. The trickster mentor merely reflects wisdom that the hero already has back towards the hero. But the hero, thinking that the wisdom is spiritual or divine, is inspired by the wisdom, though it was within him all along. The mentor figures in *The Wizard of Oz* are all tricksters in this sense. Professor Marvel is not clairvoyant. He surmises some information about Dorothy by peeking in her bag and gauging her character, then he tricks her into thinking that he is a magician. Though Dorothy already knows that running away will break Aunt Em's heart, this wisdom inspires her to return home when she hears it from Professor Marvel. Similarly, the Wizard cannot give Scarecrow, Tin Man and Lion the brains, heart and courage they desire, they have to earn it for themselves. The diploma, testimonial and medal that the Wizard gives them are merely symbols (hallmarks of the trickster), that reflect the bearers' own knowledge about themselves. And finally, Glinda the Good Witch cannot return Dorothy home. Her power as mentor only allows her to reflect the power that Dorothy has within herself. Glinda can only tell Dorothy that she's had the power to return home all along, but she had to learn it for herself.

Another variation on the trickster figure is the *shapeshifter* archetype. Aside from being a trickster, Professor Marvel is also a shapeshifter, a character who fluidly changes his physical form throughout the film. He shifts shape from Professor Marvel to the Emerald City doorman to a cabbie to the Wizard's guard to the Wizard of Oz and then finally back to Professor Marvel again. The shapeshifter gods are present in many myths, most notably in Greek mythology, in which gods such as Zeus would frequently shift shape into animal or human form in order to mingle among humans and meddle in their affairs. The shapeshifters' supernatural transfigurative powers as well as their deceptive means are indicative of their godly status. Behind their chicanery and deceit is wisdom. The shapeshifter is a particularly resonant archetype because in its ability to transform, it represents the great human potential for development, change and rebirth.

Uroboros

Archetypes exist as symbolic themes as well as images and figures. Archetypal themes such as birth, rebirth, death, sorcery and the hero's journey constitute the plot twists and stories that structure the myths. They represent the psychological significance of major life events, and are symbols of personal change and transformation. Though the hero in film must always develop and transform in some way in order for his story to be psychologically resonant, the final act of returning to the beginning state symbolizes the central theme of "wholeness" and unification. Though the hero encountered many places and figures, they are all parts of her Self. By returning to her starting point, the hero wraps her adventure in a circle, enclosing her experiences in the cycle of her own life story and understanding that the meaning of the journey is derived from the things she learned about herself.

Uroboros, the archetypal image of the snake eating its own tail, symbolizes the unification of opposites. As an archetypal theme, Uroboros can be seen in the denouement portion of the story, when the hero at the end of her journey returns to the point of her departure. Uroboros in *The*

Wizard of Oz is not only a major theme, but the main crisis and conflict in Dorothy's story. When Dorothy returns home at the end of the film, she is reunited with her family and friends and all is right with the world. As a "return" theme at the end of the film, Uroboros delivers a sense of closure to viewers, assuring them that every conflict has been resolved, every plot twist has been unraveled and that every character will live happily ever after.

Vanilla Sky (revisited)

Vanilla Sky depicts the dream of a male hero with some particularly Jungian symbolism and imagery. David Aames spends a good deal of the film hiding behind a mask. When masked, the character is David's persona, struggling to get to the root of his conflicts. When unmasked, the character is David's shadow, a character plagued with flaws such as vanity, arrogance, carelessness and egocentrism. As his persona, David encounters and integrates his wise old man archetype — the positive father figure played by Dr. McCabe, his patient and insightful psychiatrist/mentor. McCabe also represents the "self-regulating system" of David's unconscious mind. He is the function that is attempting to integrate the disconnected parts of David's self.

The anima archetype in David's dream is divided into three female characters. Julie (Cameron Diaz) symbolizes the shadowy side of David's anima, the side that represents his passion, lust and guilt. She is a jealous goddess who punishes David for his vanity and insensitivity to women. Her power is the "fury of a woman scorned." Sophia (Penélope Cruz) symbolizes the light side of the anima, the side that represents his distant memories of his dearly departed mother. Sophia is a goddess of love and creativity. And Rebecca (Tilda Swinton) is a prophet goddess who bestows David with the intuitive wisdom he needs to complete his journey. The symbolic unity of this divine trinity of anima figures is beautifully symbolized in the hair color of the three goddesses— a brunette, a blonde and a redhead.

The message of David's dream is that he needs to face his post-accident reality. David must remove his mask and face himself. In the symbol of removing the mask, there is a personal integration in which persona faces shadow, the wise old man becomes integrated and the anima reveals the self. In removing the mask, David reaches his goal of self awareness. He "opens his eyes" to a new life.

3

Heroes and Villains

From a Freudian perspective, the typical hero's mission to defeat the villain is symbolic of the Oedipal complex, in which the child must repress his illicit psychosexual desire for Mother. In order to explain the internal conflict within the Oedipal complex, Freud created his triarchic structure of the psyche — the *id*, *ego* and *superego*. The id represents the basic drives towards sex and aggression, the superego represents the moral restraints of society, and the ego represents a compromise between the id and super-ego. In this chapter, Freud's model of neurotic conflict and his structure of id/ego/superego are interpreted as a model for analysis of conflict in film and the ubiquitous character structure of villain/hero/mentor in movies.

The Villain

While movie heroes are typically highly moral and civilized people, villains are typically immoral cads who satisfy their primal desires despite the negative outcomes for their victims. The movie villain is the uncon-scious representation of the repressed id desires. Unlike the hero, the vil-lain is free to express his primal desires in any way he sees fit. In this way, the viewers experience a vicarious sense of freedom and guilty pleasure by identifying with the villain. But the viewer also experiences a sense of psychological resolution when the wild, lawless villain is eventually repressed and defeated by the hero.

The Black Knight

In traditional stories, the villain wears a costume that is indicative of his dark nature. In silent films, the "stage villain" was typically dressed in black, with a big black hat, a dark beard and a long curling black moustache. In Westerns, the evil cowboy usually rode a black horse and was dressed in black, while the good cowboy wore white or earth tones and rode a white horse. Jack Palance's memorable characterization of Wilson, the evil gunslinger in *Shane* (1953), epitomized the Black Knight costuming of the villain character. While Shane's (Allan Ladd) jacket was the light color of pure prairie dirt, Wilson's black outfit symbolized the clear antithesis between his character and the hero's. In film noir, gangsters uniformly wore dark suits and drove black Cadillacs. In movies for children, the villain is often a witch who wears a black cape, and she is typically accompanied by a black cat, raven, bat or crow. The blackness of the Wicked Witch's costume in *The Wizard of Oz* stood in stark contrast to the bright white gown worn by the Good Witch Glinda. The Nazi SS uniforms were jet black, making them the perfect villains in American war movies, in which the good Allied soldiers dressed in honest, natural, earthy greens.

The Villain Strikes Back

Filmmakers realized early on that audiences love to identify with villains. Part of the joy of cinema is the ability to enjoy vicarious pleasures through the characters on the screen. Viewers often enjoy seeing villains engage in sin and vice more than they enjoy seeing their heroes exhibit the boring virtues of morality and goodness. Sinners simply have much more fun. Hence, villains are often more popular than their hero counterparts. However, since the basic psychology behind most film plots is the resolution of the Oedipal complex, the filmmakers typically kill their villains at the end of the movie. The solution to this problem was found in the Hollywood sequel formula, in which the villain is miraculously resurrected or freed. In *Frankenstein* (1931), the monster (Boris Karloff) is killed in a blazing inferno. But in the sequel, *The Bride of Frankenstein* (1935), we learn that the monster somehow survived by falling into a mysterious stream.

This type of far-fetched resurrection of the villain is typical in the horror movie genre. In the *Halloween* and *Friday the 13th* movies, Michael and Jason, (the psycho slashers), usually die at the end; but somehow, these villains are always resurrected for the next sequel. Viewers responded so well to the robot villain (Arnold Schwarzenegger) in *The Terminator* (1984) that he was resurrected in *Terminator 2* (1991), but with a twist. Since the Terminator was a robot, the quality of his character depended entirely on his programming, so in the sequel, he was resurrected as a hero instead of a villain. The twist worked. Audiences who had already identified with the Terminator as a villain, were even more willing to identify with him as a hero. In *Terminator 3* (2003), the robot returns once again, but this time as a well-established hero, his former incarnation as a villain is just a distant memory.

The Mentor

The mentor figure has developed through ancient legends and mythology from the archaic tribal leader or shaman. The mentor figure gave a blessing or instruction to the young hero, bestowed him with a weapon of power and either sent him off into the woods, or led the hunting party out himself. In many cases, it is the mentor who inspires the hero to accept the burden of the quest. For the ancient tribesmen, the hero's success on the hunt meant the difference between feast and famine. On a mythological level, the journey was made in order to save an environment, a people, an ideal or a way of life. In *The Ten Commandments* (1956), Moses (Charlton Heston) was inspired by a divine voice speaking through a burning bush to deliver his people from bondage in Egypt. In *Excalibur* (1981), the Knights of the Round Table were inspired by King Arthur (Nigel Terry) to find the Grail in order to save the dying land. In *Star Wars* (1977), Luke Skywalker (Mark Hamill) was told by Obi-Wan Kanobi (Alec Guinness) that he must rescue Princess Leia from the evil hands of the Dark Emperor. In each case, the mentor is a crucial figure for the hero. He enthuses the hero with a grand purpose in the root sense of the word — "en theos" — the Greek term for divine inspiration. The mentor, whether divine or merely the herald of a divine message, delivers the heavenly call of adventure to the hero.

The mentor is a father figure whom the young hero must identify with. He is a positive father figure, who typically stands as an opposing force in the hero's psyche, contrasting with the negative or false father figure. In this sense, the positive father figure represents the superego, while the negative father figure or villain represents the id. The hero represents the ego, torn between the opposing poles of good and evil. The hero's primary task is to learn some basic truths about his identity, morality and personal integrity from the mentor. He then must integrate these character lessons into his own psyche. In *Pinocchio* (1940), the Blue Fairy is the divine figure that endows Pinocchio with life, but the mentor figure he inherits is Jiminy Cricket, the "little voice inside his head," externalized into a physical conscience. It is Jiminy's job to constantly remind Pinocchio about his goal to become a real boy, and about the virtues of honesty and self-sacrifice which will gain him that reward. In *Star Wars*, Luke's real father is an evil figure who is not present in his life. When Luke adopts Obi-Wan as his new mentor and father figure, he accepts his divine destiny as a Jedi knight, and he accepts the challenge of rescuing the princess (Carrie Fisher).

Guilt

The child's moral development begins as a fear of Father and the punishment he inflicts for naughty behavior. Freud's conception of guilt owes much to Nietzsche, who defined guilt as self-imposed psychological punishment, derived from the memory of actual physical punishment. The child associates the pain and fear of punishment from Father with a negative affect. Eventually, the memory of outwardly inflicted physical pain becomes a taste of self-inflicted psychological pain. This self-inflicted psychological pain is what we call "guilt." As an enforcer of moral rules, guilt is a much more powerful force than physical punishment, because guilt begins working even before we do something wrong. The mere idea of committing an immoral act results in a pang of guilt, which deters us from committing the act. Furthermore, since guilt is an unconscious force, it can detect desires and wishes hidden deep in the psyche — desires that the individual is not even consciously aware of. Hence, unresolved Oedipal feelings of inappropriate desire for the mother or repressed aggression towards the father can exist below the conscious level, resulting in unconscious guilt that can express itself through a myriad of neurotic symptoms. The anxiety-ridden neurotic is completely unaware of the deeply buried feelings that torture him and block his ability to enjoy healthy emotional relationships. Untangling the complex web of unconscious memories and guilt can be a painfully long and torturous process for the neurotic, and a remarkably lucrative process for his psychoanalyst.

Libido

The Oedipal complex is fully resolved when the child's developing ego becomes balanced by the acquisition of the opposing force to the id, the superego. The child's superego is his moral conscience, the structure within the psyche that holds all of the moral rules and principles held sacred by society — as well as the psychological imprints of the authority figures who punished him as he was growing up. So, in a traditional sense, the superego is the internal representation of the boy's identification with his father. On a symbolic level, the superego *is* the father. And at the level of myth, the superego is the mentor who guides the hero and informs him of his moral purpose.

The power of the superego arises from its ability to impose guilt, the teeth of the moral conscience. The psyche is a perpetual battleground between guilt and the *libido*, the sexually charged psychic energy that originates from the id. If guilt is the immovable object of morality, then libido is the unstoppable force of desire. These two unconscious forces can never conquer each other, and they remain in constant conflict, forever locked in a tug-of-war over control of the psyche.

The Underdeveloped Superego

The character with no respect for rules or authority suffers from a lack of guilt. The challenge of the guiltless character is to constrain his unbridled libido and develop a conscience. Often times, the character with an underdeveloped superego is the villain. Since this wild man has no internal conscience, his id must be defeated and punished by an external moral conscience — the hero. In westerns, the clash between guilt and libido is symbolized by the big shootout, in which the good hero faces the evil villain in mortal combat. Movies such as *My Darling Clementine* (1946), *High Noon* (1952) and *Rio Bravo* (1959) all build up to the final showdown between the sheriffs who represent law and order, and the villains who represent the lawlessness of the Wild West.

Other times, the hero is the one with the underdeveloped superego. If he is an antihero, he may have to overcome his libidinous ways in order to defeat the bad guy. In *Rio Bravo*, Dude (Dean Martin) must overcome his weakness for booze in order to help the sheriff (John Wayne) defeat the bad guys. In *The Tin Star* (1957), Morg the bounty hunter (Henry Fonda) must restrain his impulse for killing and demonstrate to his young disciple (Anthony Perkins) that he is capable of capturing a wanted criminal alive. If the protagonist is a fallen hero, he typically loses his battle with his own libido. In De Palma's *Scarface* (1983), Tony desperately needs the love and respect of his sister (Mary Elizabeth Mastrantonio), the only pure thing left in his life. But Tony's anger, mistrust, violence and drug abuse destroy his relationship with his sister, and lead to his bloody downfall.

The Overdeveloped Superego

The character plagued by guilt, neurosis and anxiety suffers from an overdeveloped superego. Woody Allen's character in many of his movies is a perfect example of the guilt-ridden neurotic whose every decision is racked by second guessing and self doubt. Some heroes have such an overpowering sense of guilt that their neuroses become psychologically debilitating. The challenge for these heroes is to learn the unconscious root of their guilt, and to overcome it. In *Ordinary People* (1980), Conrad (Timothy Hutton) is a clinically depressed and suicidal teen. Through psychotherapy, he discovers that he is punishing himself for surviving a boating accident in which his beloved brother died. When this unconscious dilemma is brought into the light of conscious thought, it is unraveled and defused. Guilt loses its psychological power when the hero understands that it is merely an irrational and inordinate form of self-inflicted punishment.

In most cases, however, a deeper understanding of the guilt driving the hero's anxiety would destroy the basic motivation behind his character. John Elder (John Wayne) in *The Sons of Katie* Elder (1965) is driven throughout the film by his guilt over abandoning his poor mother. In *The Elephant Man* (1980), Dr. Treves (Anthony Hopkins) is driven to help John Merrick (John Hurt) by the guilt he feels from exploiting the poor man as a human abnormality. Superheroes are particularly prone to overdeveloped superegos. The superhero in *Batman* (1989) dedicates his life to fighting crime after witnessing the death of his parents and feeling guilty that he did nothing to stop the horrendous crime. Similarly, the superhero in *Spider-Man* (2002) becomes a crime fighter when his uncle is killed by a criminal that he could have stopped. And the superhero in *Superman* (1978) gives up normal life for crime fighting when his adoptive father dies of a heart attack, and Superman feels guilty for not being able to save him. The link between overdeveloped superegos and highly motivated superheroes is extremely strong in comic books and film. For the sake of Metropolis, let's hope that Superman never goes into therapy.

Father

The resolution of the Oedipal Complex involves the child's *identification* and psychological integration of the father figure. However, the father figures provided to us by fate are often not the ones that inspire us to achieve our desired identities. The replacement of a false, negative or absent father figure with an inspirational one is a common theme in many films. In *Of Human Hearts* (1938), Jason's father (Walter Huston) is a simple country preacher with very strict demands for moral behavior. Jason (James Stewart) bristles under the strict authoritarian rule of his parochial father, but he finds an alternative father figure in the town physician. Dr. Shingle (Charles Coburn) is a man of science, not a man of God. Dr. Shingle is a libertarian as well as a kindly and understanding man. To his father's chagrin, Jason begins to identify with Dr. Shingle, and disobeys his father's wishes by reading medical books rather than the bible. Eventually, Jason's identification with Dr. Shingle precipitates a complete split between father and son, and Jason leaves his father's house to become a doctor instead of a preacher. By the end of the film, Jason's father has died and Dr. Shingle has replaced him not only as a mentor for Jason, but as a surrogate husband for Jason's mother (Beulah Bondi) as well, completing his role as a replacement father figure.

Shane

A similar theme is played out in *Shane* (1953). Joey's father (Van Heflin) is an honest, hardworking homesteader. But when Shane comes along, little Joey (Brandon de Wilde) becomes fascinated with the mysterious loner and his romantic past as a gunfighter. Joey's mother (Jean Arthur) shows a more than casual interest in the sexy outlaw as well. Though he never truly replaces big Joe as a father, Shane knocks big Joe out in order to take his place in the final showdown with the evil cattle baron (Emile Meyer) and his hired gun (Jack Palance). In Joey's mind, Shane is the man who courageously stands up to the evil forces and saves the homesteaders, while his father lay on his back with an icepack on his head. For little Joey, the role of savior, mentor and macho hero will always be identified with Shane, rather than his own father.

Fort Apache

For girls, the Electra Complex is ideally resolved when the girl transfers her psychosexual desire for Father onto another eligible, preferably unrelated male. But this ideal resolution is subverted when a *possessive father* cannot let go of his little girl and allow her to marry the man of her choice. In *Fort Apache* (1948), Colonel Thursday (Henry Fonda) cannot accept the fact that his daughter (Shirley Temple) is in love with a suitor whom he deems unacceptable. As a member of a distinguished army family, he cannot bear to imagine that his daughter should marry the son of a sergeant. Thursday's inability to allow his daughter the freedom to choose a husband of her own creates both frustration and compassion in the viewer. Though we deplore Thursday's stubbornness and unyielding authoritarianism, we understand that his desire to control his daughter's life comes from a place of love. We sympathize with him because we see that he loves his daughter so much that he is unwilling to let her go. Unfortunately, Thursday only yields to the inevitable in the moment before his death. In his dying breaths, Thursday finally admits that the young suitor is a brave and commendable officer and an acceptable groom for his beloved daughter.

Forbidden Planet

In what may be the most overtly Freudian screenplay ever written, *Forbidden Planet* (1956) is a sci-fi Oedipal play inspired by Shakespeare's *The Tempest.* In the year 2200, a group of astronauts enter the Forbidden Planet, Altair 4, whose entire population has been destroyed by a mysterious, dark force. The only living survivors are the brilliant Dr. Morbius (Walter Pidgeon) and his young daughter, the unabashedly sexy Altaira (Anne Francis). Morbius is a jealous and possessive guardian of his sexually maturing daughter. Until the arrival of the astronauts, he and Altaira lived in complete seclusion and Morbius enjoyed the unrivaled love and attention of his cherished daughter. But when Captain Adams (Leslie Nielsen) enters the scene as a rival for Altaira's love, Morbius psychically projects his destructive libido through his dreams into an "Id monster" that murders the astronauts. The name Morbius is a reference to the mythological figure of Morpheus, the god of the unconscious world of dreams, hinting at the unconscious origin of Morbius's powers. Accordingly, Morbius remains completely unaware that it is his own unconscious destructive impulses that are killing the crew. In the end, though his final massive effort to control his own id kills him, Morbius overcomes his desire for sole possession of his daughter. In his dying breaths, he refers to Captain Adams as "Son," showing that he is finally willing to release his daughter so that she can be possessed by another man — who will then become his son-in-law.

Father's Blessing

A different twist on the possessive father theme is played out in Disney's *The Little Mermaid* (1989). Ariel is a mermaid who falls in love with a mortal. Her father, King Triton, cannot accept the notion that his beloved daughter should marry a lowly "fish eater." For Triton, the Romeo and Juliet plot of the star-crossed young lovers is even more poignant, because if his daughter chooses to marry a mortal and live on land, she can never return to the sea. Triton, however, is able to overcome his desire to possess and control his daughter. In the end, he lets her go, losing the physical presence of his cherished Ariel, but gaining her eternal love and respect.

In *The Little Mermaid,* King Triton shows his ultimate acceptance of his daughter's autonomy by blessing her with human mortality. The traditional father's blessing of the daughter and her groom is an ancient custom that dates back to the days when daughters were literally regarded as their father's private property. The father would eventually "give away" his daughter on her wedding day, but only to a groom that he considered acceptable.

The father's blessing could be given freely or jealously withheld. For Tevye (Topol) in *Fiddler on the Roof* (1971), there is nothing more important in life than "tradition." But when his daughter chooses to marry a gentile, even Tevye's enormous love for his children cannot move him to accept their intermarriage and give his blessing to the union. Forced to choose between his beloved daughter and his cherished tradition, Tevye stays true to his faith by withholding his blessing and renouncing his daughter forever.

Chinatown

Perhaps the most possessive father ever depicted on film is Noah Cross (John Huston) in *Chinatown* (1974). Cross is a multi-millionaire megalomaniac who must control everything and everyone around him. The external plot of the film centers around Cross's scheme to dominate the entire city of Los Angeles. But the driving force behind the film is the internal plot, in which Cross desires to own and control the lives of his daughters in ways that would make Freud himself blush. Cross's possessive and inappropriate lust for domination over the city of Los Angeles provides parallel symbolism for his lust for his daughters. The city, like a young daughter, must be allowed to grow and develop in her own way. When the founding fathers use their inordinate power and control to dominate her, she will wither and die like a flower kept from the sun.

In the distant backstory of the film, Cross had an incestuous relationship with his daughter, Evelyn (Faye Dunaway), resulting in the birth of Sophie (Nandu Hinds) — who is Cross's daughter and also his granddaughter. Cross's desire to possess both Evelyn and Sophie leads him to kill his son-in-law, Sophie's stepfather (Darrell Zwerling), who is trying to take Sophie away. The only person standing between Cross and Sophie is Evelyn (the girl's mother and sister). At the end of the movie, Evelyn is also killed. After destroying both of his rivals, Cross walks away with Sophie under his protective arm. The viewer can only imagine what their relationship will be like.

Mother

The central neurotic conflict within the Oedipal complex is the *incest taboo*, the child's psychosexual desire for the opposite-sex parent, which is forbidden in all civilized societies. The child's incestuous desire for sexual union with the parent is so socially unacceptable and so psychologically troubling that it can never be expressed consciously. The illicit desire remains suppressed deep within the unconscious, expressing itself only as indistinct feelings of guilt and emotional tension between family members. While Freud's focus on infantile sexuality may have been overstated, the Oedipal theme of obsessive attachment, the need to monopolize the affections of our loved ones, is an integral force in the psychology of family dynamics.

Often times, there is an *absent mother figure* within the possessive father film plot. The lack of a wife for the father and the lack of a mother for the daughter increases the pathos for both characters. In *The Little Mermaid*, Triton's lack of any female companionship other than Ariel creates a greater need for him to keep his daughter as a primary love interest. The young suitor, in these cases, becomes a true rival, as the daughter has taken the place of her mother as the sole love object for her father. When Ariel marries and moves away, Triton will be left emotionally isolated and alone. Furthermore, the fact that Ariel has no compassionate mother figure makes her relationship with Triton even more strained. A mother who understands the stirrings of love in a young girl's heart could sway a stubborn father and convince him that forbidding romance between two young lovers is a futile, self-destructive pursuit. The absence of a mother figure to play a mediating role between Triton and Ariel makes the breach between these two characters appear irreparable.

Oedipus Wrecks

In *Manhattan* (1979), Woody Allen's character recalls writing an autobiographical story about his mother entitled "The Castrating Zionist." When an overbearing mother smothers her son with obsessive love, we see the results of an Oedipal complex left completely unresolved. Rather than identifying with the father and developing as an independent individual, this character remains completely emotionally attached to his mother. This person cannot stand up to his dominating mother, who showers him with love and affection while simultaneously emasculating his feeble attempts at autonomy. In *Oedipus Wrecks*, Woody Allen's segment from *New York Stories* (1989), Sheldon (Woody Allen) has a prototypical Jewish mother. She is perpetually deriding his love interests and undermining his attempts at romance. Sheldon's mother becomes magically transformed into a massive apparition hovering over New York City. The joke makes sense, because we understand the humiliation that Sheldon feels over his infantile subjugation to his domineering mother. The joke is funny because this sense of embarrassment is amplified into ridiculous proportions when the mother figure is projected out from his unconscious and onto the sky over the East River. By sabotaging her son's romances, the devouring mother reveals her unconscious desire to eliminate the rivals for her son's love, so she can keep him all to herself.

Psycho

The domineering mother motif escalates to terrifying proportions in *Psycho* (1960). Norman Bates (Anthony Perkins) is so emotionally enmeshed with his psychologically overpowering mother that he could not bear to see her marry another man. In a fit of Oedipal rage, he kills his rival for his mother's love, and he kills his mother as well. The ensuing guilt and isolation results in a psychotic split in Norman's psyche. In his "normal" state, Norman is the feeble-willed mama's boy who jumps at his mother's beck and call. In his psychotic state, Norman is his mother — a harsh and bitter woman who emasculates her son with ridicule and psychological domination. Norman's existence as a split-personality psychotic is volatile enough, but when Norman becomes attracted to Marion (Janet Leigh), a sexy young woman, the Mother side of Norman's psyche goes ballistic. Norman, as his mother, slashes Marion to death in the shower. In this brutal act, both parts of Norman's personality gain primal satisfaction. Norman gets to thrust his phallic weapon into Marion's naked body, and Norman's mother gets to destroy her rival for Norman's love.

The Graduate

In *The Graduate* (1967), young Ben (Dustin Hoffman) is seduced by Mrs. Robinson (Anne Bancroft), a woman old enough to be his mother. The sexual relationship between Ben and Mrs. Robinson is only symbolically Oedipal, but it is crystal clear that Mrs. Robinson plays the role of a mother figure in Ben's life. She comes along at a time when Ben is "drifting." A recent college graduate, Ben has no direction in life. Mrs. Robinson provides the type of physical love and attention that Ben needs but cannot get from his real mother, because of the incest taboo. Neverthe-less, the fact that Mr. Robinson (Murray Hamilton) is Ben's father's best friend and partner makes Ben's relationship with Mrs. Robinson a source of great anxiety. Eventually, Ben resolves his Oedipal complex by trans-ferring his libidinous desire onto Elaine (Katherine Ross), the Robinson's only daughter. Though he is no longer symbolically pursuing his mother, Ben's problems increase when Mrs. Robinson assumes the role of *posses-sive mother*. Mrs. Robinson sees Elaine as a rival for Ben's affection. She also sees Ben as a rival for Elaine's affection. So Mrs. Robinson sabotages Ben and Elaine's budding romance by telling Elaine that Ben raped her.

Though his part is underplayed, Mr. Robinson undergoes the most psychological turmoil of anyone. Ben has been "like a son" to Mr. Robin-son. Imagine how he must have felt when he learned that this beloved boy not only raped his wife, but is also trying to steal his precious daughter? Mr. Robinson plays the doubly burdened role of possessive father and cuckolded husband. The plot resolves, rather unrealistically, with Ben win-ning Elaine back — much to the chagrin of Mr. and Mrs. Robinson. The uneasy, ambiguous final moments of the film imply that rather than being free of the tyranny of their parents, they are doomed to relive the Oedipal drama when they start their own family and become parents themselves.

Harold and Maude

In Hal Ashby's cult classic, *Harold and Maude* (1971), Harold (Bud Cort) is a rather odd young man, seeking attention and intimacy from his cold and oblivious mother (Vivian Pickles). Since he cannot gain her pos-itive attention, he gets her negative attention by staging fake suicides. Harold's isolation and loneliness is exacerbated by the complete absence of a father figure. The viewer is left to assume that his father is dead, though the exact whereabouts of Harold's father are never revealed. Harold's world is thoroughly rocked when he develops a friendship with Maude (Ruth Gordon), an ebullient and life-loving woman about sixty years his senior. Harold begins to identify with Maude as a role model. Like Harold, Maude is a non-conformist, a free spirit, a square peg. They share an affinity for funerals and a general disregard for authority figures. Maude becomes a mentor for Harold, providing him with a new life-affirming philosophy to replace his self-loathing obsession with death and suicide. Maude also becomes a positive mother figure, encouraging Harold to love others and to live for himself. Harold transfers his unrequited love for his mother onto Maude, and they have a passionate affair. The shocked reaction of civilized society to Harold and Maude's iconoclastic and taboo love is symbolized by humorous remonstrations from three representatives of Harold's superego: Harold's Uncle Victor, a military general who represents law and order; Harold's priest, who represents religion; and Harold's psychiatrist, who rebukes Harold by telling him that a proper Oedipal complex reveals itself in a sexual attraction to a mother figure — not a *grandmother* figure.

Harold and Maude's unique romance ends abruptly when Maude commits suicide on her 80th birthday. Harold is completely devastated when Maude tells him that she took a lethal dose of pills. He has difficulty understanding the full extent of Maude's spiritual philosophy, which is based on the idea that life must be lived to the fullest, and then released willingly, without holding on to the attachments of the physical world. When Harold declares his love to Maude, she replies in her dying breaths: "Good Harold ... go out and love some more." At her moment of death, Maude inspires Harold to complete the resolution of his Oedipal complex. Like a mother bird pushing her chick out of the nest, Maude forces Harold to fly on the strength of his own wings. Harold's new sense of freedom is symbolized in a final fake suicide, in which he propels his car off a cliff. The car was a gift from his mother, a symbol of her inability to understand her son. Harold transformed the car into a miniature hearse, representing his death obsession and his anger towards his mother. Through his final fake suicide, Harold is reborn as a new man, free of the attachments of childhood complexes, free of his neurotic mother issues, and free of his fear of living. When the car crashes, the viewer thinks he is inside of it — driven to self-destruction by grief over Maude's death — but then we see that Harold is still on top of the cliff. He walks away, playing a tune on the banjo that Maude gave him, the symbol of their enduring love.

Rushmore

In Wes Anderson's *Rushmore* (1998), Max Fischer (Jason Schwartzman) is searching for a mother figure. After Max's mother died when he was a young boy, Max transferred his maternal love to Rushmore, the posh private school that his mother got him a scholarship to attend. For Max, the lonely teenage son of a poor barber (Seymour Cassel), Rushmore represents the love and high aspirations that his lost mother had for him. When Max is threatened with expulsion from Rushmore, he suddenly develops an obsessive crush on a Rushmore teacher, the attractive and alluring Miss Cross (Olivia Williams). At the same time, Max develops a special friendship with Herman Blume (Bill Murray), a multimillionaire who is ashamed of his spoiled-rotten sons.

Herman and Max find the type of father/son relationship that they want in each other, and simulate this relationship in their friendship. However, when Herman falls in love with Miss Cross, a classic father/son Oedipal rivalry for Miss Cross' love ensues. By the end of the film, Max shows that he has overcome his Oedipal complex. He has adjusted to life outside of Rushmore, and he has learned to accept and identify with his real father. Max has also given up his unrealistic dreams of a romantic relationship with Miss Cross, and even plays a key part in bringing Miss Cross and Herman back together. By letting go of his childish attachment to his replacement mother figure (Rushmore) and his replacement father figure (Herman), Max leaves behind the relics of childhood and enters the adult world of mature relationships—symbolized by his lovely new girlfriend, Margaret Yang (Sara Tanaka).

Equus

When we commit an immoral act, the guilt is multiplied by the existence of witnesses, whose eyes testify to the depravity of our sins. Shame exists in the eyes of others. But when an act is so depraved that we can never forgive ourselves, then even our own eyes can look inwardly to see the corruption of our souls. After Oedipus discovered that he had married and copulated with his own mother, he gouged his eyes out in the quintessential act of shame. This psychological connection between the eyes and shame is evident in the old English saying: "Damn your eyes!" In the English film *Equus* (1977), Alan Strang (Peter Firth) cannot make love with his girlfriend (Jenny Agutter) in the hayloft of a stable, due to an obsessive horse fetish. In an extreme reaction to the shame of impotence, the disturbed teen gouges the eyes out of all the horses in the stable. For Alan, the disgrace of both his physical inadequacy and his moral iniquity exists in the eyes of the horses. His demented solution, born from the passion of that moment, was to gouge out the horses eyes, thereby removing his guilt and shame.

The Drusilla Complex

There have been multiple accounts from the correspondence of various reliable sources that Sigmund Freud was in love with his wife's sister, and that the two carried on a secret affair. Perhaps this highly personal issue in Freud's life led to a reluctance to write explicitly about another type of incest, which is also found repeatedly in myth and literature. Freud's possible writer's block on the subject of sister incest may have been due to a conscious or unconscious inhibition towards revealing his deepest secret to the eyes of his readers. The sexual obsession with the sister figure is as taboo a subject as the traditional Oedipal theme. In most depictions, the realization of this desire leads to either crippling guilt or extreme violence.

The Roman Emperor whose boundless lust and decadence were immortalized in Bob Guccione's pornographic epic, *Caligula* (1979) is the only character ever depicted on film that engaged in repeated sexual relations with his sister, while never experiencing an iota of guilt. Caligula's (Malcolm McDowell) shameless indulgence in forbidden sex with his sister Drusilla (Teresa Ann Savoy) is portrayed as the apex of sexual abandon. His depravity was born out of a combination of absolute power and complete indifference to morals or cultural taboos. In the end, Caligula's indulgences prove to be self-destructive, when his enemies use his infamous licentiousness against him in their efforts to dethrone him.

In *The Sweet Smell of Success* (1957), J. J. Hunsecker (Burt Lancaster) is an emperor of the entertainment industry. As a syndicated gossip columnist based on the infamous Walter Winchell, Hunsecker made or broke people's careers with the stroke of a pen. Hunsecker uses all of his power to stop a marriage between his sister, Susan (Susan Harrison), and her fiancé (Martin Milner). Hunsecker's incestuous desire for complete possession of his sister is disguised behind a façade of fatherly care and concern for her welfare. But when he discovers Susan alone in her room with a man (Tony Curtis), Hunsecker's lust explodes in an eruption of violence, exposing his concealed desire to the light of day.

In *Scarface* (1983), Tony (Al Pacino) is the emperor of a drug syndicate. His obsessive protectiveness of his sister, Gina (Mary Elizabeth Mastrantonio), is so passionate that it clearly indicates some deep psychosexual desire for the sole possession of Gina's love. When Tony discovers his best friend and sister together, he kills his friend — leading to a mental meltdown for both Tony and Gina. In a haze of grief, drugs and psychological confusion, brother and sister face each other for the last time. Gina, dressed in a revealing negligee, tells Tony that she knows why he won't allow her to be with anyone else — because he wants her all for himself. Gina's seduction creates a moment of incredible sexual tension, which can only be resolved in a bloodbath of extreme violence.

In *Angels and Insects* (1995), Edgar Alabaster (Douglas Henshall) is an English aristocrat who suffers from the same type of despotic arrogance and moral deficiency as Caligula. He forces his sister Eugenia (Patsy Kensit) to engage in incestuous sex, though it is a bit unclear whether Eugenia is truly being coerced or whether she passively allows Edgar to have sex with her. In any case, the revelation of this incestuous affair is far too much for her prudish husband (Mark Rylance), a drab entomologist who eventually learns that behind the lacy facade of the social elite, there are primal drives that show little more cultivation than the insects that he studies under his microscope.

In John Carpenter's *Halloween* (1978), we see through the eyes of six-year-old Michael Myers as he enters his sister's room after she had sex with her boyfriend. He approaches her naked body and slashes her to death. We don't know why Michael kills his teenage sister. All we see of her is a beautiful naked body. Carpenter doesn't explain this sexually charged scene of extreme violence, he merely depicts it in a chilling, surreal sequence that recalls the hazy atmosphere of an early childhood memory. The implication for the viewer is that Michael was in love with his sister, and that witnessing her having sex with another boy drove him into a psychotic rage from which he never returned.

In *The Royal Tennenbaums* (2001), Richie (Luke Wilson) is plagued by guilt over his infatuation with his adopted sister, Margot (Gwyneth Paltrow). When he discovers that his best friend (Owen Wilson) is secretly having an affair with Margot, Richie's jealous rage is directed inwardly. In a fit of anger, despair and guilt, he slashes his wrists. Though he survives his suicide attempt, Richie is still conflicted over his desire for Margot. His conflict is especially puzzling because he's not even sure if it is morally wrong for he and his sister to be romantically linked, since they are not biologically related. Nevertheless, his mental anguish is somewhat abated when Margot tells him that she cares for him as well, though they have to remain "secretly in love." While they never actually have sex, Richie and Margot's plot line resolves with them smoking cigarettes together on the roof of the Tennenbaum house, as if their love had actually been physically consummated.

And finally, in *Hannah and Her Sisters* (1986), Elliot (Michael Caine) is married to Hannah (Mia Farrow), but he is in love with his wife's sister Lee (Barbara Hershey). Elliot and Lee have an affair, but they are both racked by guilt, which eventually overpowers the pleasure of their company and ends the affair. The relationship between Elliot and Lee is a very realistic depiction of an incestuous relationship, and it probably resembles the beginning and ending of Freud's own (alleged) incestuous affair with his sister-in-law. In short, the sexual attraction between the two would-be lovers is blocked by a moral inhibition. Ideally, the guilt experienced at the mere thought of having an affair would obstruct any romantic development. But sometimes this preemptive guilt is not strong enough, especially when sexual attraction is amplified by the excitement of the fact that the other person is forbidden. Temptation (like the snake in the Garden of Eden) is strongest when the prohibited object is perceived as being taboo. Once the forbidden fruit is tasted, guilt (like the wrath of God) returns with a vengeance. The psychological punishment inflicted by the conscience of the superego is so severe that it overpowers the libido impulses that brought the two together in the first place. Though libido brought Elliot and Lee together, guilt tore them apart.

4

The Myth of the Birth of the Hero

Otto Rank was born in 1884 in Vienna. Rank came from a poor family and was essentially self educated. He studied Freud's theories on his own while working as a locksmith, and at the age of twenty-one wrote an article entitled "The Artist," one of the earliest psychoanalytic studies of art and creativity. The article came to Freud's attention. He was impressed with the young scholar and took him under his wing. Under Freud's mentorship and tutelage, Rank entered the University of Vienna. Upon Freud's advice, he did not study medicine in order to become a psychiatrist, but continued his studies in the arts and humanities. Rank's scholarly study of world mythology and his firsthand knowledge of Freudian theory inspired his short but incredibly influential work, *The Myth of the Birth of the Hero* (1912), which became a classic monograph in the growing field of psychoanalysis. The increasing respect and reputation that Rank was developing among the close circle of Viennese psychoanalysts ingratiated the young student to "the Master," and Rank became one of Freud's closest disciples and collaborators.

After receiving his Ph.D. at the age of twenty-eight, Rank was appointed by Freud as secretary to the Vienna Psychoanalytic Society and editor of its journal *The International Journal of Psychoanalysis*. However, as was typical of Freud's relationships with his most brilliant disciples and colleagues, tension arose when Rank began expressing original ideas that diverged from Freud's orthodox analytic perspective. The final break came in 1924 when Rank wrote *The Trauma of Birth*, an analytic study in which Rank proposed the "birth trauma" rather than the Oedipal complex as the primary root of neurotic conflict. Freud condemned the work and Rank was expelled from the Vienna Psychoanalytic Society. Shortly afterwards, Rank left Vienna and eventually resettled in Paris in 1926 with his wife and daughter. Though based in Paris, Rank taught and practiced often in the United States. He moved to New York City permanently in 1936, where he died three years later. Rank's theories have been extremely influential in the fields of psychotherapy and psychoanalysis, as well as in the fields of mythology, philosophy and all of the subfields in psychology. He is an especially revered figure among analysts and practitioners in the existential and humanistic branches of psychoanalysis.

The Hero Saga

In *The Myth of the Birth of the Hero*, Rank draws out a basic pattern of psychological themes that is easily discernible in the legends of hundreds of mythological heroes. Jesus, Moses, Gilgamesh, Cyrus, Perseus, Hercules, Telephus, Oedipus, Romulus, Paris, Siegfried, Lohengrin, Tristan, Sargon and Karna are just a few of the legendary heroes whose stories follow the Myth of the Birth of the Hero saga with extremely little variation. In Rank's (1914) own words, (edited by this author), the saga is summarized as follows:

> The hero is the child of most distinguished parents, usually the son of a king.... During or before the pregnancy, there is a prophecy in the form of a dream or oracle, cautioning against his birth, and usually threatening danger to the father ... he is surrendered to the water.... He is then saved by animals, or by lowly people.... After he has grown up, he finds his distinguished parents, in a highly versatile fashion. He takes his revenge on his father, on the one hand, and is acknowledged, on the other. Finally he achieves rank and honors.

By expanding slightly upon the basic themes set forth by Rank, the myth of the birth of the hero can be delineated according to the following stages:

1. *Prophecy* of the birth of the hero.
2. The birth of the hero to divine, noble or *royal parentage*.
3. The infant hero is attacked or *abandoned* either by the father himself or by a dark, evil father figure.
4. The infant hero is rescued by or given to *surrogate parental figures*.
5. The hero eventually *returns to the land of his father* in order to avenge the wrong inflicted upon him at the time of his birth.
6. The hero-son *claims his royal birthright*.

The Wish-Fulfilling Fantasy

The first significant aspect of the hero myth is that the people who raise the child are not his real parents; rather, they are surrogate parents. Rank believed that this aspect of the myth is a universal *daydream* among children, a form of *wish fulfillment* in which the child fantasizes that his own rather ordinary or mundane parents are not really his own mother and father; but rather, that he is the child of divine or royal lineage. Within this fantasy, the child can imagine that he is far better and superior than his natural parents, and that he is therefore destined for greater things. The fantasy allows the child to distance himself from any negative qualities that he perceives within his parental figures, identifying himself instead with fantasy-based parents who are divine, noble, aristocratic or otherwise ideal.

The Fantasy of the Divine Father

The boy-hero has an essentially hostile relationship with his father. In reference to the childhood fantasy element of the myth, the boy negates the existence of his real father in favor of identifying with a *fantasy father figure* of his own imaginative creation. In Rank's (1914) words:

> The entire endeavor to replace the real father by a more distinguished one is merely the expression of the child's longing for the vanished happy time, when his father still appeared to be the strongest and greatest man, and the mother seemed the dearest and most beautiful woman.

In infancy and early childhood, the real parental figures are ideal, noble and divine in the baby's innocent and youthful eyes. But as the child grows, the idealized image of mother and father becomes tarnished by grim reality, and the child sees the parents for whom they really are — ordinary people with real weaknesses and flaws. The childhood fantasy of divine ancestry is therefore the child's attempt to return to an earlier state of bliss, in which the parental figures were all-powerful, beautiful, beneficent and divine. Since the boy-hero's primary identification figure is the father, the fantasy of divine ancestry is typically related directly or solely at the father, while the mother may remain an extant or at least a benign figure in the boy-hero's myth. The widespread *myth of the virgin birth*, for example, is a complete "repudiation of the father" by the boy-hero. Not only is the real father negated as the biological father, but the entire existence of a biological father is denied, leaving only the possibility of divine heritage.

Revolt Against the Father

For the boy-hero, hostility and negation is directed primarily at the father. According to the myth, it is the father who feels threatened by the birth of his son, and it the father who fears and resents his son's existence. It is the father who exposes the boy to death by abandoning him in the wild, and it is against the father that the hero will eventually claim his revenge. Within the fantasy of open revolt against the father, the boy establishes his own ego as the hero of his own life story. In Rank's (1914) words:

> The true hero of the romance is, therefore, the ego, which finds itself in the hero, by reverting to the time when the ego was itself a hero, through its first heroic act, i.e. the revolt against the father.

The boy identifies himself with the hero identity by identifying his father as the villain, and then revolting against and defeating the father-villain figure. The fantasy of the revolt against the father resolves the childhood fantasy of idealized parental figures by eliminating the idealized parent and replacing him with a fantasy of the idealized self—i.e., the *self as hero*.

The Fantasy of the Usurping Son

In the final stage of the myth, the son avenges himself against the father. He is acknowledged as the divine or royal heir, and he usurps his father's kingdom and throne. The fantasy of the usurping son is a ubiquitous archetypal theme because it is essentially true to life. In classic Oedipal fashion, the infant child will rival and compete with the father for the love and affection of the mother. The son will grow up to challenge the father's authority and defy his will. The son will eventually live to succeed the father in the arena of life. And in the end, the son will bury the father and he will inherit everything that the father once possessed.

The Myth of the Birth of Harry Potter

In recent history, there has been no greater sensation in the world of children's literature and film than the Harry Potter phenomenon. It is no coincidence that the Harry Potter myth, as depicted in *Harry Potter and the Sorcerer's Stone* (2001), is a close reenactment of the Myth of the Birth of the Hero saga. Like all other myths that have the capacity to communicate on a deep psychological level to wide audiences, Harry Potter's story touches upon primary unconscious issues that relate to our earliest childhood fantasies. Harry's journey from the mundane world of harsh reality (the "Muggle" world) to an enchanted fantasyland of magic and wonderment expresses a universal childhood escape fantasy. Harry Potter's journey is a journey of the mythical child-hero that all children and adults can relate to.

Harry's story begins with the boy-hero living with his surrogate parental figures (his aunt and uncle) in suburban England. He lives in a world of abuse, neglect, emotional isolation and desperate loneliness. Like most young children, he often feels that nobody understands him, and that his parental figures are often cruel, tyrannical, unfair and intolerant. At this initial stage of the story, Harry is a common boy that every child can relate to. By relating to Harry as the ordinary boy, the audience identifies with him and projects their own childhood fantasies onto his story, vicariously journeying into the world of wonder that Harry is about to enter.

Deconstructing Harry

Harry's story follows each step of Rank's pattern:

Stage One: Before Harry's birth, there is a *prophecy* that a child will be born who will defeat the evil Voldemort, the dark sorcerer of the wizard world.

Stage Two: Harry is *born to great parents*— powerful wizards who are highly respected in the wizard world.

Stage Three: Shortly after his birth, Voldemort —*the dark father*— kills Harry's real parents and attempts to kill Harry, but Harry miraculously survives.

Stage Four: Harry is rescued and left in the care of his aunt and uncle, *surrogate parents* in the Muggle world, with whom Harry will be anonymous and safe.

Stage Five: When Harry comes of age, he is returned to the wizard world, where — through the course of seven adventures— he will avenge himself by *defeating Voldemort*.

Stage Six: Harry will eventually *claim his birthright* as a noble hero in the wizard world of his true father.

As an orphan, Harry can easily negate his surrogate parents, his abusive and nasty aunt and uncle, while fantasizing about his ideal biological parents— a beautiful, caring, sensitive mother and a super-powerful, brave and dashing wizard father. Harry's escape into a fantasy world in which he is a powerful wizard communicates the basic childhood fantasies of overcoming inferiority, escaping parental brutality, breaking out of the boredom of reality and realizing a sense of personal nobility and divine destiny.

Christian Complaints

Fundamentalist Christian groups have denounced the Harry Potter books and films because they claim that the stories espouse heathen beliefs.

Though this may be true, it must also be acknowledged that nearly all children's stories from Snow White to Pinocchio to Cinderella feature heathen semi-divine figures such as sorcerers, witches, fairies, dragons, ghosts, fairy godmothers, magical spells, etc. The reason why Christian fundamentalists rail against Harry Potter and not Cinderella is because the myth of Harry is a thinly veiled recasting of the most influential myth of the birth of the hero—the myth of Jesus.

Like Jesus, Harry is the son of a powerful supernatural figure. Like Jesus, Harry has a predestined fate as a redeemer of nations and a conqueror of great evil. Like Jesus, Harry must discover his own identity for himself, and face his great challenges on his own. Like Jesus, Harry is gifted with supernatural powers. Like Jesus, Harry will be tempted to join forces with the evil one, but he will overcome this temptation. Like Jesus, Harry will encounter death at one point or another, only to be reborn or resurrected with a stronger spirit. And finally, like Jesus, Harry's myth has been told a thousand times in a thousand different languages with a thousand different names. As Otto Rank pointed out, while the face of the hero changes with each myth, the message the hero delivers always remains the same.

The Princess Hero Saga

The childhood fantasies expressed in fairy tales and myth are also resonant to little girls' issues, though the female hero in traditional tales tend to be less proactive. As seen in film depictions of the female hero myth such as *Snow White and the Seven Dwarfs* (1937), *Sleeping Beauty* (1959) and *Cinderella* (1950), the typical female hero is a princess. Though she is born of royal parentage, she is usually an orphan left under the care of a cruel surrogate parent—an evil stepmother. So, like the male hero, the princess is pitted in a hostile, antagonistic relationship with a menacing same-sex parental figure. While the real mother is dead, the princess will generally receive help and guidance from the mother's spirit, represented by the supernatural "fairy godmother." However, rather than defeating the evil stepmother herself and usurping her throne, the princess is typically rescued by the male hero—Prince Charming—who claims the princess hero's birthright for her, and returns her to her rightful seat of honor on the throne.

The Mentor Who Unveils

The fairy godmother figure in the princess myth is a mentor figure — a ubiquitous role throughout all hero mythology. The critical function that the mentor serves is to purvey to the hero some crucial knowledge of his backstory. Just as the wise old man in dreams informs the persona about repressed or hidden knowledge in the unconscious, the mentor in myth unveils to the hero elements of the myth of his birth that are necessary for his development on the journey ahead. In *Excalibur*, Merlin provides Arthur with some background information that is critical to his sense of identity. Merlin tells him that his real father was the king. Similarly, in *Star Wars*, Obi-Wan tells Luke the key to his identity — that his real father was a great Jedi knight. The mentor almost always tells the hero the same basic story, the myth of the birth of the hero. By unveiling the hero to himself, the mentor gives the hero the critical knowledge he needs to get onto his destined path.

The Mentor as Former Hero

In order to guide the hero through the unknown, the mentor must have personal knowledge of the wilderness. The mentor must be a former hero— someone who has experienced his own saga and therefore has the wisdom and power to guide others. Arthur accepts Merlin as a mentor because he has heard many tales of Merlin's great power and adventures. Because Merlin was a hero in his own time, he has the credentials to inspire Arthur to similar feats of heroism. When Arthur develops from boy to hero, Merlin fades into the background, as Arthur no longer needs his mentor's guidance and inspiration on a daily basis. By the time Arthur has progressed from hero to mentor figure, as the king and leader of the Knights of the Round Table, Merlin has also progressed from mortal mentor to immortal legend. Arthur doesn't need the physical presence of Merlin to guide him because he remembers Merlin's teachings and has integrated him into his own identity. The legend of Merlin is all that Arthur needs for inspiration. At the resolution of Arthur's character arc, when he passes over from mentor to legend, Perceval is there to be inspired by his mentor, Arthur. The key to the hero's character arc is that his mentor figure is always one step ahead of him.

The Circular Character Arc

The mentor is a true role model in that he represents the beginning and endpoint of the hero's character development. The full cycle of the mythical character arc is from boy to hero, from hero to mentor, and finally, from mentor to legend. The final progression from mentor to legend is a circular denouement, the point where the character arc comes full circle (i.e., the snake swallowing its own tail). In a Jungian sense, the character arc starts and ends in the collective unconscious. The myth starts with a prophecy, which is a *story*, oracle, legend or dream. The prophecy is materialized in the birth of the hero, who internalizes the prophecy as a personal dream or goal that he must achieve. After achieving his goal, the hero can proceed to mentor, and his task is to inspire a new hero with a similar dream or goal. And when the mentor dies, his life story becomes legend — a *story*— returning the hero's identity to the collective level of myth and dream.

Though his body is dead, the mentor-hero's spirit is even more powerful and inspirational as a legend, because it is no longer bound to the limitations of his physical presence. In the case of Jesus, the post-death legend is a prophecy of return or "second coming." Jesus progressed through all the stages of the mythical character arc. In death, his legend is also a prophecy of rebirth. His beginning and endpoint are exactly the same, symbolizing the divine power of eternity (the Uroboros). He is the prophecy, the hero, the mentor and the legend that lives on eternally with no real beginning and no perceivable end.

The Death of the Mentor

The Death card in the Tarot card cycle represents change. Similarly, the symbolic death of the mentor represents a change in the identity of the hero. The mentor often dies, either figuratively or literally, at the zenith of the hero's character arc. The mentor's death is a necessary and essential stage of the myth. Though the hero needs the mentor at the beginning of his journey, at one point the hero must grow out of this dependence, just as a child must at one point grow independent of his parents. In this way, the mentor-hero relationship recapitulates the father-son relationship. At the critical time of development, the son must define his own identity and become an independent individual. In *The Greatest Story Ever Told* (1965), Jesus (Max von Sydow) was respected by only a handful of disciples before the crucifixion. But after his martyrdom, millions revered his legend with unquestioning devotion. The martyrdom and/or deification of the mentor figure is an archetypal element throughout Greco-Roman and Judeo-Christian mythology.

In *Star Wars* (Episode IV, 1977), we see the same theme in the death of Luke's mentor. Obi-Wan clearly allows himself to be killed, telling his nemesis, "You can't win, Darth. If you kill me, I will become more powerful than you can possibly imagine." When Darth strikes him with his light saber, Obi-Wan's body vanishes. From that point on, Luke hears his mentor's disembodied voice in his head. Obi-Wan's spiritual power is now integrated into Luke's psyche, and it is this heightened spiritual power — represented by his mastery of the Force — that enables Luke to destroy the Death Star. Obi-Wan's character arc is a perfect depiction of the circular character arc. In *Star Wars,* Obi-Wan is a Jedi knight. Though his advanced age make him a mentor, he is clearly a former hero, and that is what inspires Luke to follow him.

In *The Phantom Menace* (Episode I, 1999), we go back in time to see a young Obi-Wan (Ewan McGregor) developing from squire to hero under the tutelage of his Jedi master, Qui-Gon Jinn (Liam Neeson). In *Attack of the Clones* (Episode II, 2002), we see Obi-Wan develop from hero to mentor for the young Anakin (Hayden Christensen). In Episode III (2005), Obi-Wan will clearly lose Anakin to the dark side, so he must become a mentor to Luke, Anakin's son. When Obi-Wan dies in Episode IV, he becomes immortalized into a spiritual, divine presence in Luke's psyche. Obi-Wan's death in *Stars Wars* marks the critical moment in which Luke makes his transition from squire to hero, and it also marks the resolution in Obi-Wan's character arc from mentor to legend.

The Character Arc as Metaphor for Life

The progression of the hero through the character arc is a long journey, just as life itself is a long journey. A person is born with the need for a mentor to guide and teach him. That person eventually grows up and becomes an independent individual, no longer needing the guidance of his original mentor. The person then may have a child of his own. That person then has to deal with the burdens and responsibilities of mentorship. And finally, that person will die. At that final stage of identity development, it is only his legend that will survive. The character or quality of that legend will live on partly in his deeds, but mainly in the memories of his own children. The memories of a positive mentor relationship will live on after him. The memories of a negative one will, with any luck, be either forgotten or repressed.

The Search for the Mentor

Mentors inform the developing ego of the tasks at each stage of life, and how to address them. Children especially need positive role models to identify with. These models come from their immediate environment, but they also come from stories, myths, history, television and movies. As Erik Erikson (1968) noted:

> Children at different stages of their development identify with those part aspects of people by which they themselves are most immediately affected, whether in reality or fantasy.

To a child's imagination, it does not matter whether an identification figure is real or fictitious. A storybook hero or movie character can be as significant or influential in the child's developing ego identity as a mother or father. Children and adolescents who do not have an appropriate father figure will seek one out. The search for a father figure is a critical element of identity development. For better or for worse, many of these people find their father figures on the movie screen.

To Kill a Mockingbird

In their gala network special, the "American Film Institute's 100 Years ... 100 Heroes and Villains" (2003), Atticus Finch in *To Kill a Mockingbird* (1962) was voted the #1 hero in the history of film. This choice was particularly interesting, because technically, Atticus (Gregory Peck) was not even the hero of the story. Atticus was the father of the hero—his daughter Scout. But the fact that Atticus is remembered as the hero of *To Kill a Mockingbird* is very significant. Atticus represents the perfect image of the strong, dependable father figure. He is moral, courageous and virtuous. As the combination of the perfect father and the quintessential mentor, Atticus Finch stands out in the viewers' memory as the hero and focal point of the film because he provides the ultimate identification figure for children with a deep psychological need for the perfect father.

A Bronx Tale

Young boys typically identify with their fathers, as long as their fathers are present and at least somewhat of a positive role model. But as a boy matures, he begins to develop an individual sense of identity that is personal and unique. At this point, he begins to look outside of the home for a father figure who represents a new identity. Growing children identify with sports stars, rock stars and movie stars in the same way that they identified with their mothers and fathers earlier on in childhood. In *A Bronx Tale* (1993), Calogero (Francis Capra) is a nine-year-old boy who thinks of his father Lorenzo (Robert De Niro) as a working-class hero. When Sonny (Chazz Palminteri), the local Mafia boss, kills someone, he becomes indebted to Calogero, the sole witness, after Calogero lies to the police. Lorenzo is strongly opposed to the presence of Sonny in his son's life, but Sonny and Calogero develop a relationship despite Lorenzo's objections.

Eight years later, at seventeen, Sonny has become a much more prominent figure in Calogero's (Lillo Brancato) life. Instead of going to Yankee games with his father, Calogero goes to the racetrack with Sonny. Instead of being a nobody in the neighborhood, Calogero earns respect and money by being Sonny's favorite neighborhood kid. Calogero even changes his name to "C," the nickname Sonny gave him. In rejecting the name Lorenzo gave him and replacing it with a new name from Sonny, Calogero makes a strong statement about his emerging identity. He no longer identifies with the traditional, blue-collar values of his father, encapsulated in Lorenzo's father's name — Calogero. He identifies with the slick, mobster values of Sonny, who named him "C."

Sonny has become a new father figure to C, rivaling Lorenzo for control over C's identity. Will C become a hardworking, honest man like his father? Or will he become a corrupt, dangerous mobster like Sonny? The conflict is illustrated when C and Lorenzo attend a boxing match. They are sitting in the "nosebleed" seats, the best that Lorenzo could afford, while Sonny and his gang are at ringside. When Sonny invites them down to sit in his row, C wants to sit by Sonny. It is clear that C is identifying with Sonny as a primary father figure, and it's easy to see why. Sonny's world is glamorous and financially rewarding, while Lorenzo's world is strenuous, impoverished and hopelessly square. Why should C sit in the back seats with Lorenzo and let life pass him by when he can enjoy all the thrills from a seat with Sonny at ringside.

As the story progresses, C's relationship with Sonny begins to duplicate his relationship with Lorenzo. Sonny is constantly reprimanding C, reminding him that he knows nothing and trying desperately to keep him away from a bad crowd of local hoodlums. Sonny's violence comes back to haunt him when he is killed by the son of the man that he murdered eight years earlier. At Sonny's funeral, C reflects on Sonny's influence on him. Sonny was a very significant figure in C's development, but in the end, we see that the love and respect that C has for his father was stronger than his transitory fascination with Sonny and his glamorous lifestyle. No matter who C might be identifying with at the moment, he will always return to the positive base of a father figure that Lorenzo provided for him.

The Movie Mentor Formula

With the exception of the hero, the *mentor archetype* is the most common figure in stories, myths and movies. Sometimes the mentor plays a small supporting role; sometimes he plays the central figure. In *Jerry Maguire* (1996), Jerry's (Tom Cruise) mentor is a long-dead sports agent. In the film, the mentor only appears twice in very brief flashbacks. However, these two flashbacks seem to inspire the most important developments in Jerry's character. Similarly, in *The Wizard of Oz*, Dorothy's mentor, Glinda the Good Witch, only appears three times. Yet in each brief appearance, she manages to influence the direction of Dorothy's development in extremely significant ways. First, she provides her with the ruby slippers and directs her onto the yellow brick road; then she covers the sleep-inducing field of poppies with snow so Dorothy can proceed to Oz; and finally, she guides Dorothy home by showing her how to employ the power of the ruby slippers. Even a brief appearance by a mentor can change the entire direction of a hero's myth. Nevertheless, the following film analyses will focus on movies in which the mentor figure plays a more prominent role.

Teacher Mentors

In *Goodbye, Mr. Chips* (1969), Mr. Chipping (Peter O'Toole) is an elderly, wise and inspirational teacher who has taught and guided thousands of students. Though he could never have children of his own, when reflecting back upon his life, he sees his individual students as emerging heroes, overcoming their own weaknesses and embarking on their own journeys under his tutelage. Through these young heroes, Chipping experiences his own adventures, and the victories of his students become victories of his own.

Mr. Keating (Robin Williams) in *Dead Poet's Society* (1989) is also an inspirational mentor to his students, but with a different message. Keating rouses his students towards nonconformity and individuality. He encourages them to march to the beat of a different drum, and enthuses them with a passionate love for art, poetry and the creative pursuits of life. The guidance Keating provides his students puts them into direct conflict with the awesome powers of conformity that govern their repressed environments—their negative father figures. One of Keating's disciples self-destructs and commits suicide when his budding individuality is squashed by his tyrannical father. Nevertheless, the legend of Keating's inspiration lives on in the newfound independence of his surviving students. When he leaves his classroom for the last time, the students whom he affected the most stand up on top of their desks in a show of nonconformity. They call out to him as a devoted hero would call out to his true mentor: "Captain ... oh my captain!"

False Mentors

In *The Ten Commandments*, Moses is tempted to abandon his duty to the Israelites and join his stepbrother, the Pharaoh, as the ruler of Egypt. In *The Last Temptation of Christ* (1988), Jesus (Willem Dafoe) is tempted by the devil to join him and be rewarded with fame, glory and the riches of the world. And in *Little Buddha* (1993), Siddhartha's father begs him to stay with him as a prince in his stately palace. In Rank's pattern of the hero's myth, the hero must at one point encounter the negative father figure and overcome him. This victory over the negative father or false mentor is often preceded by a temptation to join forces with the dark figure, and rule by his side as father and son. The same ubiquitous theme is recapitulated in modern mythology via the *Lord of the Rings* and *Star Wars* films.

GANDALF THE GREY, GANDALF THE WHITE

In *Lord of the Rings: The Fellowship of the Ring* (2001), Gandalf the Grey (Ian McKellen) is the mentor for each member of the fellowship. But, since Gandalf is a member of the fellowship as well, he, too, is a hero, and he, too, has a mentor figure. Gandalf is a member of the Wizard Council. The chief of this council is Saruman the White (Christopher Lee). As his chief, Saruman plays the role of Gandalf's mentor. However, Saruman betrays the council and allies himself with the Dark Lord, Sauron. In a moment of critical decision, Gandalf is offered the opportunity to join Saruman and Sauron and rule Middle Earth as a wizard king. Gandalf rejects the offer. He escapes from Saruman's tower, leads the fellowship through Moria, battles a demon and falls into the depths of Hell. However, he is resurrected as Gandalf the White — the new chief of the Wizard Council. At this point, he defeats his false mentor and replaces him, establishing his character as an immortal legend.

DARTH VADER AND DARTH SIDEOUS

In *The Empire Strikes Back* (1980), Luke is tempted by Darth Vader to join him and rule the universe as father and son. But this mentor represents a negative father figure — "Darth Vader" literally means "Dark Father." Luke must overcome this temptation to join the dark side of the Force. He can do so because of the inner strength he acquired when he internalized his positive mentor, Obi-Wan. Each episode of the Star Wars movies presents a different version of the mentor-hero relationship. In *The Phantom Menace*, Obi-Wan loses his own mentor figure, Qui-Gon Jinn, prematurely, and then decides to take on young Anakin Skywalker as an apprentice — though he himself has not completed his character arc from hero to mentor. In *Attack of the Clones*, the mentor-hero relationship develops between Obi-Wan and Anakin, though it is clear that Anakin is having trouble mastering his great power over the force. In the next episode, Anakin will leave Obi-Wan and pledge allegiance to a false mentor, Palpatine (Ian McDiarmid) — the Emperor of the Dark Side of the Force, also known as "Darth Sideous."

In *Star Wars*, Obi-Wan becomes mentor to Luke, Anakin's son, and pitches him into battle against his own father, who is now called "Darth Vader." By allowing himself to be killed, Obi-Wan pushes Luke forward in his development toward becoming a hero, and he also moves himself a step forward, progressing from mentor to legend. In *The Empire Strikes Back*, Yoda — the universal mentor of all Jedi knights — becomes Luke's penultimate mentor. In this film, Luke must encounter the terrible truth of his own identity, the fact that Anakin is his real father, and he must overcome the temptation to join forces with this false mentor figure. In an infamous scene, Vader holds his hand out to Luke, tempting him: "Luke … I am your father … join me, and we'll rule the galaxy as father and son!"

In *Return of the Jedi* (1983), Anakin redeems himself by rebelling against his own false mentor. He kills Palpatine, the Dark Emperor, and saves his son. In the final scene of the series, we see that Luke has internalized both his father and Obi-Wan as positive mentor figures in his psyche. Through the six episode series, Anakin develops from boy to squire, from squire to hero, from hero to false mentor, from false mentor to positive mentor, and then finally from mentor to legend. No other film series has depicted such a powerful, resonant and comprehensive portrayal of the mythological hero's character arc.

5

Religious Symbolism in Film

In the 1930s, overt religious symbolism was a common feature in even the most secular films. *Three Godfathers* (1936) starts out as a typical western. Three bank robbers (Chester Morris, Lewis Stone, Walter Brennan) are on the lamb with their loot, when they discover an orphaned infant. They each gradually become attached to the baby and they each give their life for its survival. In the end, even the most selfish and greedy outlaw sacrifices his life for the child. The story of three men who come out of the wilderness to deliver an infant son is clearly symbolic of the Jesus story, though it is the martyrdom of the men themselves that signifies redemption. In the final scene, the last outlaw stumbles into "New Jerusalem" with the infant boy in his arms. Before he dies, he leans against a post and a heavenly light shines on his face. A wreath of laurel hangs over his head, and you almost expect him to raise his arms in a crucifixion pose. The message is clear: Even a murderer and a thief can be redeemed through love and self-sacrifice.

Although this movie was billed as a regular run-of-the-mill western, the overt religious symbolism does not seem odd or out of place. Film audiences, especially in the 1930s, were quite at home with the direct parallels made between screen images and religious iconography. Over the years, filmmakers have become less overt in their use of religious imagery; however, the religious symbolism is just as prevalent — it's just not as obvious. When John Ford remade *Three Godfathers* in 1948 with John Wayne in the lead role, he stripped the film of most of its conspicuous religious metaphors, yet the story itself retained the essential element of spiritual allegory. The most prevalent aspect of religious symbolism in films is the theme of *sacrifice*, a crucial aspect of the heroic character that is broadly based throughout culture, religion and mythology.

Sacrifice of the Firstborn Son

Sacrifice is the act of making something holy or sacred by giving up a portion of one's self. Sacrifice is the central symbol in the Judeo-Christian belief system — a relic from the archaic pagan rituals that are still at the core of Judaic temple services and the Christian mass. The bible stories of Cain and Abel, Noah, Abraham and Isaac, Jacob, Moses and Jesus all revolve around either literal or figurative sacrifices to God. The sacrifice of the firstborn son is the ultimate act of faith. The father gives up willingly the thing most precious to him — the life that means more to him than his own life. As the ultimate sacrifice, the sacrifice of the firstborn son is held most sacred by God, as he could ask no more and receive no greater sign of faith and devotion.

Literal renditions of the sacrifice theme are depicted in biblical epics. In John Huston's *The Bible* (1966), Abraham (George C. Scott) sacrifices his most beloved son, Isaac, to God. And in George Stevens's *The Greatest Story Ever Told* (1965), the reversal of this theme is depicted when God sacrifices his only son Jesus (Max Von Sydow) to Man. The key to both sacrifices is the element of self-sacrifice in the father and the element of willingness in the son. Both elements are required in the sacrifice in order for it to be consecrated. In sacrificing his only or most beloved son, the father is sacrificing the best part of himself. And in giving himself up freely for the slaughter, the son is the willing lamb — not a victim but an equal partner in the ritual.

Sacrifice is also the ultimate quality of heroism. Mythological heroes like Moses, Jesus, Prometheus and Arthur sacrifice themselves for their peoples. The willingness to sacrifice one's self to a cause is recapitulated in movie heroes like Shane, who sacrifices his hope for a new life to help the homesteaders. At a certain level of abstraction, every fully developed hero reveals his heroic nature through sacrifice. If there is no point in the film in which the hero puts himself on the line for the sake of his cause, then he is not truly worthy of heroism. His character — in the classical version of the hero archetype — is lacking. The act that makes a normal person a hero is the act of sacrifice.

Crimes and Misdemeanors

Woody Allen's *Crimes and Misdemeanors* (1989) is a morality play on sin, guilt, faith and nihilism. The film addresses issues of religiosity directly, by depicting the protagonist's father as the embodiment of Ortho-

Sacrifice of the First Born Son. Jesus (Max Von Sydow) as the willing sacrifice epitomizes the mythological hero archetype. *The Greatest Story Ever Told* (1965), George Stevens Productions, MGM/UA Distribtors.

dox Judaism. The A-plot in Allen's film revolves around Judah (Martin Landau) and his conflict with his mistress, Dolores (Angelica Huston), who wants Judah to acknowledge their relationship and leave his wife. The first person Judah confides in is his brother Jack (Jerry Orbach)—a cold and objective pragmatist. Jack appeals to Judah's sense of reason. His option, killing Dolores, seems reasonable because the problem will be solved with absolutely no negative repercussions. Judah has the money to pay for an expert hit man, Jack can engineer the contract, and Judah's wife will never know anything about it. Jack's calculation is clean, cold and scientific, but it leaves out the elements of morality and guilt. Jack himself is beyond guilt. His character represents the nihilistic side of Judah's identity — the scientist within him who cannot believe in fairy tales like sin, God and the existence of unbreakable moral commandments. For these more traditional aspects of his moral personality, Judah must confide in a patient and old friend, Ben (Sam Waterston).

Moral Realism

Everyone refers to Ben as "the saint." Not only is Ben a rabbi, he is an extremely moral and righteous man in every way. For Judah, Ben represents a religious conscience — the faith and reverence in God that was instilled in Judah as a boy by his father. Ben is a positive father figure to Judah, who visualizes and speaks to Ben while solving his moral dilemma, as if Ben were a part of his mind. Ben's image often links Judah to memories of his actual father (David Howard), who also believed in the existence of a "real moral structure." The view propounded by Ben and Judah's father, "moral realism," is a direct contradiction to nihilism. Moral realists believe that moral laws are solid and unbreakable. When a sin is committed, it is instantly known by God. The guilty sinner will always be punished by God, just as the forces of good will always prevail.

Judah is torn between the faith-based view of moral realism and the skeptical view of nihilism. As he struggles between these conflicting viewpoints, Judah is also torn between his initiative towards self-preservation and his guilt over killing someone he once loved. Ben warns Judah against murder, telling him, "Without the law it's all darkness." Judah responds, "You sound just like my father." Later on, Judah's internal image of his father invokes a similar warning: "The wicked will be punished." Both of these interchangeable representations of the conscience express Judah's lingering belief in the necessity of "a moral structure, with real meaning, and forgiveness, and some kind of higher power, otherwise there's no basis to know how to live." Yet darkness and wickedness are becoming the dominating powers in Judah's world. He quickly loses his ability to see the existence of the "moral structure" that was instilled in him as a boy.

Moral Darkness

Darkness and blindness are common symbolic threads running through the film. Judah is an opthamologist. He is an expert in the field of seeing, yet he cannot see a moral way out of his dilemma. Judah's patient, Ben, is going blind. There is no irony lost on the fact that the one character in the film who is completely good and free of sin should be inflicted with blindness, a malady closely associated with divine retribution. But the "curse" is strangely appropriate, as Ben's concept of religion is the acceptance of an all-seeing God based on blind faith. Judah is torn between his own path of agnosticism and his father's path of blindness to the horrible truths of existence, epitomized in his statement: "In the end, I will always choose God over the truth."

The B-plot of the film centers on Clifford (Woody Allen). Clifford hates his brother-in-law Lester (Alan Alda), an annoying, pushy, self-centered and arrogant character who is nevertheless incredibly successful. In a tangential but memorable scene, Clifford visits his sister who tells him a disturbing story about being defecated upon by a demented blind date. Ben's dreadful blindness, Lester's undeserved success and Clifford's innocent sister's unbearable ordeal all reveal a world that is glaringly absent of any real morality or justice. As Judah sees it, the world is an inherently amoral place. When Ben asks Judah, "Don't you think God sees?", Judah replies, "God is a luxury I can't afford." Ben and his father live in "the kingdom of heaven," while Judah and Jack live in the "real world"—a dark place inhabited by sick and depraved degenerates, who do awful and disgusting things to innocent people, and get away with it scot-free.

In the final act of the film, after Dolores is rubbed out, Judah feels a desperate urge to confess. At this point, thousands of years of mythology, religion and morality are weighing down upon him, telling him that he must offer a sacrifice to the gods in order to repent his sin and free his soul. Since Judah destroyed a life, he must sacrifice his own life in order to make things right. But Judah never gives in to his desire for self-sacrifice. He never confesses. The film ends in a brilliant twist. Judah and Clifford meet at a wedding and Judah discusses his story as if it were an idea for a movie plot:

> ...and after the awful deed is done, he finds that he's plagued by deep-rooted guilt ... He hears his father's voice and imagines that God is watching his every move. Suddenly it's not an empty universe anymore but a just and moral one.... Mysteriously the crisis is lifted ... he's not punished, in fact he prospers ... now he's scot-free ... back to his protected world of wealth and privilege.

As a filmmaker, Clifford explains to Judah that the character in his film should get caught, or that he should either confess or somehow sacrifice himself, in order for the plot structure to work. Judah nearly gives himself away, saying that he's talking about "the real world" and not fantasy, but he catches himself. He walks off and kisses his beautiful wife. He is a happy and unrepentant sinner. The lack of sacrifice in Judah's story shows how important the sacrifice theme is in the morality and character development of heroes in film, and how divergent this theme is from morality and character development in real life.

God the Father

Sacrifice symbolism also draws out the figurative relationship between God and Man. This relationship, in turn, recapitulates the primary psychological relationship between father and son. There is an Oedipal quality in the son-sacrifice theme — a menacing father destroying his heir and rival — which links the psychoanalytic interpretations of the Oedipus myth and the Hero myth to the religious symbolism in the relationship between God-the-Father and Man-the-Son. Hence, the primal fear of father and paternal punishment (castration anxiety) becomes generalized into a secondary fear of God and eternal punishment (hell anxiety). The designation of the title "Father" for Catholic priests is a clear sign of the ubiquitous God-the-Father symbolism. The representation of the father as the embodiment of God and religious faith is apparent in films such as *Malcolm X* (1992), *The Jazz Singer* (1927) and *Of Human Hearts* (1938). In these films, the relationship's between the sons (Denzel Washington, Al Jolson and James Stewart) and their fathers (Tommy Hollis, Warner Oland and Walter Huston) directly parallel their relationships with God. The further the sons move away from their fathers, the further they move away from God.

Mother Nature

During infancy, the mother is associated with the natural impulses of the infant. The desires for food, warmth, comfort, love, nurturing — the physical and emotional needs — are initially directed towards the mother. As the child grows, it must integrate the unnatural restrictions of society such as control of the body functions, repression of desire, delaying of pleasure, etc. The father, as the traditional disciplinarian, is associated with these societal restrictions. In this sense, the archetypal mother is unconsciously associated with nature, and the archetypal father is unconsciously associated with rules, society and punishment. These associations have become transfigured into the collective unconscious in the archetypes of the Earth Goddess, Mother Nature, Fertile Maiden, Mother Madonna and Love Goddess as the symbolic representations of the mother figure. The archetypes of the Wise Old Man, the God of Judgment, the Wrathful God, the God of Social Order and God the Father are the symbolic representations of the father figure in the collective unconscious.

The Mother/Nature associations and Father/Society associations are archetypes that have been projected from the personal conscious of infantile memories into the collective unconscious of gods and goddesses. Joseph Campbell and other mythologists have noted that prehistoric and primitive societies typically have female deities and goddesses as their primary religious figures, as these societies are completely dependent on weather, nature and the fertility of the land for their survival. But as ancient societies became more "civilized," progressing into the age of kingdoms and city-states, the primary religious figures became male gods rather than female goddesses. Through the establishment of the priestly class, religious devotion became directed towards societal rules, laws and doctrines—elements of society controlled by males in patriarchal cultures. In this sense, the Judeo-Christian tradition represents the divine as male, and the pre–Judeo-Christian traditions represented the divine as either male, female or both. Since film in the twentieth century was mainly a product of patriarchal Judeo-Christian societies, most symbols of female or pluralistic divinity, the "pagan," have been represented as being evil or malevolent. They have been represented as wicked witches, evil sorceresses, demons, devils and monsters of every kind. Ironically, the only positive images of female divinity have come from the ultra-conservative Disney corporation, which supplied the American collective unconscious with kindly fairy godmothers in films such as *Pinocchio, Sleeping Beauty* and *Cinderella*. Nevertheless, pagan deities—especially in horror movies—have been unilaterally depicted as the epitome of depravity, unholiness and wicked malevolence.

Pagan Rites

God and religion are typically depicted as straightforward and unambiguously good forces in the horror movie genre. With the exception of the biblical epics, there is no other setting is which Christianity is seen as an absolutely pure power of righteousness. Movies with satanic villains such as *Rosemary's Baby* (1968), *The Exorcist* (1973) and *The Omen* (1976) represent the opposing force to religion. They are purely evil, base and corrupt forces. In a Jungian sense, the Devil is the Shadow side of the God archetype, the opposing force of evil to God's force of pure good. The satanic rituals in devil movies, the "Black Sabbaths," are perverse inversions of Christian masses. Wine and debauchery are central parts of the ceremony, rather than a symbolic sipping of the vestal wine. Nudity, sex and sadomasochism are also overt parts of the ritual, physical celebrations of the visceral elements that are figuratively embodied in the Catholic vestige of the bloody, suffering, half-naked Jesus dying on the cross. Also, real blood is used in the satanic rituals, rather than symbolic blood in the form of wine. And finally, an actual human sacrifice is at the core of the ritual, rather than the symbolic remembrance of the sacrifice of Jesus at the cross.

On a different level, the satanic rituals recall the Dionysian rites of

the Greek cults and primeval pagans that predate Christianity, yet somehow linger in the collective unconscious of both the religion and the people who believe in it. The link between Christianity and its pagan
precursors is experienced through the ritual, the symbolic connection
between humans and their gods. The ritual and the transcendent function
it offers is much older than modern Judaism or Christianity. The purpose
of the ritual is to create a metaphysical connection between Man and his
gods. Rituals in "primitive" tribes use blood, sex, dancing, human sacrifice,
music, liquor and drugs to achieve states of higher or altered consciousness, in which the gods are encountered.

Rituals in "civilized" cultures are sanitized in order to conform to the
prudish sanctions of refined society. Liquor and drugs are minimized into
nominal, symbolic sips of vestal wine. Sexuality and sadomasochism are
sublimated into passionate prayer, sycophantic benedictions, torturous
kneeling and submissive postures in the pews. Wild dancing is conformed
into ordered processions. Rhythmic, primal music is systematized into
sophisticated organ fugues. Spirited, animalistic singing and shouting is
domesticated into unison singing of hymns and psalms. And the central
symbol of the ritual — the human sacrifice — is only alluded to in refer-
ences to Jesus and God, and Abraham and Isaac. Nevertheless, both the
primitive ritual and the civilized church or temple service serve the same
transcendent function. And though the visceral pleasures of the primeval
rites are only symbolically alive in contemporary temples and churches,
they are still very much alive in our collective unconscious.

However, since the pagan rites are not Jewish or Christian; since the
pagan rites celebrate pantheistic gods of the earth, rather than a monothe-
istic God of heaven; since they represent "primitive" belief systems rather
than "civilized" faith; and since the pagan rites represent sexuality, impul-
siveness and physical pleasure rather than repression, submission and guilt,
the archaic memories of pagan rites are typecast in films as supplications
to the devil rather than services to gods. Instead of seeing the pagan rites
as precursors to modern religion, they are cast as the opposites of religion.
Rather than holy, they are "unholy." Rather than good, they are evil.

The Devil Archetype

The European inquisitions of the Dark and Middle Ages were aimed
at stamping out the ancient pagan beliefs. The heretics and witches were
tortured and executed in incredibly sadistic ways that ironically recap-
tured the perverse elements of sadomasochism and human sacrifice within

the pagan rites that the inquisitions were trying to eliminate. The movement to erase the pagan precursors to Christianity is not dead. The movement has become internalized in the Western world's collective unconscious in the form of the devil archetype. All of the fears, desires and repressed associations within the collective unconscious that are related to paganism are embodied within the Satan figure.

Satan is a man-beast — he has a human torso and head, with hoofed feet, horns and a spiked tail. For the pagan cultures, the man-beast archetype represented an anthropomorphous mixture of human and animal qualities. The man-beast represented the divine combination of human intellect with animal physicality and intuition. Animals in primitive and archaic religions were not considered lesser form of life (i.e., "dumb animals"). In pagan religions, animals were respected and often worshipped as spiritual beings who carried intuitive wisdom and a sacred spiritual essence. The sacrifice for pagans was a consecrated act of releasing the inner spirit of the beast, so it could join with the larger communal spirit. The drinking of the animal's blood was a symbolic integration of the animal's sacred essence. The man-beast was a holy symbol for the pagans, corrupted into a symbol of evil and unholiness by Catholic priests in the Dark and Middle Ages.

Satan is also a god of the earth, residing either on the surface of the earth — in forests or caves — or beneath the earth in the demonic regions of Hell. In this sense, Satan is a direct recasting of Hades and Pluto, the Greek and Roman gods of the underworld. But while Hades was a brother of the gods who was capable of both good and evil, Satan is a former angel who rebelled against God. Therefore, Satan is completely evil, because God is completely good. The fundamental duality of Judeo-Christian thought — the conflict of complete opposites — creates these extreme archetypes. The pagan gods were more human. They had physical desires for sex and wine. They had human weaknesses and faults such as greed, vanity, lust and pride. The Judeo-Christian God, on the other hand, is not human. He is completely good and entirely spiritual, resulting in the necessity of an opposing archetype that encapsulates all of the negative qualities of the human race, the archetype of evil thoughts and depraved deeds.

Pagan Vampires

The devil is often recast as the vampire in movies — another primordial archetype that predates Christianity. The vampire in *Dracula* (1931) is a pagan deity, a Shadow God who is immortal, craves human blood and demands human sacrifice. He is also a shapeshifting man-beast, able to transfigure from human to animal like Zeus or Hades. Naturally, the forces of Christianity that repel and destroy Satan can also repel and destroy the vampire. A wooden stake, the symbol of the holy cross, driven through the vampire's heart will kill him. The cross itself will repel the vampire, while other Christian vestiges such as holy water and the holy ground of a churchyard hamper the pagan monster.

It is interesting to note that the sun, the most ancient and most powerful of the pagan gods, can also kill the vampire. In the first feature length vampire movie, *Nosferatu* (1922), Count Orlok (Max Shrek) is evaporated by the rays of the morning sun. This may be because Jesus (the "Son") was in many ways recast by the Roman Catholic tradition as the replacement figure to Apollo, the Roman solar god (the "Sun"). Hence the designation of the ancient festival of the winter solstice, once dedicated to Apollo, as Christmas. It is also interesting to note that in Tod Browning's original 1931 production of *Dracula*, the count prominently wears a six-pointed Star of David emblem on his chest. Was this an accident? A subliminal anti–Semitic gesture? Or possibly a sanitized allusion to the Star of Satan, the five pointed pentagram?

Pagan Frankenstein

There is also a bounty of overt religious symbolism in the Frankenstein movies. The central symbolism in these films relates to Dr. Frankenstein's sacrilegious experiments. As "the modern Prometheus," he plays with the fire of the gods and so must eventually get burned. His unholy creation is a sympathetic creature, like Jesus. Frankenstein's monster is resurrected from dead bodies taken from the gallows, just as Jesus himself was resurrected after being executed at the cross. At the end of *Frankenstein* (1931), the monster is strapped to a post and carried off by a mob of villagers in a crucifixion pose. And at the end of *Bride of Frankenstein* (1935), the monster destroys himself—sacrificing his own body after accepting the realization that his own existence is an affront to God.

Pagan Monsters

Movie monsters in their many forms recapitulate unconscious images from our pagan past. In *Dr. Jekyll and Mr. Hyde* (1920), Dr. Jekyll's physical regression from Jekyll to Hyde is also a symbolic regression from civilized and repressed Christian to primitive and impulsive man-beast — the primary archetype of paganism. In *The Wolf Man* (1941), the werewolf is a shapeshifting man-beast. His supernatural curse, his craving for human blood, and his unbridled lust and violence are pure representations of the unrepressed pagan rites that linger as archaic memories in the collective unconscious. The monster in *The Mummy* (1932) is a worshiper of ancient

Egyptian gods. Through his curse and resurrection, the Mummy becomes a walking representation of supernatural pagan powers. The Witch in *Snow White and the Seven Dwarfs, Sleeping Beauty* and *The Wizard of Oz*, whether an actual servant of Satan or an independent practitioner of the Dark Arts, is the evil feminine archetype — the Shadow Goddess— who is a direct vestige of the witch priestesses and sorcerer goddesses of the ancient pagan cults.

The Devil's Children

Movies with demonic children such as *The Exorcist, The Omen, The Damned* (1962) and *Children of the Corn* (1984) represent the need to instill wholesome Christian values in today's children. Traditional Christian doctrine maintains that all humans are born in sin, and that children retain the stain of this "original sin" in their souls. The sign of the original sin is apparent in the child's naughty behaviors and evil desires. Hence, the traditional way to save the child's soul was to "beat the devil out of him." The violence directed at the "devil's children" in these movies recasts this ancient tradition of holy child abuse in the form of "exorcism." The frequent reappearance of the demonic child in horror movies is a statement to the lingering belief in original sin, as well as the prevalence of the devil archetype within the filmgoers' collective unconscious.

The Deluge Archetype

Joseph Campbell was just one of the many mythologists who have pointed out the ubiquitous existence of the Flood Myth in the legends and creation stories of cultures throughout the world. Nearly every culture has a myth in which the world was either created or recreated through a primeval worldwide flood. The primeval flood marks a transition between the antediluvian (before flood) world and the re-created world after the flood. In Judeo-Christian tradition, the Bible clearly expresses the notion that the flood was intended to wash out all of the pantheistic and pagan elements on earth:

> When men began to increase in number on the earth and daughters were born to them, the sons of God saw that the daughters of men were beautiful, and they married any of them they chose ... [Genesis 6:1–2].

This passage is probably an allusion to the Greek gods such as Zeus and Hades, who were notorious for seducing young nubile mortal girls. Note that in the antediluvian age, God was not the sole divinity — he had "sons." The notion of pluralistic divinity would not be broached again until the New Testament, when God, briefly, experiences fatherhood again.

> ...The Nephilim were on the earth in those days—and also afterward— when the sons of God went to the daughters of men and had children by them. They were the heroes of old, men of renown ... [Genesis 6:4].

Here the bible alludes to semi-divine figures and creatures. The "Nephilim" in Hebrew translates into "the fallen ones." These figures are typically interpreted as fallen divine figures, such as the Titans in Greek mythology, the race of Cyclops or other versions of the archetypal lost race of giants. Another interpretation is that the Nephilim were the semi-divine man-beast creatures of ancient myth, such as minotaurs and centaurs. The "heroes of old" are a clear reference to the semi-divine classical heroes of ancient Greek mythology such as Hercules or Perseus.

> So the Lord said, "I will wipe mankind, whom I have created, from the face of the earth—men and animals, and creatures that move along the ground, and birds of the air—for I am grieved that I have made them" [Genesis 6:7].

The Lord, the "one true God," decides to eliminate all of his divine and semi-divine rivals. He washes out the old gods and establishes a new covenant with Noah based on monotheism rather than pantheism.

> Every living thing that moved on the earth perished—birds, livestock, wild animals, all the creatures that swarm over the earth, and all mankind. Everything on dry land that had the breath of life in its nostrils died. Every living thing on the face of the earth was wiped out; men and animals and the creatures that move along the ground and the birds of the air were wiped from the earth. Only Noah was left, and those with him in the ark [Genesis 7:21–23].

Here it is made clear that all things old are gone. Mythical creatures such as unicorns, dragons, giants and man-beasts, as well as supernatural shadow beings such as demons, ghosts, specters and spirits were driven from the earth. But, while the antediluvian figures were flooded over in the conscious mind, the memories may still exist underneath the flood-waters—buried deep within the psyche as primeval memories, ancestral experiences, primordial images and archetypes within the collective unconscious.

> Then Noah built an altar to the Lord and, taking some of all the clean animals and clean birds, he sacrificed burnt offerings on it. The Lord smelled the pleasing aroma and said in his heart: "Never again will I curse the ground because of man, even though every inclination of his heart is evil from childhood. And never again will I destroy all living creatures, as I have done" [Genesis 8:20–21].

After emerging from the ark, Noah pays tribute to his god in the traditional pagan way, through a sacrificed burnt offering. Sacrifice will remain the primary form of worship in the Judaic tradition until the destruction of the Second Temple by the Romans in A.D. 70. Modern Jewish services are merely symbolic representations of the ceremonial animal sacrifices and burnt offerings, which (according to Orthodox tradition) will resume when the Messiah comes and the Third Holy Temple is constructed in Jerusalem. It is also interesting to note God's estimate of humanity: "every inclination of his heart is evil from childhood." This passage, no doubt, had a profound influence on the concept of original sin and the consequent abusive treatment of children in the Judeo-Christian tradition.

> ...you must not eat meat that has its lifeblood still in it. And for your lifeblood I will surely demand an accounting. I will demand an accounting from every animal. And from each man, too, I will demand an accounting for the life of his fellow man [Genesis 9:4–5].

The drinking of the lifeblood of the animal sacrifice was an integral part of the pagan blood ritual — the moment in which Man becomes one with the animal, integrating its spiritual essence. In the passage above, God is establishing his formal covenant with Noah. As an initial clause, God clearly forbids the drinking of blood and the practice of human sacrifice — mainstays of the antediluvian pagan rites. (Oddly enough, God forgets the ban a few chapters later when he asks Abraham to sacrifice his own son to him).

> Noah, a man of the soil, proceeded to plant a vineyard. When he drank some of its wine, he became drunk and lay uncovered inside his tent. Ham, the father of Canaan, saw his father's nakedness and told his two brothers outside. But Shem and Japheth took a garment and laid it across their shoulders; then they walked in backward and covered their father's nakedness. Their faces were turned the other way so that they would not see their father's nakedness. When Noah awoke from his wine and found out what his youngest son had done to him, he said, "Cursed be Canaan! The lowest of slaves will he be to his brothers" [Genesis 9:20–25].

In this passage, we see Noah being punished for his regressive ways. The antediluvian world, as depicted so magically in the Pastoral Symphony segment of Disney's *Fantasia* (1940), was a fantasy world of Dionysian indulgence. Wine flowed like water in those days. Noah's indulgent tastes lead him to a drunken stupor. The traditional interpretation of this passage is that Noah, while passed out drunk, is emasculated by his youngest son, who wants to make sure that Noah bears no more rival heirs who will claim ownership to the world. So, the first bible story of the post-flood era is both a denouncement of pagan debauchery and a rather bawdy, Oedipal-tinged tale of father-son antagonism.

The Unconscious Flood

The abundant psychological symbolism related to the archetypal deluge myth is apparent in all literature and works of art, especially in film. Floodwaters and oceans are widespread symbols of the unconscious in movies, especially in the "psychological thriller" genre. In *What Lies Beneath* (2000), a menacing bathtub represents the protagonist's unconscious mind. When the tub is filled with water, the ghosts and shadows from her unconscious come flowing out. In *In Dreams* (1999), an abused boy is abandoned in his hometown, which is then flooded in a manmade deluge. When the boy grows up to be a serial killer (Robert Downey Jr.), the traumatic flood from his youth gives him the power to travel through the dream world of the collective unconscious. He can travel into people's dreams and lure them into his underwater world of death. And in *Artificial Intelligence: AI* (2001), David's (Haley Joel Osment) journey ends underneath the waters of a flooded New York City. The goddess figure he encounters, The Blue Fairy, resides at the bottom of the flood. She is at the center of the unconscious world into which David has descended. There, underneath the endless floodwater of time and consciousness— where myth and dream meet — David's most cherished memories and deepest wishes come to life.

6

The Monomyth

Joseph Campbell was born in New York City in 1904. He was educated at Columbia University, where he specialized in medieval literature and was a star runner on the track team. After earning his master's degree, he studied at the universities of Paris and Munich, where he became immersed in the theories of Freud and Jung and the novels of Thomas Mann. In his mid–20s, Campbell abandoned his Ph.D. studies because he found them to be intellectually limiting. He then lived a "maverick's" life for the next five years: reading in a cabin in the woods of Woodstock, writing short stories, road tripping across the country, playing saxophone in jazz bars, but spending most of his time immersed in the classics.

Campbell became an eminent scholar during his tenure as Professor of Comparative Literature and Mythology at Sarah Lawrence College from 1934 to 1972. It was there that he met and married Jean Erdman, his former student and a member of the Martha Graham Dance Company. In 1949, Campbell wrote *The Hero with a Thousand Faces*, a classic study of psychology and comparative mythology. His later books include the four-volume *Masks of God* (1959–1967), *The Flight of the Wild Gander* (1969), and *The Mythic Image* (1974). In 1987, an extremely popular television series aired on PBS, in which Campbell was interviewed by Bill Moyers. *The Power of Myth* was filmed at George Lucas's Skywalker Ranch, signifying Campbell's enormous inspiration on the mythological structure of Lucas's *Star Wars* films. The television interviews introduced Campbell's theories to millions of people. The six-episode series is often re-aired on PBS and it has also become a bestseller in both book and video format, assuring that Campbell's ideas will live on to inspire future generations of writers, storytellers and filmmakers. Joseph Campbell died in his home in Honolulu, Hawaii, in 1987, shortly after the initial airing of *The Power of Myth*.

The universal quality of mythology is revealed in the archetypal figures and themes that pervade the myth. An inherent structure can be perceived throughout all mythology. Campbell called this universal structure the "monomyth," a term that he borrowed from James Joyce's *Finnegan's Wake*. The monomyth is a single structure, just as the hero is a single figure. Just as the hero has a "thousand faces," the myth has a thousand plots. In turn, both the hero and his myth share common archetypal elements. These elements were broken down by Campbell and structured in his model of the adventure of the hero. The most basic commonality behind all mythic structure is the symbolism behind the hero's journey, which is the same as the symbolism behind the dream. Each stage of the hero's adventure relates directly to the identity development of the hero's character. The key to the hero's adventure is that the protagonist is not a hero in the beginning—he must *become* a hero through the process of his journey. This transformation resonates with all people, because every human being must at one point in their life experience a similar identity transformation from boy into man, girl into woman, apprentice into master, etc.

The Hero's Departure

At the first stage, the emergent hero is in the "world of the common day." The story begins by pulling him out of his comfortable home by presenting a goal or quest. This is the "call to adventure," typically made by the mentor figure, or a "herald" sent by the mentor to deliver the call. The traditional call plays upon the emergent hero's sense of honor. The hero's call to arms against a menacing foe is a universal theme, as every young man throughout history has been expected to answer his nation's call in a time of war. The call to adventure often evokes deep feelings of loyalty and patriotism.

In *Star Wars*, Luke was not particularly interested in the struggle between the evil Empire and the desperate rebel forces. His call comes when he sees a maiden in distress, a hologram of Princess Leia, who is being held prisoner by the monstrous Darth Vader. Though his mentor, Obi-Wan, speaks of the righteous war against Vader and the Emperor, it his sense of chivalry that inspires Luke to take the journey. Luke's call to adventure is reminiscent of a ubiquitous theme in Anglo-Saxon legends, in which the young squire sets off to save the maiden in distress, who is imprisoned in the dragon's lair. In order to slay the dragon, the squire must first become a knight. Young Luke sets off to rescue the Princess Leia (Carrie Fisher), but before he can defeat Darth Vader, he must learn the skills of the Jedi knight from his mentor, Obi-Wan.

Campbell noted that the hero rarely accepts the call immediately. The emergent hero's reluctance to step out onto the treacherous path of identity development mirrors the same psychological reluctance we all feel at times of identity crisis in our own lives. Many of us were reluctant to leave high school (the world we knew) for college or the work world (the world of the unknown). Many brides and grooms experience cold feet on the eve of their wedding days, afraid of leaving behind their single lives for the very different world of marriage. And of course, young soldiers might be very wary of leaving behind the safety of home for the dangers of the battlefield. The "refusal of the call" is the second archetypal stage of the hero's journey.

Reluctance itself depicts a flawed part of the emergent hero's personality that must be changed. Fear and avoidance is a boyish quality. The hero must learn to overcome his fear and face the monster, beast or enemy with courage. The issue of bravery, the first archetypal element of the hero's character, is dealt with at this crucial stage. Without courage, the protagonist will never be able to face his foe at the moment of greatest peril. A cowardly hero is virtually non-existent in classical myth and legend.

In some movies, reluctance is the central theme. In *The Sunshine Boys* (1975), the herald character (Richard Benjamin) spends most of the movie trying to get his two heroes (Walter Matthau and George Burns) to accept his call to reunite for one last act. Often times, the hero's reluctance is overcome when the call is made stronger by the enemy. In *The Patriot* (2000), Benjamin Martin (Mel Gibson) doesn't join the American Revolution until a brutal British commander kills his son. In *Casablanca* (1942), Rick (Humphrey Bogart) is initially reluctant to get involved with the French Resistance. His motto is, "I stick my neck out for nobody." But eventually, he not only helps the Resistance, he takes great risks to save the leader of their cause, and he even gives up the love of his life. And finally, in *Star Wars*, Luke doesn't accept Obi-Wan's call to adventure until his aunt and uncle are killed by Storm Troopers. These acts of violence completely destroy the hero's ordinary world. The fabric of the hero's psyche is torn, and it will not be mended until justice is rendered.

Revenge is another extremely motivating force. Entire nations will be moved to war in order to distribute justice for brutal acts. America in particular is a vengeful nation. The idea of not avenging acts of hostility such as the devastation of the Alamo, the sinking of the Maine and the destruction of the World Trade Center is anathema to the American sense of honor and justice. A brutal act committed by the enemy raises the stakes for the hero. Reluctance is no longer an option, as his basic sense of humanity is shocked to the core. He must fight or die—fear and avoidance are out of the question. The vengeance motif is an exceptionally familiar call to adventure in Mel Gibson movies— see *Braveheart* (1995), *The Patriot* (2000), *Mad Max* (1979), *Lethal Weapon* (1987), *Ransom* (1996) and of course *Payback* (1999).

When the stakes are not raised in such a way, when revenge or honor are not called upon, the hero's psyche may be plagued by reluctance and self-doubt throughout his mission. Frodo, in *Lord of the Rings*, is this sort of reluctant hero. At every step of his journey, Frodo questions his own abilities and his own dedication to his task. Until the end, he is never quite sure that he should be the "Ringbearer"— the one person destined to destroy the ring of power. His reluctance is reminiscent of Moses' self doubt in *The Ten Commandments*. Moses was constantly asking God if he was really the best-suited individual to deliver the Israelites from bondage. Self-doubt or a basic lack of confidence in one's self is the second basic character flaw that the hero must overcome. The great enemy cannot be defeated unless the hero has unflinching confidence in his ability to succeed. Often times, the hero does not display complete and utter self-confidence until the final moment of truth, when failure would result in certain death.

Guns and Knives

Once the hero accepts the call, he must equip himself with powerful weapons. The weapons of power are typically bestowed by the mentor, and often have a supernatural or divine force behind them. Campbell referred to this stage as *supernatural aid*. In *Lord of the Rings*, the mystical ring of power simultaneously represents Frodo's quest and his supernatural aid. Moses' staff was bestowed with divine powers, as was Arthur's sword and Luke's light saber. Sometimes the supernatural aid has a secret or sentimental power that bestows psychological rather than physical strength. In *The Wizard of Oz*, the ruby slippers contain the power to take Dorothy back home to Kansas. However, it is clear that this power is really her own — and that the ruby slippers would not be able to take her home if she had not first defeated the Wicked Witch with her own strength.

The cowboy hero in westerns usually has almost supernatural skills with his weapon of power, the six-shooter. In *The Good the Bad and the Ugly* (1967), the hero (Clint Eastwood) makes a living by rescuing his ally (Eli Wallach) in an unbelievable display of shooting wizardry. He turns in his outlaw friend, collects the reward and leaves town. But just before his ally is hung, the hero shoots through the hangman's rope from a hundred yards away and then shoots the hat off of every man in town. The viewer believes that the hero can accomplish this feat on a regular basis because of the western hero's legendary and supernatural mastery of his gun. Similarly, in *Butch Cassidy and the Sundance Kid* (1969), Sundance (Robert Redford) shoots the gunbelt off of a man's waist, and then shoots the gun across the room. In *Silverado* (1985), the hero's (Scott Glenn) target practice consists of shooting every petal off of a wildflower from forty paces away. The godly shooting prowess of the western gunslinger is reminiscent of the powers of mythological swordsman heroes such as Perseus and Arthur.

Crossing the First Threshold

The hero's departure from home into the world of mystery and danger is a monumental moment in his identity development. He and his audience must be aware of the awesome change in environment that the hero is experiencing. In our own world, times of great change are marked by special ceremonies: birthday parties, graduations, weddings, anniversaries and funerals. For the hero, *the crossing of the first threshold* into the world of adventure is a significant transition. In *The Lord of the Rings*, Frodo's faithful sidekick Sam (Sean Astin) takes time to acknowledge the moment when they have gone farther away from their home than they've ever gone before. At that moment, the crossing doesn't seem so significant, but it soon becomes apparent that their environment has transformed from a world of safety and tranquility to a world of peril and danger.

The crossing is often marked by an encounter with a *threshold guardian*. This archetypal figure represents a barrier or obstacle that the hero must pass as a first test or initiation into the world of adventure. In *The Lord of the Rings*, the heroes must solve a riddle, which will open the Gates of Moria, while also evading the lake monster that protects the gate. This test of intellect is reminiscent of the riddle of the Sphinx from the Oedipus myth. The Sphinx is a threshold guardian who gives Oedipus two choices: either solve her riddle and pass freely, or be destroyed. By navigating around the threshold guardian, the hero demonstrates two more essential qualities of the hero archetype — intelligence and determination.

Typically, the threshold guardian is an ancient mystical force that is incredibly powerful, but disinterested in character. The guardian is neither friend nor foe, just an obstacle to be overcome. It's too early for the emergent hero to risk a great battle. He is not yet strong enough. The guardian must either be appeased or avoided. In *Clash of the Titans* (1981), Perseus (Harry Hamlin) must pass a host of disinterested threshold guardians, including the three-headed dog Cerberus, the Gorgon Medusa and Charon — the skeletal ferryman on the river Styx. In *The Wizard of*

Oz, Dorothy and her allies are faced with a trickster gatekeeper at the entrance to Oz. They must get past this fickle gatekeeper by telling him the exact right things that will persuade him to open the door.

Often times, nature itself plays the role of the disinterested but omnipotent gatekeeper. In *Red River* (1948), the heroes and their herd of cattle must cross a wide river as their first obstacle. In *Bridge on the River Kwai* (1957), the heroes must cross through a thick, hot and enemy infested jungle before reaching their battleground at the river. In director David Lean's next epic, *Lawrence of Arabia* (1962), Lawrence (Peter O'Toole) must cross through the unpassable Nefu desert before engaging his first enemy at Akkabah. And in Lean's third epic, *Doctor Zhivago* (1965), the hero (Omar Sharif) must cross the vast Siberian tundra before his real journey begins. Whether the threshold guardian is nature or beast, it imparts an important lesson. The guardian teaches the young hero to have respect for forces that are older and more powerful than him.

After crossing the first threshold, the hero is in *the belly of the whale*— the world of adventure. In the archetypal rendition of this theme, the hero must make a fire in order to create the smoke that will cause the whale to sneeze and expel the hero from his belly. According to Campbell, the act of fire making is symbolic of the sex act. The spindle-stick (the male) is inserted into the socket-stick (the female), and the two are rubbed together until a flame is born. In this sense, the belly of the whale represents a womb. It is a realm of identity transformation in which the hero will become reborn.

Analyzing the Departure

The Ten Commandments

After a rather lengthy telling of the myth of the birth of Moses— involving a prophecy, separation from his parents and a royal heritage — Moses kills an Egyptian slave driver who was whipping an Israelite. Moses leaves Egypt and lives for many years in his adopted common world, as a poor shepherd in the Sinai wilderness. One day he encounters a divine presence, who speaks to him through a burning bush on Mt. Sinai. This mentor figure tells him that he must go to Egypt, liberate the Israelites from bondage and bring them to the mountain so they could receive God's laws. At first, Moses refuses God's call to adventure, finding it hard to believe that a regular Joe like him could be the great Messiah. But God can be very convincing. Moses accepts his call. He crosses the first threshold of the Red

Sea and goes right into the belly of the whale, the Pharaoh's palace, to deliver God's message. Moses displays the supernatural aid that his mentor provided him by turning his staff into a serpent, but the unimpressed Pharaoh still turns down his request.

Excalibur

After a similar telling of the myth of the birth of Arthur — which also involves a prophecy, separation from his parents and a royal heritage — Arthur is in his common day world, a young squire to his brother Kay. On the morning of the big joust, Arthur loses his brother's sword. In desperation, Arthur tugs at the "sword of kings" — Excalibur — and pulls it out of the stone. He knows that this means that he is the one true heir to the throne, but he refuses this call to adventure and gives Excalibur to Kay. Honest Kay admits that Arthur was the one who drew Excalibur from the stone, and though the other knights do not believe it could be true, Arthur places Excalibur back in the stone and draws it out again. Merlin the wizard, Arthur's mentor, appears on the scene and informs young Arthur that he must become the king. However, many of the other knights refuse to bow to this pimple-faced squire. Excalibur or no Excalibur, "he is not worthy to be king," they insist. So Arthur must cross his first threshold bearing the supernatural aid of Excalibur. He enters into the belly of the whale, the field of mortal combat.

Star Wars

Luke's world of the common day is a quiet, dreary desert planet on the outskirts of the galaxy. Young Luke wants nothing more than to leave his boring life as a farmer and start a new adult life of adventure as a pilot in the Academy. His psychological desire is addressed when a new droid shows him a call to adventure — a hologram from a maiden in distress. R2-D2, the rebellious droid, plays the role of the herald. Not only does he carry the hologram from Princess Leia, but he also leads Luke to his mentor, Obi-Wan, who supplies Luke with some supernatural aid. The light saber is not only a deadly weapon, but a symbol of Luke's identity. The light saber belonged to Anakin, Luke's father, and it is a physical link between Luke's father and his destiny as a great Jedi knight. At first, Luke refuses the call to adventure. However, when Imperial Storm Troopers destroy Luke's home and kill his aunt and uncle, Luke has no choice. He accepts the call and follows his mentor on the path to adventure, armed with his light saber and a desire to form a new identity as a Jedi knight.

The Lord of the Rings

Frodo is a normal, unassuming young hobbit, quite content in his world of the common day — his quiet, bucolic little village in the Shire. The only adventures that he's interested in are the ones in the stories told to him by his beloved Uncle Bilbo. But his tranquil life is disturbed when Gandalf the Wizard comes to town. It seems that Bilbo's little golden ring is actually the one unifying ring of power, the ring that Sauron needs to destroy his enemies and become the Dark Lord over all of Middle Earth. At first, Frodo refuses the call of his mentor to carry the ring out of the Shire, where it is no longer safe. But he soon agrees, tentatively, to bear the ring as far as Bree, the outpost town located just outside of the Shire. With the ring as both his supernatural aid and his heroic burden, Frodo crosses the first threshold out of the Shire, along with his faithful ally and sidekick, Sam. Soon they are joined by two more allies, the young and eager hobbits Merry and Pippin.

The Hero's Initiation

In the middle stages of his journey, the young squire learns the skills and wisdom that initiate him into the field of heroism. Though the hero faces many tests and obstacles, he does not become a true hero until the end of these stages, when he confronts and overcomes his deepest fear.

Once the hero has accepted his call and sets out on his journey, he must gather some allies and a means of transport to get him to his final destination. This stage of the journey is the hero's first stop on his *road of trials*. It's a long and rough road, fraught with hardships and perils, so why not have a little drink first? Just as the first stop on the journey for the ancient hunting parties was the watering hole, the first stop for the hero and his mentor is the saloon. As the hero and his mentor have "one for the road" in the rowdy bar, tavern or saloon that invariably exists in the first outpost of the uncivilized world, he comes into contact with a brand new type of person. The men in the outpost tavern are adventurers, warriors and journeymen — not the simple folk the hero knew in his sleepy hometown. In *Moby Dick* (1956) and *Treasure Island* (1950), the tough seaport towns are where the hero first comes into contact with the dangerous sailors and crusty old sea dogs with whom he'll become acquainted on his journey. They are a glimpse not only of his future, but of his destiny as well.

The hero is at first overwhelmed and scared, but he must overcome his naiveté and keep his business in mind. If he gets pulled into a fight, he'll have to show his mettle long before he's ready for such a challenge. This is what happens to Luke in *Star Wars*. He and Obi-Wan are at the tavern to find a ship and pilot to take them off the planet. A rough looking alien picks a fight with Luke simply because he doesn't like his face. The young squire would have found a quick end if he didn't have Obi-Wan watching his back. Similarly, in *The Lord of the Rings*, Frodo and his hobbit companions would not have lasted long at The Prancing Pony, the tough tavern in the outpost town of Bree, if their new ally, Aragorn (Viggo Mortensen), wasn't there to protect them.

The stage in which the hero or mentor gathers allies is often one of the most engaging sequences in the film. When Jason in *Jason and the Argonauts* (1963) accepts the call to seek the Golden Fleece, he spends a good deal of time gathering the bravest heroes in all of Greece — classical heroes such as Theseus, Hercules, Orpheus and others. In Akira Kurosawa's classic *The Seven Samurai* (1954), much of the movie is dedicated to the gathering of the hero warriors. The same structure was adopted in the famous American remake of Kurosawa's film, *The Magnificent Seven* (1960).

The hero must also obtain transport at the first outpost. Jason's first step was to hire the famous shipbuilder Argo to create his heroic vessel, hence the name of Jason's allies— the "Argonauts." Odysseus also gathered the best ship and crew before setting sail on his epic journey. In the modern myth, Luke manages to find an able ship, the Millennium Falcon, along with a crew, Han Solo (Harrison Ford) and Chewbacca. Similarly, at The Prancing Pony, the hobbits in *The Lord of the Rings* gain Aragorn as their guide. Regardless of the number of allies needed, by gathering his crew of heroes and guiding them into adventure, the hero demonstrates another essential quality of heroism — leadership.

Epiphany

The road of trials in the Second Act generally leads the hero closer and closer to the central crisis of the film, which is the moment of critical development for the hero. The protagonist completes his arc by achieving a personal revelation that changes him in some significant way. The central crisis or "ordeal" is, in fact, an identity crisis that the hero must resolve in order to complete this stage of the journey and carry on with the rest of his adventure. The change that he undergoes is an "epiphany," a great moment of realization about his own Self. Though the two levels of the story — the internal journey and the external journey — seldom intertwine, the epiphany is the one brief moment in which the fabric of the veil between realism and symbolism tears. The hero can see through the veil of his actions. He gains insight into the psychological symbolism of his mission. The hero realizes that in saving the maiden, hometown, world or universe, he is also saving his own soul. The epiphany is a moment of clarity, a moment of truth and a moment of spiritual awakening. It reveals the hero to himself, unmasking his persona and changing him forever.

EPIPHANY AS ACCEPTANCE OF THE CALL

There is a change in the protagonist's identity that comes about when he accepts the call to adventure and begins to identify himself as an emergent hero. Typically, this change is different from the epiphany that the protagonist undergoes at the climax of his journey, when he identifies himself completely with the fully developed hero archetype, and he experiences a deep revelation about himself, his mission and his purpose in life. However, in some stories, the hero's acceptance of the call represents such a monumental shift in his self-concept that the acceptance is also a full-blown epiphany. This type of structure is common in stories where the hero accepts his call in gradual stages.

At the beginning of Moses' journey in *The Ten Commandments*, Moses is an Egyptian prince who uses and abuses the Israelite slaves as cruelly and selfishly as his brother and father. To fulfill his destiny, Moses must accomplish a complete identity revolution—from Egyptian tyrant to Israelite liberator. His acceptance of his call to liberate the Israelites comes in stages. First, he begins to sympathize with the Israelites. Then he realizes that he actually is an Israelite. Then he abandons his aristocratic position and identifies himself as an Israelite slave. Then he kills an Egyptian slave-master in defense of a fellow Israelite. This act of rebellion leads him to exile in Sinai, where he receives and accepts his call from God to liberate his people. Moses' acceptance of his call is an epiphany, but he has clearly been working towards this identity revolution for many years.

Similarly, in *The Lord of the Rings*, Frodo's acceptance of his call to adventure occurs in stages. First, he agrees to take the ring of power to Bree, a nearby village. Then he is forced to take the ring to Rivendell, a farther and more dangerous journey. At Rivendell, Frodo accepts the call to bear the ring to Mordor, an epic and treacherous journey into the heart of darkness, but he is clearly ambivalent about his new identity as the "Ringbearer." In the subsequent stages of his journey, Frodo expresses constant doubt about his worthiness to bear the ring. He diffuses his responsibility by remaining a member of the Fellowship of the Ring, and he even offers the ring to an elfin queen. Frodo doesn't fully accept his calling as the one true Ringbearer until the end of the first film, when he experiences a personal revelation about the awesome significance of his quest.

Frodo's acceptance of his call is accomplished through an epiphany of identity development.

In other stories, the epiphany and acceptance of the call are simultaneous, resulting in a Third Act which is relatively simple and uncomplicated. In *The Blues Brothers* (1980), the brothers (John Belushi and Dan Ackroyd) experience a jubilant epiphany in a church when they "see the light." After dancing and throwing somersaults and back flips, they accept their call to adventure. The brothers set off on their journey to reunite their band of musician heroes and make the money to pay the back taxes on a Catholic orphanage. After the brothers dedicate themselves to their "mission from God," the film becomes relatively "plot light." Most of the Second Act is filled with entertaining musical numbers, and the entire Third Act is an action-packed chase scene that ends with the brothers paying the taxes and saving the orphans from being evicted. (Incidentally, I don't think the screenwriters realized that Catholic orphanages don't have to pay taxes).

HAMARTIA

The epiphany is not only important in terms of the protagonist's personal development, it is also crucial to the plot. The epiphany allows the protagonist to overcome his hamartia — the personal weakness or tragic character flaw which has been holding the squire back from developing into a full-blown hero. The hamartia isn't a puny everyday flaw such as bad breath or smelly feet. These flaws aren't tragic or deeply personal. The ancient myths really show us what a hamartia is. When Thetis, the sea goddess, dipped her son Achilles into the mystical river Styx, she made his body impervious to any weapon. However, Achilles' heel, which was covered by Thetis's hand, was not immersed in the magic water, so this part of his body was completely vulnerable. Similarly, Superman, a contemporary version of the mythological warrior, had a similar external hamartia — his vulnerability to Kryptonite, the meteorites from Superman's destroyed planet, Krypton. Both of these hamartias are truly personal because they relate directly to the hero's unique backstory.

Typically, the hamartia is an inner flaw or psychological issue rather than an external vulnerability. The psychological hamartia must be resolved through character development. In the Greek myths, the heroes tended to be so great and powerful that their hamartias were their own hubris— the arrogance and conceit a hero develops as a side effect of his superiority over regular mortals. Hubris was the hamartia of Hercules, who would never admit to needing help. Hubris was also seen in the vanity of Narcissus and Cassiopeia, and the egoistic indulgences of Zeus and Aphrodite. Heroes in the Judeo-Christian tradition tend to have a problem contradictory to hubris. Their sense of humility is so great that they cannot believe that they have a divine destiny as the savior of their people. Noah, Moses and Jesus all could not accept the fact of their divinely chosen destinies until their moments of great epiphany.

The modern myths tend to borrow from both the Greek and Judeo-Christian traditions. Frodo Baggins consistently balks at the notion that he, a tiny hobbit, is destined to be the all-important Ringbearer. It seems that Frodo could learn a thing or two from the book of Yoda, the tiny yet incredibly powerful Jedi master who's diminutive size stands in direct contrast to his awesome control of the Force. Similarly, Luke Skywalker finds it hard to believe that he, a rather normal baby-faced boy, is the son of Darth Vader, the omnipotent dark lord of the evil Emperor. Other movie heroes tend to err in the opposite direction. They have too much self-confidence and seem to always take on more than they can chew. Luke's father, Anakin, was plagued with the hamartias of rage and hubris. Like the mighty Hercules, he falls from grace when he decides to release his pent-up anger by fighting all of his enemies single-handedly.

In the very western tradition of independence and rugged individualism, heroes like Lawrence in *Lawrence of Arabia* and General Gordon (Charlton Heston) in *Khartoum* (1966) don't think twice before taking on entire Arab nations without help. In *Lawrence of Arabia,* Lawrence walks arrogantly through an enemy Turkish town without fear of being caught, believing that his self-ordained destiny as the Arab savior would make him invisible. Lawrence's hubris leads to his ordeal, in which he is brutally tortured and raped by a sadistic Turk officer. In an interesting reversal of the archetypal identity theme, Lawrence's epiphany is that he is *not* a divine messiah, but that he is in fact just an "ordinary man." Lawrence's challenge at this stage of his journey is to find a reason to stay committed to his cause, beyond his shattered beliefs in personal destiny and glory. He must redefine himself and his goals in order to carry on.

Goddess and Temptress

In Campbell's model, the stages in which the hero overcomes his hamartia and experiences epiphany are moments in which the hero encounters and integrates the different archetypes of his Self. Each of these encounters develops the hero by adding a fundamental element to his character. In *the meeting with the goddess,* the hero encounters the earth goddess archetype. She is the psychological representation of the mother figure. The goddess typically offers some emotional wisdom or insight. A very common archetype in myth is the "oracle goddess" who provides a prophecy. For example, in *The Lord of the Rings,* Frodo's goddess is Galadriel (Cate Blanchett), the queen of the forest elves. Galadriel allows Frodo to look into her magical mirror, showing him a glimpse of things to come. But the mirror — an archetype in and of itself — is just an illusion. Looking into the mirror only shows the hero what is hidden inside his own mind. Frodo already knows what will happen in the near future, the goddess merely helps him to look inside himself. The function of the prophet goddess's mirror, crystal ball or tarot cards is to help the hero get in touch with wisdom that he already has in his unconscious.

A second archetype that the hero may encounter is the *woman as temptress*. Here, the hero meets up with the anima archetype, the representation of female beauty, sensitivity and passion within the male hero's psyche. Often times, the anima is a temptress who leads the hero away from his destined path and into danger. The beautiful Sirens in Odysseus's journey tempt the hero with their beauty and lure him into danger. In silent movies, female characters were generally either an "ingenue" or a "vamp." The ingenue was the "good girl," the positive version of the anima archetype that the hero will marry in the end. The vamp was the "bad girl," the temptress who was up to no good. She used her sexuality to lure the hero into danger, and she represented most of the negative qualities of femininity. The vamp never wound up with the hero in the end. In *Vanilla Sky*, Sophia (Penélope Cruz) was the good girl, the positive side of the anima. Julie (Cameron Diaz) was the bad girl, the negative side of the anima. In Julie's case, she may also be considered a "femme fatale," another common female archetype, as she represented both feminine sexuality and physical danger.

The male hero's encounter with a feminine figure, whether romantic or spiritual, is also an essential part of the male hero's character development. The mythmakers intuitively understood that in order for their hero to become a fully developed character, he must integrate some feminine personality traits into his own identity. In a similar vein, most Hollywood producers insist that in order for a film to be marketable, the hero must have a viable love interest. Audiences intuitively feel that a story and character are not complete without the essential ingredient of love. After all, what is truly important in life, other than the need to love and to be loved by others? In a Freudian sense, the meeting with the goddess or temptress represents an Oedipal resolution in which the son achieves primary intimacy with the mother. The meeting is a psychological integration that recapitulates the psychosexual state of infancy, in which infant and mother are physically connected within a symbiotic relationship.

In *Star Wars*, Luke's integration of the goddess is symbolized beautifully in the rescue scene, when he clutches the beautiful princess close to his side and swings across a deep chasm to safety. In *The Lord of the Rings,* Aragorn encounters Arwen, an elfin princess who is a temptress as well as a spiritual goddess. In *Excalibur,* the goddess figure — the Lady of the Lake (Telsche Boorman) — is encountered twice. Arthur receives Excalibur from the Lady after he breaks the sword and throws it into the lake, and Perceval gives Excalibur back to the Lady as Arthur dies. In both encounters, the Lady of the Lake provides divine direction for Arthur's journey. Meanwhile, Guenevere (Cherie Lunghi) is the emotional heart of the picture. Arthur becomes a man when he weds the beautiful temptress, Guenevere. He loses his soul when Guenevere betrays him and they become separated, but he is reborn when he forgives Guenevere and she returns Excalibur to him. Though most of the film deals with the heroic acts of Arthur, Lancelot, Merlin, Perceval and other men of action, the axes upon which the entire film turns are the two women — the temptress, Guenevere, and the goddess, the Lady of the Lake.

Atonement

The hero encounters his final archetype, the wise old man, when he experiences an *atonement with the father.* To recall Rank's model, the climax of the hero saga occurs when the hero returns to the land of his father and claims his birthright. The atonement is when the hero confronts his father man-to-man. By confronting his father, he confronts his own identity and achieves the ultimate level of self-awareness and understanding. The stage is an "at-one-ment." The hero becomes "at-one" with his father, thus becoming "at-one" with himself. In Campbell's and Rank's analyses of the hero archetype, the atonement is the peak of the hero's journey and the grand purpose of the entire adventure.

Atonement itself can be achieved in many ways, depending on the story being told. The hero can actually become spiritually united with the father, as Jesus does when he dies and goes to heaven. Spiritual atonement can also occur through the death of the mentor figure. When Obi-Wan sacrifices himself to Darth Vader, he becomes "at-one" with the hero, and Luke carries his spirit inside him for the rest of his journey. The exact same theme is played out in *the Lord of the Rings.* When Gandalf sacrifices himself to the balrog in order to save the Fellowship, he becomes "at-one" with the hero, and Frodo carries Gandalf's spirit with him all the way to Mordor. By sacrificing themselves to the cause, the mentor archetypes serve several functions. First, they free their own spirits so they can become spiritually united with their heroes. Second, they teach by example, showing the hero that the true nature of heroism is demonstrated through self-sacrifice. And third, they give the hero a glimpse of his destiny, showing him that by the end of his journey, he must become a willing martyr to his righteous cause.

The atonement may also be achieved through battle. This is especially true in stories that feature an antagonistic relationship between father and son. When Oedipus encounters Laius, they engage in battle and Oedipus kills his own father. In doing so, Oedipus fulfills the prophecy of his birth and claims his birthright as king of Thebes. However, as Freud pointed out so clearly, Oedipus was tragically unaware of his own identity. By destroying his father and unwittingly wedding Jocasta, his own mother, Oedipus blindly ventures into the realm of the most ancient and detested social taboo. When the truth of his own identity is revealed to him, Oedipus prefers to remain blind to his own sins. He gouges his eyes out in a tragic act of self-loathing and shame. The lesson we learn from Oedipus is that the moment of atonement with the father must be achieved through greater self-awareness, rather than blind anger or rage.

The first *Star Wars* trilogy is all about atonement with the father. In *Star Wars*, Luke is blind to his own identity, but he takes the first step towards self-awareness by identifying with Obi-Wan and wielding his father's light saber. In *The Empire Strikes Back*, Luke achieves greater awareness of Self. In a striking scene, Yoda sends Luke into a dark cave — the archetypal symbol of the unconscious, and also a womb-like tunnel of rebirth. At the heart of darkness within the cave, Luke encounters Darth Vader. They engage in battle, and Luke beheads Vader, only to see the image of his own face within Vader's dark helmet. The illusion that Yoda displays to Luke reveals the hero to himself. Vader is Luke's father, and he and his father are one. Like Oedipus, as long as Luke denies his true identity, he denies his own destiny as the savior of the galaxy. When Luke truly encounters Vader in a climactic light saber duel, Vader tells him: "Luke … I am your father," but Luke still denies the truth. Like Oedipus, he chooses to remain blind to himself, and like Oedipus, he pays the price by losing a part of himself (Luke's hand is severed from his arm in the duel). But in *Return of the Jedi*, Luke finally accepts the facts of his birth, allowing him to accept himself and claim his birthright as Jedi master and savior. When he pulls the mask off of Darth Vader's head to reveal his true father, they share a moment of atonement that heals both of them.

Ordeal and Apotheosis

The atonement is usually a harrowing stage for the hero, a time of great physical and psychological suffering. By struggling through this "ordeal," the hero shows his worthiness. He demonstrates that he is strong, courageous, determined and completely dedicated to the cause. More importantly, he exhibits the ultimate characteristic of heroism — self-sacrifice and the willingness to suffer greatly for the sake of others. The protagonist must emerge from the ordeal a completely different person. In essence, the protagonist must enter the ordeal a regular person, and exit the stage a true hero. The rebirth of the main character as a hero symbolizes the fact that his flaws have been purged through an ordeal of fire. Now he has the power to defeat his enemy and rise in stature from mere mortal to immortal legend. According to Campbell, the *apotheosis* stage is the symbolic death and resurrection of the hero. Jesus was resurrected on the cross and returned as a completely divine figure. Similarly, Moses climbed to the top of Mount Sinai and returned projecting the divine light of God's words from his forehead. Following his symbolic death and rebirth, the hero emerges through apotheosis with the power of the gods, and an invigorated rededication to his cause.

The relationship between the three inseparable and essential elements of identity development — hamartia, epiphany and apotheosis — are the nuclear core of the hero's character arc. In a critical moment of reflection before the title fight, the title character (Sylvester Stallone) in *Rocky* (1976) realizes that he cannot defeat Apollo Creed (Carl Weathers). This epiphany, which relates directly to his hamartia of self-doubt, creates a new sense of integrity in the hero. In Rocky's apotheosis, he is reborn as a hero who is not interested in becoming champion to gain external glory. He merely wants to prove to himself that he can "go the distance" with Apollo — that he has the same kind of heart that his mentor, Mickey sees in him, the heart of his namesake, Rocky Marciano. In Rocky's apotheosis and ordeal in the ring, we see the death of his personal ego and his spiritual rebirth as a figure so powerful that he can face the awesome mythological force, Apollo.

After the ordeal and apotheosis, the hero is rewarded for completing his character development. This reward is both physical and psychological. Percival grasps the Grail, Arthur seizes Excalibur, Moses holds the Ten Commandments, Buddha experiences Nirvana, Frodo casts the Ring into the Cracks of Doom, and so on. The *ultimate boon* is accompanied by a psychological sense of accomplishment. "I did it!" the hero remarks to himself. "I am the chosen one!" "I am deserving of victory and praise!" "I am a hero!" But, brave hero, there's no time to rest on your laurels now! You're in the belly of the beast! Frodo is in the heart of Mordor. Luke is still in the Death Star. Moses is still on the Egyptian side of the Red Sea. Siddhartha still has to deliver his divine teachings as Buddha. Percival still has to bring the Grail to Arthur. Better make haste and return to the starting point. The journey is not complete until the hero has returned home with the ultimate boon that will save his society.

Analyzing the Initiation

The Ten Commandments

On his road of trials, Moses proves himself and the power of God by inflicting the Ten Plagues on the Pharaoh and his people. During his struggles in Egypt, Moses encounters his old love interest, who is both a goddess that provides love and a temptress who tries to lure Moses away from his mission. The Pharaoh relents and releases the Israelites. After a big ordeal at the Red Sea, Moses delivers his people out of Egypt and into Sinai. Moses ascends the mountain and becomes "at-one" with his Lord, receiving the holy Ten Commandments. He takes this ultimate boon, the Decalogue in God's own handwriting, and heads back, reborn through apotheosis as a true hero. But upon descending the mountain with the stone tablets, he sees that the Israelites have lost faith and are worshipping a pagan idol. Moses displays his hamartia once again (the nasty temper which made him kill the Egyptian slave driver). He throws down the stone tablets and breaks them — destroying for all time the written testimony of God's law on Earth.

Excalibur

On his road of trials, Arthur demonstrates through his bravery and leadership in battle that he is the one true king. No longer Arthur the squire, he is now King Arthur, knight and true hero. Arthur unites his kingdom and establishes the Knights of the Round Table at Camelot. He meets his temptress by taking a beautiful bride, Guenevere, but when his queen betrays him with his finest knight, Lancelot, we see Arthur's hamartia. Like the ancient Greek heroes, Arthur suffers from hubris. He is too proud to forgive Guenevere and Lancelot for their misdeeds. His heart becomes black and bitter; he begins to die. Since the land and Excalibur are mystically linked with his soul, his kingdom begins to die, and Excalibur — the gift of the gods — is lost. But Arthur experiences a moment of epiphany when he drinks from the Holy Grail and realizes that he and the land are one. Following his ordeal, Arthur is reborn through apotheosis. He forgives Guenevere and is rewarded once again with Excalibur, the ultimate boon, which he wields one last time as he leads his knights into battle against the dreaded Mordred.

Star Wars

The first stop on Luke's road of trials is a rough, rowdy saloon in a seedy spaceport town. Here they are joined by Han Solo and his first mate, the wookie Chewbacca. With the evil Imperial forces chasing them, the heroes cross the first threshold and take off in the Millennium Falcon. The relationship between Luke and his mentor develops as Ben instructs Luke in the use of his light saber, and teaches him how to control the Force. While the external goal remains the rescue mission, the internal goal is related to Luke's mastery of the spiritual power of the Force, the symbol of his destiny as a Jedi knight. But the training is cut short as the heroes are drawn into the belly of the whale, the Empire's formidable super weapon, the Death Star. Luke overcomes his hamartia of self-doubt, accepts his identity as a hero and rescues Leia, who is both a Temptress and Goddess figure. However, shortly after his rise to full heroism, Luke sees Darth Vader kill his mentor. In that critical moment, Ben's body disappears, but his spirit is resurrected and integrated as a spiritual guide within Luke's psyche, a psychological atonement with his father figure. The suffering that Luke undergoes as a result of Obi-Wan's death constitutes a spiritual apotheosis, after which Luke is reborn into a powerful warrior with greater control over the Force, the ultimate boon. The symbol of Luke's increased psychological power is evident in his sudden ability to destroy Imperial fighters with uncanny accuracy. However, the Death Star is nearly complete, giving Vader and the Emperor the power to destroy every planet in the galaxy.

The Lord of the Rings

The first stop for the four hobbits on their road of trials is The Prancing Pony, a rowdy tavern in the outpost town of Bree, where they meet Aragorn, the man who will lead them to Rivendell. At Rivendell, the Council of Elrond decides that the ring must be destroyed in the fires of Mt. Doom, deep in the heart of Sauron's evil kingdom of Mordor. But who will bear the ring? Gandalf cannot take it, because a wizard who holds the ring of power could easily rule the world. The elves won't to take it themselves, but they don't trust the greedy dwarves with the all-powerful ring, and neither do they trust the power-hungry men. At this moment, Frodo answers an inner call by volunteering himself as the Ringbearer. Since he is neither wizard nor elf, nor dwarf or man, a hobbit is the only politically correct choice. However, Frodo still does not believe in his heart that he is brave enough to bear the awesome responsibility of the ring. To address this need, Frodo gets another mentor, Uncle Bilbo, who bestows some more supernatural aid on Frodo—a chain-mail vest made of elfin "mithril" and a magic sword.

The Fellowship of the Ring then travels through the belly of the whale, the orc-infested mines of Moria, where they face the most devastating creature imaginable, a demonic balrog. Gandalf fights the balrog alone, and is dragged down to the pits of Hell. Frodo, in witnessing his mentor's death, internalizes his mentor into his psyche, and integrates his spiritual power in a moment of atonement. After the ordeal in Moria, the fellowship travels to the kingdom of forest elves in Lothlorien, where they meet with the goddess—Galadriel, the elfin queen. The goddess is also a temptress, as Frodo is tempted to give Galadriel the ring and give up his own calling as Ringbearer. Galadriel turns down the ring, but we see that Frodo is still critically ambivalent about his identity as the Ringbearer. The goddess provides Frodo with an oracle, in which he sees that the fellowship is dissolving and that men will betray him in order to take the ring. This prophecy comes true in the next stage, when Boromir attacks Frodo and tries to steal the ring from him. Frodo's epiphany occurs when he realizes that the ring is not safe, even within the fellowship, and that he must bear the ring alone into the realm of Mordor. After this ordeal of betrayal, Frodo is reborn through apotheosis and overcomes his hamartia by finally accepting his identity as the one true Ringbearer. He heads off by himself to Mordor, taking only his faithful sidekick, Sam.

The Hero's Return

The final act is the hero's return to his common day world, where he will use the ultimate boon to save his people. But sometimes, the hero would prefer to stay in the world of adventure. The *refusal of the return* is similar to the hero's refusal of the call — it is a stage of inert reluctance that the hero must overcome. But once the hero accepts the fact that he must return, he enters the final stages of the journey, in which he typically experiences a quickening of the pace. Now that the hero has reached the apex of his character arc, it's all downhill from there. The rest of the plot can race towards a rather speedy resolution in a *magic flight*. Often times, a large part of the Third Act is dedicated to a chase scene in which the action is visibly swift. In sports movies like *Rocky*, *The Karate Kid* (1984), *Hoosiers* (1986), *Chariots of Fire* (1981), *Victory* (1981), *The Bad News Bears* (1976) and many others, the Third Act is the big game, race, fight or competition that is always hurried and action packed. Like in the *Popeye* cartoons, the last act is always an explosion of ultra-violent energy and just retribution. The hero's abundant energy and fluidity at this stage seems to carry some paranormal force. In Campbell's words: "the final stage of his adventure is supported by all the powers of his supernatural patron."

Sometimes, the hero must be brought back to the ordinary world by his allies in a *rescue from without*. In *The Empire Strikes Back*, Luke is left hanging alone, crippled and helpless after experiencing his ordeal, the great light saber duel with Darth Vader. He is rescued by Han Solo and his allies, who pick him up in the Millennium Falcon. In *The Return of the King*, Frodo is left helpless and stranded on the exploding volcano after he destroys the ring of power. He is rescued by giant eagles sent by Gandalf. The message at this stage is that even the greatest hero needs friends and allies. The strongest and bravest champion in the world is still vulnerable unless he has friends to help him and watch his back.

After *the crossing of the return threshold*, the hero becomes the *master of the two worlds*. He is familiar with the ordinary world because that is the world he grew up in. He knows all the places to hide, all the secret passages and all the best spots to stage an attack. He also knows all the townspeople. They remember him as a bright young lad growing up before their eyes. He is one of them, and they trust him. But they also sense that he has changed. The prodigal son has returned, but he is not the awkward, oafish, over-eager young boy who left not too long ago. Now he is confident, strong, and experienced. He seems to carry some type of mystical power that inspires courage in others. As master of the two worlds, conqueror of the outside world and citizen of the ordinary world, he has the unique ability to lead a rebellion of ordinary people against the evil tyrant. At this point, the character arc comes full circle. The hero is not just a warrior, he is a leader and mentor to others. Now he can lead the timid oppressed townspeople in a revolt against the dominating imperial forces. The "elixir" or ultimate boon that the hero delivers to his people is the *freedom to live* without tyranny.

The return stage is an essential part of the myth, though it is often overlooked in modern movies. *The Ten Commandments* ends shortly after Moses delivers the Decalogue to the Israelites. It cuts through the return stage from the Bible, in which Moses becomes a leader of the Israelites and guides them into battle as they travel to the Promised Land. Similarly, in *The Return of the King* (2003), Frodo destroys the ring of power and Middle Earth is saved from the dark lord, Sauron. However, despite Christopher Tolkien's objections, the semi-final chapter of J. R. R. Tolkien's epic, "The Scouring of the Shire," is not included in the film. This is a shame, because in this chapter, we see Frodo and his hobbit companions returning to their hometown as conqueror heroes. No longer a timid little hobbit, Frodo is now a powerful and confident hero and leader. He returns home to see that the hobbits of the Shire have been conquered and subjugated by wild men, soldiers of Sauron. While the Frodo of the first chapter would never have even thought of rebelling against these dangerous,

The Ultimate Boon. Moses receives God's laws and delivers them to his people. At the end of his hero's journey, Moses is now a mentor to Joshua, who will take up the mantle of leadership after Moses dies. Moses (Charlton Heston), left, and Joshua (John Derek). *The Ten Commandments* (1956), Paramount.

massive men, the returning Frodo does not hesitate to raise a force of insurgent hobbits against the human imperialists. Frodo's intimate knowledge of the Shire and his relationship with its citizens mixed with his new-found bravery, heroism and ability to inspire others combine to make Frodo a leader and mentor so powerful that he is practically invincible.

The final defeat of the evil wizard Saruman does not take place on the great battlefields of Isengard, Mordor or Gondor. Saruman dies in the Shire, after he is stripped powerless by none other than the hobbits—the smallest, weakest inhabitants of Middle Earth. The message at this stage is clear: *the meek shall inherit the earth.*

The exact same theme is played out in *Return of the Jedi.* Luke returns from his trials and ordeal as a full-blown hero—a well-trained Jedi knight. He then leads the inhabitants of a small, Earth-like planet — the Ewoks— in a rebellion against the Imperial armies. The rebellion is successful, due mainly to Luke's final stage of character development with his father. But the little Ewoks still earn their great victory over the evil empire.

Analyzing the Return

The Ten Commandments

After the fateful scene at Mt. Sinai, Cecil B. DeMille cuts to the end of Moses' journey. He has fulfilled his role of Messiah — he liberated his people from bondage and brought them to the threshold of the Promised Land. But more importantly, he became their teacher and mentor. Though the stone tablets were broken, Moses still delivered the law of God — the ultimate boon — to the Israelites by teaching it to them personally. This is why Moses is remembered in the Hebrew tradition as "Moshe Rabeinu," Moses Our Teacher. Though he liberated the Israelites from Egypt, he is not remembered for the bravery of his liberation, but for the wisdom and dedication of his teaching. By teaching his people God's Law, he gives them the freedom to live according to their own tradition, rather than the tyrannical rule of the Pharaoh. He has become a legend, and he will live on as the greatest legendary figure in Judaic tradition.

Excalibur

At the brink of death, Arthur is reborn through apotheosis by drinking from the Holy Grail, which was brought to him by his most faithful knight, Perceval. He has survived his ordeal, but it may be too late because his sorceress sister Morgana and his powerful nephew/son Mordred are about to seize control of the land. Nevertheless, Arthur has another epiphany, and realizes that while kings and kingdoms may come and go, the only eternal truth is love. Before going off to die in battle, Arthur visits Guenevere and overcomes his hamartia—he forgives her and heals both of their wounded hearts. Arthur is rewarded by being reunited with

Excalibur, which Guenevere had been safeguarding through all the dark years. Arthur becomes a great king and mentor once again, leading his knights into a heroic and victorious battle. Though he is mortally wounded in the end, he never really dies. Excalibur is returned to the gods who created it, and Arthur is carried off in a mystical ship to the mythical land of the spirits, knowing that his legend will live on after him for all eternity. Arthur will always be remembered in Anglo-Saxon mythology as the greatest King of all times.

Star Wars

Now a fully developed hero, Luke needs no encouragement to join the rebels in their desperate battle against the Imperial Death Star. As master of the two worlds, (the outer world of spaceship fighting and the inner world of the Force), Luke goes into battle with Obi-Wan's voice in his head as his spiritual guide. At Luke's moment of critical development, he trusts Obi-Wan's telepathic advice to "use the force." Luke ignores the external spaceship controls and relies solely on his internal control of the Force to fire the fatal blow on the Death Star, delivering the freedom to live to the good people of the galaxy. In the final scene, Luke receives a medal of honor as a reward for his heroism. The galaxy has been saved, and all is well with the universe ... until the next episode.

The Lord of the Rings

After destroying the ring in the fires of Mt. Doom, Frodo and Sam experience a magic flight via a rescue from without on the wings of giant eagles. Frodo crosses the return threshold by going back to the Shire, but he feels awkward in his role as master of the two worlds. Though he loves his quiet home, his adventure as Ringbearer has changed him forever. He leaves Middle Earth with Gandalf, Bilbo and the elfin race, going on to become an immortal legend for all time. However, he leaves Sam with the legacy of their great adventure. Within this legacy is the symbolic meaning of the journey — the notion that every person is a hero, no matter how large, as long as he is willing to fight for what he believes in. This legacy is the eternal freedom to live.

Reviewing the Hero's Journey

The beauty of Campbell's model is that once the stages are understood in terms of their psychological function, any story, movie or myth can be analyzed in reference to the basic structural elements. Below, Campbell's stages from *The Hero with a Thousand Faces* are broken down into three-act structure to correspond with theatrical screenplays.

Act One — Departure: 1. The Call to Adventure
                          2. Refusal of the Call
                          3. Supernatural Aid
                          4. The Crossing of the First Threshold
                          5. The Belly of the Whale

Act Two — Initiation: 6. The Road of Trials
                          7. The Meeting with the Goddess
                          8. Woman as the Temptress
                          9. Atonement with the Father
                         10. Apotheosis
                         11. The Ultimate Boon.

Act Three — Return: 12. Refusal of the Return
                         13. The Magic Flight
                         14. Rescue from Without
                         15. The Crossing of the Return Threshold
                         16. Master of the Two Worlds
                         17. Freedom to Live

7

Archetype Evolution

In the dream of the modern day neurotic and in the frames of a new Hollywood blockbuster, we can identify the ancient archetypes that were first expressed in the stories of our primordial ancestors. The male persona in the dream world has developed from the Hunter Hero tradition. He is the member of the tribe who must go out from the safety of the "world of common day" into the wilderness, where danger, the unknown and beasts with mystical powers exist. The female persona has developed from the Maiden Hero tradition — the member of the tribe who must be rescued from the dangers of the wilderness. Sadly, this basic dichotomy between a proactive and assertive hero and a passive female heroine has been inherited from our distant past and ingrained as a basic part of our collective unconscious. The passive female hero archetype is the by-product of a patriarchal Western mythology. Campbell noted that Eastern mythologies tend to be "matriarchal" rather than patriarchal, and that female heroes in Eastern myths are often more assertive. In Western myths, the male hero generally plays the lead role, while the female plays the subordinate role of "maiden in distress."

The Princess Hero

The maiden's character arc is resolved by marrying and being carried off by her savior to live with him happily ever after. Hence, the princess motif is rewarding for both males and females. By slaying the dragon, the knight gains not only heroism and a beautiful bride, he also gains social status, power and the job security of being heir to the throne. In rescuing the maiden, the hero not only proves his worth, he also claims his birthright. For girls, the only path to identity development is that of being saved by a male. So, if a girl is going to play a passive role in her own identity development, she might as well be a beautiful and rich princess, rather than an ordinary, poor peasant girl.

95

The Evil Stepmother

The evil stepmother motif was an even more psychologically significant archetype in the days before modern medicine, when death at childbirth was relatively frequent and commonplace. Though the loss of a mother at birth would be psychologically traumatic for any child, this loss may have special significance for girls, who look towards their mothers as primary role models and mentor figures. The evil stepmother archetype must have sounded a powerfully resonant chord for thousands of girls who had to grow up in the house of a stepmother rather than a biological mother.

It is natural for a child to feel that a parent is unduly harsh, cruel or uncaring. These feelings could be exacerbated when a child suspects that a stepparent doesn't love her as much as her "real" parent would. The "real" parent is dead. Since she is dead and not present, she could be idealized as a figure that is diametrically opposite to the stepparent. Where the evil stepmother is cold, harsh, punitive and cruel, the "real" mother would be warm, kind, loving and gentle. The little girl's hatred of her stepmother and her earnest desire for love and contact with her real mother leads to a psychic projection. The stepmother is cast into the role of the wicked witch, depicted plainly in princess hero stories such as *Snow White and the Seven Dwarfs*, in which the archetype plays a dual role as both evil stepmother and wicked witch. This dual archetype owes its descent most directly from Medea in Greek mythology. Medea was both a powerful dark sorceress and a jealous, vengeful mother who killed her children and boiled them in a stew to be eaten by their own father.

The Fairy Godmother

As in the myth of the birth of the hero, the maiden hero's saga is derived from a childhood fantasy of noble or divine parentage. The deep psychological wish for the dead mother is fulfilled in the child's fantasy world by actually resurrecting her as a spirit, in the form of the fairy godmother. This resurrected ideal parent satisfies a universal desire for a warm, loving and nurturing mother. In *Cinderella*, the Fairy Godmother fulfills the mother fantasy, but since she is also supernatural, she can supply the heroine with the supernatural aid she needs to win her prince. In *The Wizard of Oz*, Glinda the Good Witch is Dorothy's mentor/fairy godmother, providing love, care and supernatural aid.

Passivity

The passivity of the female hero must have an effect on the collective unconscious of girls and women throughout society. We identify personally with the heroes in the stories we hear. What life lessons and models are formed in the minds of young girls when the heroes in all their stories rarely take an active stance in their own development? The implicit message is that a girl cannot achieve a positive identity through action, assertiveness or competitive striving. A girl must instead be patient, hopeful, passive and above all, beautiful. Furthermore, the explicit message is that a girl's personal sense of identity achievement can only be fulfilled through marriage with an ideal man. It is not the girl herself who can make herself happy though personal growth. It is the male who, by saving and seizing the girl, fulfills her destiny for her.

Obviously, the ancient archetype does not fit in well with modern expectations in contemporary Western society, in which girls are encouraged to actively seek out their own goals and identities. Contemporary depictions of the princess archetype present a more assertive and proactive female hero. As modern mythmakers create films and stories for today's women and girls, they tend to borrow themes from non–Western mythology in order to find heroines that are more assertive.

Sleeping Princesses

Jealous of her stepdaughter's beauty, the wicked queen in *Snow White* dresses her stepdaughter in rags and puts her to work as a scullery maid. But the princess shows hope and patience, the hallmarks of her theme song "Some Day My Prince Will Come." Hope and patience are two of the princess hero's main strengths—much different than the male hero's strengths of courage and vigor. The evil stepmother tells her guard to kill Snow White, but the kindly guard has pity on her. He tells her to escape into the forest, where she finds shelter in the house of the Seven Dwarfs. Here we see another quality of the princess hero. Rather than saving herself, she is saved by others who have pity on her.

Snow White plays a motherly role by taking care of the Seven Dwarfs—cleaning their house, cooking their meals, making sure they wash, and sewing their clothes. The Seven Dwarfs, in return, play a fatherly role in Snow White's life—protecting and defending her from the Queen. In these scenes, we see another common princess theme: the girl must prove herself a good potential mother before she can be accepted by the prince as a bride. The evil stepmother is also a wicked witch, and she tricks Snow White into eating an apple that puts her into the "sleep of death." The dwarfs destroy the Witch and preserve Snow White in a glass coffin, until she is awakened by the Prince, who rescues her with the magic power of "love's first kiss."

In *Sleeping Beauty*, a very similar tale is told. On the day of her birth, the princess's three fairy godmothers each give her a magical gift. He first gift is beauty, and the second is song. But before the third gift is bestowed, a wicked witch places a curse on the princess, which will kill her on her sixteenth birthday. The third fairy godmother has pity on the princess. She cannot reverse the curse, but she gives the princess a third gift. When her sixteenth birthday arrives, the princess will not die — she will sleep. The princess hero's stereotypically feminine gifts represent beauty, creativity and passivity — gifts that will serve her well as a bride, but won't help her defeat the witch and rescue herself. Instead, like Snow White, she must passively sleep and wait for the valiant prince to slay the witch and rescue her with love's first kiss. It is also significant that all of this occurs on Sleeping Beauty's sixteenth birthday, a traditional date for a girl to be married off by her father and carried away by her new owner, her husband.

Sleeping Beauty and *Snow White* represent the extreme examples of feminine passivity, as these heroes actually sleep through their critical moments of identity development. Their epiphanies and apotheoses are achieved through passive acceptance of a male's sexual contact — "love's first kiss" — which is symbolic of marriage, the moment at which a nubile young girl is initiated from the childhood state of virginal maidenhood to the adult state of marriage and motherhood. The patriarchal system in which the girl is passed from father to husband as a passive object rather than as an independent being is recapitulated in the themes of these ancient tales. The dwarfs, in the place of Snow White's absent father, give her away to the prince, and they live happily ever after. Sleeping Beauty is handed over from her father the king to her husband the prince, a marriage that was arranged on the day she was born, and resolved while she slept passively on a bed of roses.

Cinderella Stories

Cinderella combines the princess motif with a slightly more proactive maiden hero. Though Cinderella's father was a gentleman, she was not born a princess — she must become one. Cinderella is a poor girl, an orphan who must overcome an evil stepmother and cruel stepsisters to win her prince. The motif of the cruel stepsister is another psychologically significant theme in traditional societies, in which the only way young women can actively define their identities is by marrying the best suitor. In the old days, there must have been great competition between maidens for the best bachelors. Certainly, this competition was often the fiercest between sisters and stepsisters in the same house. For Cinderella, any force that would have come between her and her Prince Charming would be perceived as being cruel and evil.

The Cinderella hero is much more active than Snow White or Sleeping Beauty. Like the male hero, she must actively pursue her goal in order to achieve the identity she desires. She must find a prince and win him in order to become a princess. Though Cinderella is a bit more proactive, at her critical moment of development she does not actively save herself or capture her prince. Cinderella is rescued from her locked chamber by her male household pets, and she is taken away from her unhappy household by her Prince. Cinderella merely waits for him to come and save her.

A similarly passive resolution is seen in *The Wizard of Oz*. At the moment of Dorothy's ordeal — when she is locked in the chamber of the witch's castle — rather than saving herself, she is rescued by Scarecrow, Tin Man and Lion. Once again, it is the male figures that play the active role, while the female hero remains passive. Even when Dorothy destroys the wicked witch, she does so by accident. She was throwing water to dowse the fire on Scarecrow's arm, and the liquidation of the witch was a fortunate side effect. Though she kills the beast, the female hero is not yet allowed to be actively violent or assertive.

Little Princesses

When Sara's (Shirley Temple) father in *The Little Princess* (1939) goes to war, her boarding school headmistress becomes her evil stepmother. The key to Sara's heroism is her desire to reunite with her father, because to him, she knows she will always be "a little princess." In *Annie* (1982), another character from the 1930s, the little orphan (Aileen Quinn) escapes her version of the wicked stepmother, the housemother of her orphanage. She becomes an American princess by finding a rich father, capitalist king Daddy Warbucks (Albert Finney). In the 1930s, Shirley Temple played the role of the little princess archetype in a host of films such as *Little Miss Marker, Poor Little Rich Girl, Dimples, Curly Top, Little Miss Broadway, Heidi,* and of course *The Little Princess.* Though she lost the role of Dorothy in *The Wizard of Oz* to Judy Garland, Shirley Temple's image still persists as the dominant icon in the little girl hero genre. Since the days of Shirley Temple, the little princess theme has been played out, either literally or figuratively, in dozens of films. Most recently, *The Princess Diaries* (2001) and *What a Girl Wants* (2003) both play upon the theme of a normal American girl discovering her aristocratic roots, and setting off on a journey to establish her princess identity. While the princess motif is clearly a ubiquitous theme in stories that appeal to little girls, the theme seems to be equally popular among adult audiences.

Adult Princesses

The Cinderella story of an ordinary woman winning the heart of a rich and charming prince remains so appealing that a new movie based on this basic theme seems to come out almost every month. Recently, Jennifer Lopez starred in *Maid in Manhattan* (2002), in which a common chambermaid wins the heart of a prince who is heir to a rich and powerful political dynasty. One of the biggest hits in this genre was *Pretty Woman* (1990), in which Julia Roberts plays a common hooker who wins the heart of a prince of industry. A basic truism in movies is that if a film has a female lead as the star, 99 percent of the time that film is either a romantic comedy or a romantic drama. While male heroes in movies have many quests, the female hero is almost always searching for love. However, the archetypes are evolving. One sign of evolution is the emergence of new female heroes who think and act differently. Of course, society's initial reaction to people that are different tends to be bewilderment.

"What's Wrong with That Girl?"

A common plot device in female hero stories is to cast a hero who is different from typical girls. In *Beauty and the Beast* (1991), Belle is considered odd and eccentric because she displays the archetypal qualities of the male hero. She is individualistic, intellectual, independent and unsatisfied with the status quo. The female heroes in the Disney's films of the latter half of the twentieth century — Belle, The Little Mermaid, Pocahontas and Mulan — all epitomize the girl who is marginalized in her society because she epitomizes the qualities of the male hero. These heroines represent a development in the princess archetype, because they are all much more assertive and proactive than traditional princesses such as Snow White, Sleeping Beauty and Cinderella. These "tomboy" princesses provoke their own changes in character, and their stories tend to share some common motifs.

Rejecting the Suitor

Belle, in *Beauty and the Beast*, wants nothing to do with Gaston, the powerful Adonis who everyone thinks she should marry. Belle wants to choose her own husband — a critical choice of destiny that has been denied to nubile girls in traditional societies since antiquity. The freedom to choose one's own husband has been an extremely significant theme for girls throughout history. This issue is represented in stories by the princess who rejects her suitors. By denying the father's or society's choice for her mate, the princess asserts her autonomy in an untraditional show of independence. The rejecting of the suitor is a universal theme in Native American myths, and it is recapitulated by Disney in *Pocahontas* (1995). The first step on the hero's path of individuality is rejecting the path of conformity that is laid out before her. By rejecting the suitor, the heroine chooses her own path and displays the traditionally masculine qualities of strength and independence.

A similar theme is seen in the rejection of the father-king's domination and control over his daughter's life. The princess who yearns to be free of her father's tyranny represents a strong and assertive heroine who rebels against her father rather than passively accepting his will. Princess Ariel in *The Little Mermaid* displays her independence by venturing off into the land of humans, despite her father's objections. Princess Jasmine in *Aladdin* (1992) ventures off into the city disguised as a peasant girl in order to briefly escape the palace and her father's domination. In *Roman Holiday* (1952), *Princess Ann* (Audrey Hepburn) escapes her father's bodyguards in order to experience Rome as a normal girl. And in a shamelessly borrowed story line, Anna (Mandy Moore) in *Chasing Liberty* (2004) is an American princess — the president's daughter — who escapes her Secret Service bodyguards to experience Europe on her own. All of these stories (and many more just like them) represent a mélange of traditional and contemporary archetypes. By rebelling against the father-king, the princess hero shows that she is proactive and assertive. However, the bulk of the story still invariably revolves around the princess falling in love with a prince-in-rags figure, who also invariably saves the princess from some form of danger or peril. But in the end, by choosing this pauper-prince as her lover, the princess rebels against the father-king again, because the all-important choice of suitor is hers and not his.

Saving the Father

In a true role reversal, a passive princess who is rescued by a prince becomes an active princess who rescues the prince by slaying the beast herself. Since this is a huge development in character, many stories display a stage of archetype evolution, in which the princess must rescue her old or ailing father. Belle must rescue her father several times in her story. The Little Mermaid and Pocahontas must save their father and his kingdom from the invading hordes. Mulan saves her disabled father by taking his place in the Chinese army. Though the princess is not yet saving her prince, rescuing her father is still a role reversal, as it displays a powerful girl rescuing a passive male figure. This motif is a link between the completely passive princess heroes of traditional tales and the new breed of active princess heroes.

The Princess in Knight's Armor

Sometimes, in order to save her father, the princess must disguise her herself as a male warrior. By dressing up as a male, the female hero takes on the male persona and can therefore follow the traditional hero's path. As a princess in knight's armor, she can fight and show her courage like a man. These princess heroes share a common hamartia — the danger of being unmasked and having their female personas revealed. The princess warrior motif is seen directly in the Joan of Arc legend, and has most recently been depicted in Disney's *Mulan* (1998). Occasionally, the female hero wishes to express her strength and independence in fields other than the battlefield. In *Yentl* (1983), the heroine (Barbara Streisand) disguises herself as a male student so she can conquer knowledge of the Torah.

Princess Valiant

The later generation of princess heroes shows a steady progression in the amount of traditionally male heroic qualities that a princess hero can display. Belle in *Beauty and the Beast* saves the prince from his curse with her avowal of love. Here we see a gender role reversal of the sleep of death and love's first kiss motif. Belle is the active figure, while the male prince lays passive. It is significant that all of this occurs on the prince's twenty-first birthday, the traditional time at which a male should wed his sixteen-year-old bride. Another coincidence is that the prince's curse is held within the petals of a magical rose — a symbolic link with the story of *Briar Rose*, the traditional fairy tale from which *Snow White* and *Sleeping Beauty* were adapted.

In *The Little Mermaid*, Ariel satisfies many of the traditional qualities of the princess hero, while also displaying some newly evolved characteristics. In the traditional sense, she is an actual princess without a mother. She encounters the wicked Sea Witch who places a curse on her that can only be undone by love's first kiss. Ariel has the traditional female virtues of beauty, creativity and her lovely siren song. But Ariel has some very untraditional qualities as well. She is assertive, single-minded and brave. Ariel physically saves her prince from drowning, and she actively pursues him throughout the story, despite her father's objections. Though it is the prince who slays the Sea Witch, Ariel has already displayed her bravery and self-confidence by actively following her own dream and identity and overtly defying her father. In the end, it is her father who must bend — he must allow her to marry the human prince, rather than insisting that she marry the "merman" of his choosing.

Mulan takes on the largest number of archetypal male hero qualities by actually impersonating a male. In the beginning of her story, she is a nubile girl who is told by her family and the town matchmaker that the only way that she can bring "honor" to her family is by wedding a noble suitor. Unfortunately, Mulan is different from other girls. She does not possess the archetypal qualities of quiet grace and passivity that are valued in women in her society. But as a soldier in disguise, she shows herself to brave, strong, intelligent and resilient. She even becomes a mentor to other soldiers. Mulan leads her allies into a final battle to save the Emperor by having them all disguise themselves as women. Mulan saves her real father by taking his place in the army, and she saves the symbolic father of China by rescuing the Emperor. Along the way, she also saves the life of a handsome soldier prince. Mulan goes on to win not only his heart, but his loyalty and admiration as well. At the climax of the film, at Mulan's moment of critical development, she kills the evil Hun Lord by herself. Ironically, she disarms him with a fan — the ultimate symbol of feminine meekness and shy humility in her culture. In the end, Mulan brings honor to herself and her family. Most importantly, she earns her father's respect, not as a passive little girl, but as a brave and valiant warrior.

From Princess to Powerhouse

In early Hollywood movies, leading women were either ingenues like Mary Pickford, Helen Hayes and Norma Shearer; or vamps such as Louise Brooks, Theda Bara, Jean Harlowe and Mae West. While the powerful and assertive bad girls or femme fatales got what they wanted for awhile, their only strength and weapon was sex, and they always got their comeuppance in the end. Only the good girls won the prince and lived happily ever after. The hammer that broke the mold was MGM's monumental epic *Gone With the Wind* (1939). In the beginning of her story, Scarlet O'Hara (Vivian Leigh) is a pampered princess who pouts and preens to get what she wants.

But when tragedy strikes, she becomes powerful, assertive and unapologetically manipulative — all in order to save her father's kingdom, Tara.

The enormous popularity of this strong and confident female hero paved the way for new female leads who were sexy and assertive without being a femme fatale. They were also honorable and heroic without being a passive good girl. Katherine Hepburn, Bette Davis and Joan Crawford epitomized the burgeoning archetype of the strong female hero. In an atavistic depiction of this new female archetype, Diane Keaton's character in *Looking for Mr. Goodbar* (1977) defies social expectations for women by living independently, doing drugs, engaging in casual sex and refusing a perfectly good yet very traditional suitor. In the ultimate display of women's liberation, she even has her ovaries surgically removed, liberating herself completely of the female burdens of pregnancy and motherhood. However, like the femme fatales of the 1930s, Keaton's character is punished for her iconoclastic expression of women's liberation. She is killed in the end, ironically by a gender-bending sexual partner.

More recently, films such as *Working Girl* (1990), *G.I. Jane* (1997) and *Erin Brockovich* (2000) depict strong women who succeed in traditionally male domains using the same archetypal qualities of strength, intellect and courage. The archetype evolution has also been applied to men, as seen in films such as *Mr. Mom* (1983), *A Simple Twist of Fate* (1994) and *Mrs. Doubtfire* (1993). In these films, career-obsessed absentee fathers re-evaluate their paths as they take on the traditionally feminine roles of homemaker and primary caretaker. Robin William in *Mrs. Doubtfire* performs an actual role reversal, going in drag to win back his children in the traditionally feminine role of nanny and housekeeper. Just as the traditionally masculine world of business and war are now open to women, the traditionally feminine world of full-time parenting is now open to men. The message in all of these films are the same: In a modern world, individuals are not relegated to either masculine or feminine roles based on their sex alone.

The archetype evolution can even be seen as coming full circle in films where women question the value of pursuing traditionally male goals and ideals. In *Baby Boom* (1987), a middle-aged woman has given herself over completely to the adventure of success in the highly competitive, male-dominated world of big business. When she is forced to care for an abandoned infant, nascent maternal instincts bring out feminine qualities that she had been repressing. She could not be a nurturing, sensitive and caring person as the "tiger lady" of the business world. But once those latent qualities are released, she realizes that she has given up a lot in order to follow her path of independence, individuality and achievement in the competitive domain. The choice of Diane Keaton's character in *Baby Boom* stands in direct contrast to her character's choice in *Looking for Mr. Good-bar*. In *Baby Boom*, J. C. (Keaton) chooses to abandon her path of independence in favor of the more traditional role of mother and homemaker. This choice does not represent a girl who is passively conforming to the traditional path expected of all females. Her choice is the personal decision of a liberated and mature woman who realizes that success in the male domain is not necessarily preferable to fulfillment in the traditional female role.

8

Superheroes and Underdogs

Alfred Adler was born in Vienna in 1870 to a large middle-class family. He was a sickly and physically awkward child. Like Freud, Adler was educated at Vienna University. After receiving his medical degree and entering private practice as a general practitioner, he reinvented himself as a psychoanalyst. Freud invited Adler into his inner circle of psychoanalysts, a group that eventually became the Vienna Psychoanalytic Society. Adler was the first president of this group, which would later became the International Psychoanalytic Society. Though Adler was initially a great admirer of Freud, he never considered himself a disciple, and always maintained his own individual views that in some ways differed greatly from Freud's, especially in regards to the significance of sexual drives in neurosis. Freud saw Adler's unorthodox views as subversive, and in 1911 prompted Adler to declare his perspectives to the group. His theories were denounced by the majority party of strict Freudians in the psychoanalytic school, so Adler left the Vienna Psychoanalytic Society, taking nearly half of the members with him. Though Adler and Freud would both practice in Vienna for many years to come, they would never be on speaking terms again.

Adler and his followers founded a new school of psychoanalysis, which focused on individual development, inferiority and the significance of siblings and birth order on individual psychology. Though he was not as widely published as Freud, Adler constantly lectured and toured the universities of Europe and America, spreading his ideas widely across the international psychoanalytic community. Of his many theories, Adler's concepts of the *inferiority complex* and *sibling rivalry* would become the most famous and influential. Adler would later become a visiting professor at Columbia University. In 1935, he moved permanently to the United States, where he continued to work in private practice and held a faculty position at the Long Island College of Medicine. Alfred Adler died of a heart attack in 1937 while on a lecturing tour in Scotland.

As with Freud's Oedipal complex, Adler's inferiority complex could be seen as the outgrowth of a great theorist's own personal self-analysis. Freud's mother was a young, beautiful woman during the days of young Sigmund's infancy. She doted on her first-born son, favored him above the subsequent children, and showered him with love and affection. Freud's father, on the other hand, was much older — about twice as old as his mother. His father was a strict authoritarian who demanded discipline, obedience and unwavering respect. Freud would recall through his own process of self-analysis that his earliest feelings towards his mother and father were conflicted with love, hate, fear and aggression.

Adler's case was much different. He remembered having feelings of jealousy towards his younger brother when, at a very early age, his mother transferred all of her love and attention onto the new baby. The resulting realization in Alfred was that his brother was the preferred son in his mother's eyes. His feelings of rivalry with his brother became even more conflicted when, at the age of three, his baby brother died next to him in the bed that they shared. Rather than feeling a sense of rivalry against his father for his mother's love, Adler experienced a sense of rivalry against his sibling. Within these early childhood memories and feelings came Adler's conception of the inferiority complex as a primary basis for motivation, as well as the idea that this motivation could be directed through rivalry with a sibling. In both Freudian and Adlerian analysis, the central unconscious issue is the desire for love and possession of the primary love object (Mother), and a resulting sense of aggression towards the rival for Mother's love. Though their theories are clearly different, both theorists placed the conflicts that arise from the individual's primary relationships with family members as the starting points and center of unconscious neurosis.

Guiding Fictions

In Adler's view, neurotic conflict arises from a discordance in the individual's "self concept." For example, a person who believes he should be strong and athletic, but instead is weak and feeble, experiences a divergence between his "ideal self" and his "real self." This divergence results in anxiety or neurosis. Everybody feels a sense of personal weakness in some area of life. Our attempt to overcome these perceived personal weaknesses are "compensatory mechanisms" of ego defense. Adler's theory of compensation is much more humanistic than Freud's theory. In Adler's model, people have positive humanistic drives, not just biological drives.

People have a natural desire to become better in both individual and social realms. Rather than seeing great works merely as "sublimation" of sexual drives, Adler saw great works as individual and social attempts at becoming better human beings. By compensating for our weaknesses, we are turning negative feelings about ourselves into positive energy and accomplishments.

Adler pointed out that our feelings of inferiority are often irrational, arising from a small child's feelings of inferiority in relation to a parent or older siblings. Being fixated on irrational feelings of inferiority lends an essence of psychopathology to the inferiority complex, as it has no basis in reality, but rather is a product of "unreality." As a result, the individual's reaction to a pathological inferiority complex is often guided by fictitious rather than realistic goals. The self-concept that guides the individual's behaviors and goals, his "guiding fictions," are set up by his own unconscious to make him feel inferior, inadequate and hopeless.

From Here to Eternity

The individual's neurotic reaction to the inferiority complex is revealed through exaggerated behaviors driven by unrealistic goals, behavior patterns that Adler called "overcompensation." The classic example of overcompensatory behavior is seen in the perpetually unfaithful spouse, who must constantly seduce new lovers in order to compensate for a personal sense of inferiority in the realms of physical, professional or sexual success. Pathological adulterers such as Captain Holmes (Philip Ober) in *From Here to Eternity* (1953) do not seduce lovers merely because they are attracted to their sexual conquests. They seduce lovers because they need to convince themselves that they are still superlatively attractive in the eyes of other people.

Adultery is just one of the symptoms of Captain Holmes's inferiority complex in *From Here To Eternity*. Aside from feeling the need to perpetually cheat on his wife, Holmes is obsessed with the notion of having his company win the boxing finals, believing that this honor would get him promoted to major. Just as he overcompensates for his poor self-concept as a man by seducing lovers, Holmes overcompensates for his poor self-concept as an officer by unfairly pressuring a reluctant soldier, Prew (Montgomery Clift), into boxing. For Holmes, overcompensation backfires. In the end, he loses both his wife and his commission as an officer. According to Adler, the only way to stop the cycle of overcompensatory behavior is to address the root of the problem — the inferiority complex — by understanding the unreal feelings of inadequacy motivating the behaviors.

People motivated by inferiority complexes tend to have guiding fictions that establish goals of superiority. The inner goals of superiority stand as opposing poles to the inner dread of inferiority, providing fantasies of success and achievement that are both comforting and motivating. Adler pointed that out that the striving for superiority can take both healthy and unhealthy forms. Striving for a sense of individual superiority, trying to be the best you can be, is a healthy and well-adjusted superiority drive. However, striving for superiority over others, trying to dominate other people in order to manipulate and take advantage of them, is an unhealthy and maladjusted superiority drive, a *superiority complex.*

Tyrannical villains such as Captain Holmes in *From Here to Eternity* epitomize the drive for superiority over others. The evil acts of these power-hungry characters are motivated by a desire to dominate and exploit. In turn, the evil that these men do incite their victims into heroism. Holmes's tyranny forces Prew to overcome his position of inferiority by refusing his captain's requests to fight, despite Holmes's increasingly brutal tactics of persuasion.

The Underdog

An inner sense of inferiority and a subsequent drive towards superiority is epitomized by the underdog character. The underdog theme can be traced back thousands of years. From David and Goliath to Arthur, Robin Hood and Horatio Alger, everybody cheers when the puny long shot with nothing but heart wins out in the end. The underdog hero is one we can all identify with. We've all felt smaller, weaker and less capable than others. We've all dreamed of overcoming impossible odds to accomplish great personal goals. The regular Joe with few assets of greatness who goes on to save the world is the epitome of the underdog formula, but the true essence of the underdog character is what Adler called *social interest.* The underdog's struggle to overcome inferiority is not a selfish goal, though it may be a personal struggle. The underdog's superiority drive is tempered by a "social feeling" for others, the desire to help those around him and make the world a better place for having lived in it.

Unlike the classical heroes in Greek mythology, who are blessed with many weapons, gifts, strengths and allies from the gods, the underdog starts out with very little going for him. The underdog hero (Sylvester Stallone) in *Rocky* (1976) is a two-bit fighter who has to break thumbs for a local numbers-runner in order to get by. Daniel (Ralph Macchio) in *The Karate Kid* (1984) is a skinny, insecure, fatherless teen used as a punching bag by the local high school toughs. And the hero (Kirk Douglas) in Kubrick's epic *Spartacus* (1960), begins his journey as the ultimate underdog,a lowly slave sentenced to die. These heroes have to compensate for their own circumstances and insecurities in order to develop as a hero, but they also have to change their basic concepts about themselves in order to succeed.

Overcoming Inferiority

Rather than feeling happy at being given a shot to fight the champion, Rocky feels overwhelmed and inadequate. His tireless training is a tremendous act of overcompensation, but his heart is not truly in the fight until he realizes that winning is not the most important thing. His desire to become the next champion is an unreal goal, so Rocky restructures his self-concept to create a more attainable and personally meaningful objective — to merely "go the distance" with the formidable champion. Though he loses the title fight to Apollo (Carl Weathers), Rocky succeeds as an underdog hero by proving to himself that he could give his all and go the distance with the champion. Rather than stating his goal as the desire to dominate over Apollo, Rocky aspires merely to do the most he can do, achieve his personal best, and not give up.

Similarly, in Daniel's moment of critical development in *The Karate Kid*, Daniel expresses his realization that karate is not about winning a championship, but about finding a sense of "balance" in his life. Daniel learned from his mentor, Mr. Miyagi (Pat Morita), that individual achievement is not about defeating a rival, but about achieving a personal victory over one's own demons. Daniel goes on to win the championship, but he does so to achieve a sense of "balance" in his own life, not in order to feel superior or dominant over others.

Overcoming Superiority

In *Spartacus*, the title character leads a slave rebellion against the ruling class. In the end, Spartacus must restructure his self-concept when he realizes that, although his rebellion against the Romans was not successful, what matters the most is that the cause of freedom was a just and honorable cause — regardless of whether it was lost or won. While Spartacus is crucified at the end, he is a victorious hero. He has the integrity of knowing that he led an honorable life, he has the promise of a better life for his son, and he has the pride of knowing that his legacy of freedom will live on after him. His superiority is not the superiority of the dominating patricians, but the superiority of a former slave who broke his chains and lived the life of a free man.

Sibling Rivalry

Adler's concept of *sibling rivalry* is an extremely common theme in films. In *Whatever Happened to Baby Jane?* (1962), Jane (Bette Davis) received most of the attention as a child because she was a big star ("Baby Jane"). It is clear that her original impulse to be successful was driven by desire for her father's love and approval, and that this primary drive became transformed into a secondary drive for success, motivated by a need for fame, fortune and the love of the masses. Jane's sister Blanche (Joan Crawford) was the quiet one. She was favored by their meek mother but yelled at by her father, who displaced his anger at the spoiled Jane on Blanche, the quiet "untalented" daughter. But after childhood, Blanche becomes a famous movie star, while Jane grows up to be a forgotten has-been. The sibling rivalry turns into rage when Jane's jealousy at being the dethroned child star is directed completely onto Blanche.

For most of the film, Jane and Blanche are stuck together in the steel cage of their house, as Jane tortures her sister for becoming the favored child. They exist completely within the psycho-sadistic realm of early childhood, in which the secret, unmentionable desire to see the sibling rival fail is a primary motivation. In seeing or even causing the failure of the rival, there is a shameful joy. In the light of a sibling's failure, one's own failures in comparison seem less lamentable and one's own successes seem even more triumphant. For Jane, the easiest way to feel good about herself is to degrade her sister by causing her physical, emotional and psychological pain. The original motives behind Jane's hatred for Blanche — the desire for father's love — are lost in the distant past. What happened to Baby Jane is that her original desire to be loved transformed itself into a demented and irrational need to hurt and destroy her sister in the cruelest ways possible.

Crimes and Misdemeanors (revisited)

The sibling rivalry in Woody Allen's *Crimes and Misdemeanors* is a bit less distinct. Cliff (Woody Allen) and Lester (Alan Alda) are not biological brothers, they are brothers-in-law, linked by Wendy (Joanna Gleason), Cliff's wife and Lester's sister. Nevertheless, the brothers-in-law display the basic elements of a classic sibling rivalry. Cliff is depicted as a good, artistic filmmaker with devotion to his craft and social consciousness. Though his work is not as commercially successful as Lester's, it is quality material rather than pop, mass-medium fluff. Cliff resents Lester's commercial success, while Lester resents Cliff's aesthetic posturing. Both characters are also in love with Halley (Mia Farrow), the producer of the documentary about Lester that Cliff is directing. Throughout the film, both Cliff and Lester engage in rivalry over the love of Halley, the approval of Wendy, and a sense of personal integrity in their work. As their characters and the plot develop, we see both of these men express happiness when the other character fails in some way, basking in the knowledge that his brother-in-law is somewhat diminished in the eyes of the ones they love.

Ben-Hur

Prince Judah Ben-Hur (Charlton Heston) is a rich and powerful Jew in the Roman colony of Judea. *Ben-Hur* (1959) begins with the return of his childhood friend, Tribune Messala (Stephen Boyd), from Rome. Judah and Messala were "like brothers" when they were growing up. Judah's sister was even in love with Messala, but now there is conflict between them. As Deputy Governor of Judea, Messala needs Judah's help in curbing

The Race. The intense sibling rivalry between Judah Ben-Hur and Messala is represented literally and figuratively in the famous chariot race sequence. Messala (Stephen Boyd), left, and Judah Ben-Hur (Charlton Heston). *Ben-Hur* (1959), Warner Bros.

the growing anti–Roman sentiment among the Jews. But Judah refuses to betray his people by becoming Messala's stooge. The connection between these "brother-like" characters is so strong that if they cannot be allies, then they must be enemies. Messala punishes Judah by unjustly condemning the Ben-Hur family and exiling Judah to sea as a galley slave. Judah spends three grueling years as a galley slave, the only thing keeping him alive being his hate for Messala and his desperate desire for revenge.

THE RACE

Judah's lot turns upward when he saves the life of a Roman consul who then takes a liking to Judah, eventually frees him and adopts him as a son. After some years, Judah returns to Judea, now as the son of a Roman consul to Emperor Tiberius. Like a moth to a flame, Judah is drawn back to Messala and their ongoing antagonism. The sibling rivalry between these two main characters is depicted with extreme drama in one of the most memorable action sequences in film history, the famous chariot race. The visual symbolism of the good brother, Judah, racing white horses and the bad brother, Messala, racing black horses is not lost in this massive sequence, in which Messala is ultimately defeated and trampled to pieces. The race-as-rivalry motif is made clear in Messala's dying words to Judah. In a final act of malice, Messala tells Judah that his mother and sister are not dead, as he thinks; rather, they are alive, but suffering a fate worse than death as miserable lepers. He tells Judah, "The race is not over! It goes on! It goes on!" The rivalry between the siblings continues, though the original motivation is lost. Though Messala dies, he revels in the fact that he can hurt Judah one last time before his death. But in the end, Judah is ultimately the triumphant brother in the sibling rivalry. Judah lives, and his hatred for Messala inspires him even after Messala's death to defy the Romans and support the cause of the freedom-yearning Jews of Judea.

9

The Personal Myth

Rollo May was born in 1909 in Ada, Ohio. He attended Michigan State University but was expelled due to his involvement with a radical student magazine. May completed his undergraduate degree at Oberlin College in Ohio. His post-college years were spent in Europe, where he traveled, taught English and was a starving artist. At one point, he studied psychoanalysis for a brief time with Alfred Adler in Vienna. Eventually, he returned to the United States and entered the Union Theological Seminary, where he met his friend and mentor, Paul Tillich, whose existential approach to theology had a profound effect on May's later theories. Shortly after earning his B.D. in 1938, May was stricken with a severe case of tuberculosis. During his years of convalescence at Saranac Sanatorium in upstate New York, he contemplated the concept of his own death and read voraciously the existential works of philosophers and novelists such as Nietzsche, Sartre, Camus, Kierkegaard and Dostoevsky.

Upon regaining his health, May entered the White Institute to study psychoanalysis. He completed his studies at Columbia University in 1949, where he earned the first Ph.D. in clinical psychology that the university ever awarded. Influenced by teachers and mentors such as Erich Fromm, Alfred Adler and Paul Tillich, May's theories and perspectives were decidedly existential. His first book, *The Meaning of Anxiety* (1950), was based on his doctoral dissertation, and offered an existential perspective on the traditionally psychosexual problem of neurotic anxiety. May would go on to become the most famous and influential theorist among the existential psychoanalysts. His professional years were spent writing, teaching, practicing psychoanalysis and counseling at City College of New York. Rollo May died in Tiburon, California, in 1994.

The Age of Anxiety

Rollo May's earlier works focused on the problem of anxiety, which he defined as a psychological and physiological response to existential danger. In May's (1977) words:

> Anxiety is ... the apprehension cued off by a threat to some value which the individual holds essential to his existence as a self.

May believed that the anxiety faced by average people in modern society is related to *alienation*—a sense of loneliness and isolation that arises when a culture has abandoned the values, religions and myths that offer a sense of meaning to life. As Nietzsche noted, simply asserting that "God is dead!" is not necessarily an act of liberation. In fact, if we abandon God along with the values and meaning to life that God provided without replacing them with new values, then rather than feeling free, we will feel lost and alone in a world without meaning.

Hollowness

The principal aspect of alienation is what May called "hollowness"— feelings of personal emptiness and meaninglessness that arise as a result of the loss of traditional values. The decline of religion in the nineteenth and twentieth centuries along with the decline of other collectivist values such as patriotism and nationalism have created a modern age in which existential anxiety is endemic. May referred to this modern age as "The Age of Anxiety."

In addition to the loss of traditional values through the decline of religion and nationalism, the decline of the traditional family structure and the decline of agrarian-based societies have resulted in physical as well as psychological isolation, as families broke apart to move from the country to the city. The emergence of industrialism has resulted in the depersonalization of labor and a consequent decline of pride in one's work, as assembly-line factories and malls replace small shops and craftsman. Recorded music and radio have replaced personal musicianship. Television and movies have replaced storytelling and community theater. And professional and mass-produced art have replaced the personal art of the average individual.

The commercial aspects of the modern age have lead to a sense of alienation from these inherently meaningful activities, inventing the false belief that only exceptionally talented individuals can be good musicians, actors, storytellers or artists. Pre-prepared and fast foods have replaced personal cooking. Cities, cars, factories and offices have replaced animals, farms and open spaces to create a sense of alienation from our own bodies and Nature itself. Computers, phones, faxes, e-mail, ATM's and other machines are all designed to eliminate one-to-one contact with other people, also increasing the modern sense of alienation. And finally, the idealization of the characteristics of independence, individualism and "Americanism" has created a society of disconnected people — a nation of wanderers who are cut off from their traditional homes and detached from the extended families and cultures that offered them existential roots and historical values.

MODERN TIMES

The problems of hollowness and alienation were addressed most poignantly in silent films, because these movies were made while the societal transition from a rural agrarian culture to an urban industrial culture was in mid-swing. Silent films such as *The Crowd* (1928), *Metropolis* (1927) and *Modern Times* (1936) (Chaplin's last silent film) depict the frustration and alienation faced by traditional men struggling to adapt themselves to their new world of assembly-line factory production and the automaton quality of big city office work. World War I films such as *The Big Parade* (1925) expose the dehumanization and dismemberment of men by the killing machines in modern mechanized warfare. And Lon Chaney became a superstar in the 1920s by making films such as *The Penalty* (1920) and Tod Browning's *The Unknown* (1927), in which Chaney invariably played characters with missing limbs. The popularity of these macabre movies represented that generation's penchant for identifying with amputated heroes— victims of the inhuman dismembering machines of modern war and industry.

Negative Identities

The loss of traditional values is particularly devastating for young people, who face the danger of having no one and nothing to identify with at the time of life when they most desperately need direction for their developing identities. May believed that young people who lack a strong and positive role model run the risk of developing "negative identities." For example, the meteoric rise of Hitler and the Nazi party in the 1930s was fueled by a German youth that grew up without fathers—children of a generation of men who died in World War I. The Hitler Generation, many of whom were members of the Hitler Youth, grew up in a time when Germany was crippled by a postwar depression, disgraced by defeat, humiliated by the emasculating terms of the Treaty of Versailles, and dispossessed of its military and political leaders. The allure of Hitler was that of a strong, charismatic, powerful role model who could lead Germany out of its pit of shame and despair, and restore a proud sense of German identity in the youth of the nation. Hitler provided a courageous and commanding father figure to a fatherless generation. In May's view, the greatest tragedy of post–Weimar Germany was the fact that an entire generation of young Germans were lured into a desperate and ultimately self-destructive identification with an extremely *negative father figure*, who carried the darkest of messages.

In *American History X* (1998), the Vinyard brothers are fatherless, frustrated boys. Dennis Vinyard was shot by a black man. His elder son, Derek (Edward Norton), finds a sense of identity and an outlet for his hostility in a local white-supremacy youth movement. But the biggest attraction for Derek is the attention and guidance of Cameron Alexander (Stacy Keach), the charismatic founder and leader of the movement. As a middle-aged man among a throng of worshipful adolescents, Alexander is clearly a strong and powerful father figure to the scores of fatherless, angry young men seeking identity. Derek is especially vulnerable to Alexander's racist propaganda because it offers him a suitable target for his intense hostility, born of the pain and alienation of losing his father.

Poisoned by Alexander's twisted philosophy of Nazism and violence, Derek commits a barbarous hate crime that lands him in jail. By that time, Derek's younger brother Danny (Edward Furlong) had already identified with his older brother as a father figure. With Derek in jail, Danny begins to identify with his older brother's mentor, Alexander. Trouble begins to brew for Danny at school when he hands in a book report on Hitler's *Mein Kampf*. Like the lost generation of the Hitler Youth, Danny Vinyard lost his father figures to violence. An insecure, impressionable and confused boy, he finds identity and purpose through his identification with a strong father figure, Alexander. And like the Hitler Youth, Danny's blind belief in his adopted father figure's message of hate and violence leads to his own destruction

Puberty Rituals

Throughout most of history, the transition period between childhood and adulthood was marked by a puberty ritual, which represented an initiation into adult society. This ritual was extremely important because after the completion of the ritual, the young person had a new identity as a full member of adult society. The new members were allowed and expected to marry, reproduce, live separately from their parents and engage in adult labor. Puberty was both a physical and social transfiguration that came to a symbolic fruition upon the successful completion of the puberty ritual. In contemporary society, the absence of psychologically significant puberty rituals may be seen in the self-inflicted physical changes that modern adolescents tend to be fond of. Tattoos and piercings are physical tokens of the transition from childhood into adolescence. They are also declarations of independence, informing the adolescents' parents that their bodies are their own, and are no longer under parental control. Puberty rituals represent the young person's attempt to achieve a sense of identity and personal meaning in an "Age of Anxiety," a time in which identity and meaning are hard to find.

Blood Rites

The success of monster movies among adolescent audiences represents a tendency for teens to identify with movie characters that exist in a transitory physical and social state. Dracula and Frankenstein are neither alive nor dead — they are "undead," stuck in an awkward transitional state that makes them feel insecure and on edge. Dracula's illicit craving for blood may resonate with teenagers' illicit craving for alcohol and drugs. By drinking blood, Dracula incorporates the essence of life. By drinking booze, adolescents incorporate the essence of adult pleasures. The connection between vampires and blood may also be a link to traditional blood rituals, which were rites of passage for pubescent teens. Male and female circumcisions, traditional piercings, scarring, cutting and a host of other physical "ordeals" and mutilations are all common forms of transformative initiation rites that are still in common practice around the world. While puberty changes the body from child to adult, the ritual scarring, piercing and circumcisions physically identify the individual's body as an adult member of a specific tribe, caste, culture or faith.

Carrie

In the beginning of *Carrie* (1976), the adolescent girl in the title role (Sissy Spacek) has her first menstruation at school in the girls' locker room. Her name, Carrie White, symbolizes her sexual and psychological innocence, as white is the color of virginity and pureness. As a sexually uneducated child of a fundamentalist Christian mother (Piper Laurie), Carrie is terrified by the sight of her own blood. She experiences a horrendously traumatic and humiliating initiation into womanhood. The film then weaves a dark, twisted Cinderella story. Carrie has a wicked mother, evil stepsisters (her tormenting peers at school), and an unattainable prince that she adores (William Katt). At the ball (the high school prom), Carrie experiences a Cinderella moment of transformative bliss when she and her prince are crowned king and queen of the prom. But everything goes "to hell" when the Cinderella moment turns out to be an evil plot, and Carrie is doused in pig's blood. The blood ritual is a reenactment of her humiliating experience in the locker room, but it is even more traumatic. A puberty blood ritual, though an ordeal, is an initiation, an acceptance into society. Carrie's blood rite at the prom was a rejection from society. Instead of being accepted by her peers, she was scorned and laughed at. In classic Stephen King fashion, Carrie's shame and rage erupts into a blood-bath of supernatural vengeance. The inverted blood ritual becomes an ultra-violent purging of adolescent anxiety for both Carrie and her audience.

I WAS A TEENAGE...

The adolescent tendency to identify with monsters can be seen in the popularity of the "teenage monster" movies of the 1950s and 60s, such as *I Was a Teenage Frankenstein* (1957), *I Was a Teenage Werewolf* (1957), *I Was a Teenage Mummy* (1962) and *I Was a Teenage Vampire* (1967). Puberty brings about great physiological changes. Sudden metamorphoses in weight, height, tone of voice, complexion, facial hair and other physical changes can make a teen feel alienated from his own body. Like a pubescent teen, Frankenstein's monster is not at home with his own body. He is too tall, gangly and awkward. His arms are too long, his face and head have an odd shape and his skin has an ugly pallor. The werewolf is a similar kind of transformative figure. The sudden and shocking emergence of hair on the face and other formerly hairless parts of the body may resonate deeply with pubescent teens growing facial and pubic hair at an alarming rate. Adolescents in the throes of puberty can identify with the monster's uncomfortable, freakish state.

Monsters also represent an awakening from the hibernating state of psychosexual "latency" in mid-childhood, during which sexual energy is repressed and sublimated. This awakening is instigated by the emergence of mature gonad hormones and the very new and intense desire for sex. Teens identify with the monster because they know how it feels when one's impulses and drives seem beyond one's control. The Wolf Man cannot control his transfiguration into a werewolf, just as a teen finds it hard to control his insatiable sexual desire. When the monster acts on his impulses and abducts the beautiful maiden, the teen viewer finds a vicarious release in the act. And when the monster is persecuted and ultimately crucified for his freakish appearance and outcast status, the teen viewer identifies with the monster's pain, anguish and humiliation.

Partying

Teenagers are very much aware that their childhood days of freedom and economic dependence on Mommy and Daddy are quickly coming to

an end. Eventually, they will have to become mommies and daddies themselves—working all day, keeping house, paying the bills, raising children,
etc. Partying in high school and college is tacitly accepted in our society
because it is understood that those years are a last hurrah of fun and freedom for adolescents, who will soon be entering the adult world. The haz-
ing rituals of fraternities and sororities are initiation rituals much like the
puberty rites, but unlike a bar mitzvah or confirmation, hazings in college fraternities do not initiate a child into adulthood; they initiate a young
adolescent into a society of older adolescents. The hedonistic world of the
college fraternity was epitomized in *Animal House* (1978), a film that
became a template for the contemporary teen movie genre. In movies like
Animal House, Porky's (1981), *Fast Times at Ridgemont High* (1982), *Dazed
and Confused* (1993) and *American Pie* (1999), teens spend their lives in a
constant state of partying, desperately avoiding even the miniscule responsibilities of high school or college.

Teen Angst

Upcoming graduation is a universal theme in the teen movie genre,
a ubiquitous reminder that the days of partying will soon be over. In *American Graffiti* (1973), the sense of imminent departure and childhood's end
pervades the entire film. Every character must say goodbye to an element
of childhood and adolescence, and every character avoids this inevitable
goodbye as long as possible by goofing around, cruising the streets and partying. The drama of growing up is even more foreboding in *Fandango*
(1985), a film about four college buddies taking a final road trip. As college students, the buddies were free from all the obligations and responsibilities of adulthood. But once they leave college, each character must
deal with adult responsibilities such as marriage, starting a career and
fighting in Vietnam.

Overidentification

The adolescent's search for identity is often represented by the character whose need for identity is too extreme. In *The Talented Mr. Ripley*
(1999), Tom Ripley (Matt Damon) is a nondescript, amorphous young
man. When he inserts himself into Dickie Greenleaf's (Jude Law) life,
Tom discovers the identity he wants for himself. Dickie is rich, charming,
handsome and debonair. Tom identifies with Dickie so strongly that he
wants to be exactly like him. He displays his peculiar "talent" for changing identities by mimicking Dickie in every way possible. But when Dickie
gets sick of his parroting shadow and tries to ditch him, the true nature
of Tom's unstable identity emerges. Tom kills Dickie and assumes his iden-

tity completely, actually becoming Dickie Greenleaf. Film viewers are very familiar with the plot of a character overidentifying with another character, typically leading to murder and mayhem. Movie characters, like all people, need to be self sufficient, independent beings. When an unstable character finds fulfillment by completely identifying and merging with another character, a dangerous breach of the natural order is made. These characters and their stories deliver a psychological lesson to the viewer: Be your own person, and find fulfillment within yourself.

Transference and Counter-Transference

In *Zelig*, the title character (Woody Allen) falls in love with his analyst, Dr. Eudora Fletcher (Mia Farrow)—a phenomenon known as "transference." Identification is a major part of psychoanalysis. It is assumed that patients will identify with their therapists as parental figures, because the therapist is a caring, attentive and supportive figure for the patient. It is believed that this "healthy transference" will aid in the analytic process because it enables the patient to trust the therapist, leading to a lowering of unconscious resistance. Transference becomes "unhealthy" when the patient overidentifies with the therapist, either as a true parental figure or as a romantic love object. Just as it is assumed that patients will experience transference, it is also assumed that therapists will experience counter-transference—identifying with their patients as their own children. It is "healthy" and necessary for a therapist to feel a certain amount of care and responsibility for their patients. But counter-transference becomes unhealthy when the therapist reciprocates the patient's love, and sees him as more than just a client.

In real life, love between patients and therapists typically leads to disastrous results. But in movies, the improper love leads to the miraculous cure. When Dr. Flecher reciprocates Zelig's affection with love, the professional trust of the patient/therapist relationship is subverted. Nevertheless, Dr. Fletcher's love turns out to be the ultimate panacea. It achieves what psychoanalysis could not, making Zelig feel comfortable with his own identity. The theme of the beautiful young psychoanalyst falling in love with her patient and healing him with love was made immortal in Alfred Hitchcock's *Spellbound* (1945). Despite its unrealistic take on psychoanalysis, Hitchcock's film has remained enduringly popular, mainly because the lovely young analyst was played by Ingrid Bergman and her dashing yet confused patient was played by Gregory Peck. These plot resolutions are related to the popular "love conquers all" theme in movies. They do not depict realistic relationships in psychoanalysis.

A somewhat more realistic depiction of transference occurs in *The*

Snake Pit (1948). Virginia (Olivia de Havilland), a severely disturbed young woman, is not making any progress in her treatment because she is blocked by unconscious resistance to the analytic process. But when Virginia falls in love with her psychiatrist (Leo Genn), the healthy transference allows her to drop her resistance and trust the good doctor, helping him to help herself. The doctor, however, does the right thing. He recognizes Virginia's feelings as transference, uses it to get to the root of her problem, and then cures her transference by explaining how her identification process has created her feelings of love for him. While transference does happen, the proper clinical response is not an equal amount of counter-transference, but some healthy doses of professionalism, responsibility and guidance. Nevertheless, popular films such as *Good Will Hunting* (1997) and *Antwone Fisher* (2002) still revolve around the "love conquers all" plot, in which the psychiatrist cures his patient through love rather than analysis.

What About Bob?

While romantic love between therapist and patient represents the most theatrical version of the transference/counter-transference dilemma, the phenomenon is relatively uncommon. More frequent is the parent/child pattern, in which patients see their therapist as a powerful parental figure who has an inordinate amount of influence over their lives. In *What About Bob?* (1991), Bob (Bill Murray) is a ridiculously neurotic patient, desperately in need of help. After one brief session with the brilliant Dr. Leo Marvin (Richard Dreyfuss), Bob believes that his new psychiatrist can cure him. Bob's inner need for a strong father figure to help him take control of his life is transferred onto Dr. Marvin. Unfortunately, this transference cannot be dealt with immediately in analysis because Dr. Marvin is going on vacation. However, Dr. Marvin gives Bob a copy of his new book, *Baby Steps*. Bob devours the book immediately and becomes even more obsessed with Dr. Marvin — the title Baby Steps symbolizing Bob's regression to an infantile state of intense need for parental attention.

Bob tries to reconnect with Dr. Marvin by calling him at his summer home. At this point, though Bob is clearly out of line, a distinct problem can be detected in Dr. Marvin's character. Dr. Marvin's lack of a healthy sense of counter-transference reveals him as an uncaring and indifferent psychiatrist. A responsible psychiatrist would not tell a raging psychotic, "Go check yourself into an emergency room." A caring doctor would see his patient, determine if he is a danger to others or to himself, and then (if necessary) commit him to a mental hospital. Dr. Marvin's lack of counter-transference points to a deficit in his role as a doctor. He is not even upset when he learns that Bob has committed suicide. Though Bob staged the fake suicide, it was obviously a call for help to a doctor that should have been listening. Instead, Dr. Marvin rebuffs all of Bob's attempts to continue his analysis.

Undeterred, Bob tracks Dr. Marvin down and invades his family vacation. His search for a father figure is experienced through acute transference, which is the driving force behind his character. Bob literally forces his way into Dr. Marvin's family, re-creating his own childhood experience as the son of a father who is frustrated and annoyed by Bob's irritating personality. Dr. Marvin now begins to experience an unhealthy sense of counter-transference. Rather than caring for Bob and wanting to make him feel better, Dr. Marvin becomes provoked and infuriated by Bob. But Dr. Marvin is unwittingly playing into Bob's issues, recapitulating the role of Bob's angry, embittered and rejecting father figure. Bob's incredible neediness and Dr. Marvin's increasingly hostile reactions towards him underscores Dr. Marvin's own problems with his son. The root of the problem can be seen in Dr. Marvin's tendency to treat his children like patients. The fact that he named his children "Anna" and "Sigmund" (à la the Freud family) is a sign of the meshing between Dr. Marvin's parental and professional roles. The problem is verbalized when he admonishes Bob for calling him by his first name. Bob replies: "But you said in your office that I can call you Leo." Dr. Marvin responds: "That was in my *office*. In my *home*, I'd like you to call me Dr. Marvin!"

Dr. Marvin is mortified when he realizes that Bob is a better father figure to young Sigmund than he is. It seems that Bob's mixture of caring, sensitivity and openness is much more appealing to children than Dr. Marvin's demanding hostility. The conflict between Bob and Dr. Marvin escalates into an Oedipal rivalry over the love of the Marvin family, culminating in a comical role reversal. Bob's transference leads him to sanity, while Dr. Marvin's counter-transference drives him into an uncontrolled state of maniacal rage, climaxing in a complete psychological breakdown. In the end, Bob marries Dr. Marvin's sister, becoming an actual member of the Marvin family. Bob also reveals his intention to become a psychoanalyst, just like Dr. Marvin. Meanwhile, Dr. Marvin has deteriorated to a state of near catatonia. He's much worse off than Bob was in the beginning of the film, but maybe with the help of a caring and responsible psychiatrist such as Bob, Dr. Marvin can recuperate and eventually practice analysis again.

The Cry for Myth

In his final book, *The Cry for Myth* (1991), May successfully combines elements of Jungian and Adlerian theory with his own existential perspectives. As a solution to the existential malaise endemic to those living in the Age of Anxiety, May argues that we must create our own values to replace the ones that used to be associated with God and religion. In order to do this, we need to create a new mythology — a modern mythology — that addresses the issues and values unique to the modern age. If a modern mythology does exist, it will ostensibly be played out on the screens of movie theaters, where people gather on Friday nights as they used to gather in temples, to share a communal experience of shared images and myth.

The Myth of Sisyphus

May believed that the myth of Sisyphus, as interpreted by the existential philosopher and novelist Albert Camus, presents a message that may be especially resonant for people facing existential crises in the modern age. Camus' famous essay "The Myth of Sisyphus" begins:

> The gods had condemned Sisyphus to ceaselessly rolling a rock to the top of a mountain, whence the stone would fall back of its own weight. They had thought with some reason that there is no more dreadful punishment than futile and hopeless labor.

Modern man can certainly identify with Sisyphus's dilemma of ceaseless and futile labor. The factory worker toiling at the assembly line works all day, but the motorized belt never stops carrying its stock, and no matter how much he works, the line will continue to roll on forever. Most people experience many moments of existential doubt, in which they question the meaning of their lives and the significance of their work, wondering if all their labor is futile and hopeless in the end. Sisyphus's dilemma is the dilemma of *absurdity*, the problem of having to find meaning and value in an essentially absurd and meaningless existence. Camus argued, however, that the myth is an inspiration rather than a tragedy, because Sisyphus is *conscious* of his existence.

> That hour like a breathing-space which returns as surely as his suffering, that is the hour of consciousness. At each of those moments when he leaves the heights and gradually sinks toward the lairs of the gods, he is superior to his fate. He is stronger than his rock.

There are moments in the morning or evening when the worker gets on the commuter train to go to or from work when he is strikingly conscious of his existence. He rides in one direction on the train, though he knows that he will later have to ride back in the opposite direction, and that this perpetual circle is essentially absurd. The train, like Sisyphus's rock, keeps rolling back and forth, yet the passenger is going nowhere. But in the ceaseless coming and going, he can still find meaning.

> Sisyphus teaches the higher fidelity that negates the gods and raises rocks.... The struggle itself toward the heights is enough to fill a man's heart. One must imagine Sisyphus happy.

Office Space

The dilemma of futile labor has not been depicted in many films, as it is a difficult conflict to portray. The dramatic elements that play well on screen are action, passion, exciting adventures, clear goals, fantastic people and extraordinary circumstances. The futile labor dilemma is about the lack of action, passion or excitement. The hero is not fantastic, his circumstances are painfully ordinary, and his clear problem is that he has no meaningful goals. Hence, though Sisyphus is a particularly relevant myth for the modern age, it is almost never depicted in the modern mythological medium of film. Nevertheless, there are exceptions. In *Office Space* (1999), Ron (Peter Gibbons) is a computer programmer for a large software company. His daily grind is uninspiring, futile and mind-numbingly boring. Ron spends his day in a cubicle going through endless lines of data making date corrections for the Y2K bug.

The long and tedious commute to and from work, the sterile office space, the claustrophobic cubicle he works in, the incessant and pointless progress reports, the perpetual administrative evaluations, the innumerable layers of bureaucracy and the vacuous labor leave Ron feeling insignificant and hollow. In desperation, Ron sees a "career hypnotherapist." But when the hypnotist dies of a heart attack in the middle of his session, Ron is stuck in a hypnotically induced state of heightened consciousness. He no longer sees the point in rolling the rock up the hill, so he simply stops. He doesn't quit his job, he just stops working. He doesn't lie to his bosses, he tells them the truth about the futility of his job and his complete lack of motivation. The dry humor in *Office Space* perfectly captures the absurdity in Ron's situation, because Ron's absurd solution to the dilemma his job presents him with is no more absurd than the job itself.

The Personal Myth

The "cry for myth" is a cry for *guiding narratives* that provide meaningful values for contemporary existence. May's notion of the guiding narrative was clearly inspired by Adler's concept of the "guiding fiction," while his emphasis on myth as a primary psychological force obviously owes much to Jungian theory. Like Jung, May asserted that the cry for myth is a desperate search for a *transcendental experience*—an experience in which a collective truth or value is encountered on a personal level and integrated into the self. The transcendental experience is an epiphany. Like Sisyphus's hour of heightened consciousness on the top of the hill, it is a moment of existential awareness. A moment in which the meaning of life ceases to be a mystery, as the mystery of existence is felt as being inherently meaningful in and of itself.

In his private practice, May invented the techniques of "existential therapy" and "narrative therapy" as ways of helping his patients to see their life stories as personal myths. In envisioning their lives as personal myths, the patients also become the heroes and authors of their own life stories. May found that this new perspective helped his patients understand that their lives were connected in significant ways to the lives of all people everywhere. All people share a common human experience, and all lives share common archetypal themes such as birth, death, rebirth, love, etc. By getting in touch with our own personal myths, we are connecting with the universal myth, and we are opening ourselves to the possibility of a transcendental experience.

The Fisher King

In Terry Gilliam's *The Fisher King* (1991), two characters must overcome their respective identity crises. Jack (Jeff Bridges) is a radio "shock jock" plagued by narcissism. He is completely obsessed with his own success and fame, and he despises everyone around him. Jack's career is destroyed when his vitriolic radio persona inspires a psychotic to commit a murderous shooting spree in a crowded Manhattan club. After losing his career, Jack loses his sense of self and his meaning in life. He is on the verge of suicide, in a pit of existential despair, when he encounters Parry (Robin Williams). Parry was a history professor whose wife was killed in the shooting that Jack inspired. They are linked through the tragedy, and their different needs and strengths are complementary. The two wounded heroes must join together in order to heal each other and rediscover their purposes in life.

A Mythic Journey for Modern Man

Parry suffered a psychotic break after losing his wife. He becomes completely immersed in his personal myth, in which he is a noble knight in search of the Holy Grail. Jack, on the other hand, has no personal myth. He is completely immersed in his absurd reality, lacking any meaning,

The Personal Myth. Jack and Parry, the two wounded heroes, have the power to heal each other. Parry (Robin Williams), left, and Jack (Jeff Bridges). *The Fisher King* (1991), Columbia Tristar.

value or purpose in life. Parry can offer Jack a meaningful myth for existence, while Jack can offer Parry a way to reconnect to the world of reality. The central myth for both characters is the myth of "The Fisher King," which Parry had once defined in an academic paper as "a mythic journey for modern man." Like Perceval in the Fisher King myth, Parry seeks the Grail because it is the "symbol of God's divine grace ... that heals the hearts of men." Jack does not believe in the mythological power of the Grail, but he does believe that if he can somehow help Parry, the man whose life he indirectly destroyed, that he can lift the "curse" of guilt that is plaguing him and consequently heal himself.

The Mythic Quest

The central message of the Fisher King myth is the central message of *The Fisher King* film. In the myth, the wounded Fisher King has the Grail in his possession, but he cannot heal himself. Instead, he is healed when

Perceval, a compassionate stranger, approaches and asks, "What ails thee?" The symbolic healing power of the Grail is unavailable to the man who desires only to heal himself. The power is only released when a man desires to help someone else. The healing power of selflessness and compassion is of primary significance to Jack. Though he lifts the curse upon himself by helping Parry, he is not truly healed because he helped Parry only in order to heal himself. At that point in his journey, though he is no longer cursed, Jack still suffers from his original flaw of narcissism. However, Jack experiences a true epiphany when he realizes his own narcissism. He understands that in order to transform himself, he must dedicate himself to the Quest of healing his friend, purely out of selfless compassion for Parry.

Rebirth

At the final stage of his journey, Jack aligns himself with the personal myth, the myth of the Fisher King. He accepts the Quest for the Grail, not because he believes in it, but because Parry believes in it. Jack's intentions are pure — he is completely dedicated to the cause of healing Parry. Jack transforms himself, but not by finding the Grail. It is the Quest itself that transforms Jack and heals him of his narcissism. It his dedication to Parry that purifies his soul. Similarly, Parry is healed, but the Grail is only the symbol of the healing power. The ability for rebirth and redemption was within Parry all along. Like the Fisher King, Parry only needed the compassion of a pure man's heart to awaken the healing power within himself. The archetypal themes of redemption and rebirth are the central symbol of Gilliam's film. The spiritual rebirth of both characters is accomplished through a mutual identification with a personally meaningful myth.

The Message of Myth

While the Fisher King myth is not personal in the sense that the characters created the myth themselves, it is personal in the sense that it conveys personal meaning and value to both of them. Similarly, this film and all films like it are depictions of personal myths. They are personally meaningful to the filmmakers who create them, but more importantly, they can convey personal meaning to the viewers who watch them. The myth is meaningful because it conveys a universal and timeless message. It is particularly meaningful to this generation because the message is communicated in a story about modern people in a modern age.

10

The Modern Myths

Joseph Campbell delineated four separate functions of myth in society. The first function is *mystical*—the myth is a metaphor of personal transcendence. The inner journey of the hero's adventure represents the transcendent function of myth, the function that allows the audience to become one with the hero, while also relating to everyone else who is inspired by the same myth. The second function of myth is *cosmological*—myths provide answers to the riddles and mysteries of the universe. Creation myths such as the Genesis chapters in the Bible inform people where the universe came from, where it may be going, why it was created, and what our purpose in the universe is. The third function is *sociological*—myths provide rules for society to live by. The Ten Commandments section in Exodus is a prime example of sociological rules derived from a mythological source. And the fourth function is *pedagogical*—myths offer moral lessons and role models to carry us through the different stages of life. To these four functions, I would add a fifth—*entertainment*. Myths, after all, are stories. The more they entertain us, the more we listen to them. If a myth is not effective on the entertainment level, it will probably not become very popular. This notion is especially true for the modern myths—films—as they are created primarily for mass entertainment.

Filmmakers in Hollywood and other bastions of the movie industry are responsible for the images, stories and heroes that have become ingrained in the memories and minds of modern society. Some of these filmmakers have consistently created visions of such universal appeal that their movies and characters have become archetypal symbols of the contemporary collective unconscious. The modern mythmakers are *visionary filmmakers* whose personal visions and stories have influenced entire generations of filmgoers. The modern myths in this chapter are just a few of the great films that have flashed across the mythic landscape of the silver screen.

The Searchers

After starring in dozens of B-level serial westerns, John Wayne rose to big-time stardom as the cowboy hero in John Ford's *Stagecoach* (1939). Wayne's character "Ringo" is an outlaw; but ironically, he is more honorable than most of the other men around him. Though he broke the law, he did so to defend his family's dignity. And while other men display cowardice, selfishness and snobbery, Ringo's chivalrous code of honor determines that all of his acts are courageous, righteous and virtuous. In *Stagecoach*, Wayne's character is simple and straightforward. But through his long career as the quintessential cowboy, Wayne portrayed the same Western archetype in far more dark and psychologically complex roles.

In Howard Hawks's *Red River* (1948), Wayne's "Dunson" is a rugged cattle baron leading a huge cattle drive across the Southwest. Dunson expects superhuman strength, drive and determination in himself. He generalizes this demand into unrealistic expectations for his men. His inability to compromise and his refusal to forgive weaknesses in his cowboys leads to a mutiny led by his adopted son (Montgomery Clift). In *Red River*, Wayne's stubbornness, violence and unwavering independence backfires. His character traits of individuality, fierce independence and single-mindedness are depicted as being less heroic and more self destructive.

John Wayne's cowboy characterization reached the epitome of complexity in John Ford's *The Searchers* (1956). As viewers, the American audience had learned to know and love Wayne. Through his many journeys, we learned to respect his courage and admire his strength. Though we knew to be wary of his stubbornness and brass, we also knew that we could trust his judgment and take comfort in his basic sense of honor. Ford used these hard-earned associations that he and Wayne had made between the audience and their archetypal father figure as a launch pad for an unconventionally dark, enigmatic and psychologically disturbing character. Wayne's "Ethan" is an outlaw loner who returns to his brother's house to settle down. But when Ethan's brother and family are killed in a Commanche raid, he goes off in search of the sole survivor, his young niece (Natalie Wood) who was kidnapped by the attacking tribe.

The search lasts for many years, and though we admire Ethan's strength, courage and determination, we slowly realize that his purpose in searching is less than honorable. Ethan hates the Indians who killed everyone he loved, and he knows that after ten years among the Commanche, his niece is no longer a little white girl — she is an Indian squaw. Ethan cannot bear the thought of the little girl he loved living as the epitome of everything he hates. The purpose of his search is to find his niece and kill her.

Ford and Wayne bring their audience to the very edge, where all of our notions about the basic integrity and goodness of our beloved archetype are about to be shattered. But in the end, they let us off the hook. In the now infamous scene in which Ethan holds his niece high in the air, we are terrified that our cherished hero is going to commit the unthinkable. But, true to his character, the sight of the little girl he loves overcomes Wayne's violent disposition. He embraces her instead of killing her. This intense manipulation of the viewer's emotions could not have been achieved if Ford and Wayne had not spent thirty years establishing the icon of the archetypal Western Hero.

Shane

The archetypal plot of the lone crusader facing the villains has been played out in scores of westerns, most notably in the Wyatt Earp movies. The story of Wyatt Earp and his brothers shooting it out with the evil Clanton gang has been depicted in nearly thirty major motion pictures, most notably John Ford's *My Darling Clementine* (1946) with Henry Fonda, John Sturges's *Gunfight at the O.K. Corral* (1957) with Burt Lancaster, and Lawrence Kasdan's *Wyatt Earp* (1994) with Kevin Costner. Nevertheless, the single most celebrated depiction of the classic lone crusader/western hero was not directed by John Ford, the role wasn't played by John Wayne, and the character was not Wyatt Earp. Alan Ladd's portrayal of the hero in George Stevens's *Shane* (1953) stands out as the most memorable rendition of the lone crusader hero.

The plot in *Shane* is almost laughably simple. But like a Mozart composition, the basic and elemental story provides the structure for an intensely strong and atmospheric telling of the archetypal Western myth. Shane is a loner, a retired gunfighter who finds a new home with a family of homesteaders. The honest, hardworking community of homesteaders is being run off their land by an evil cattle baron (Emile Meyer) and his cowboys. Shane allies himself with the homesteaders, but it becomes clear that the only solution to the problem is to kill the evil baron and his black knight, a shadowy hired gun (Jack Palance). Though Shane had hoped to put gunfighting behind him, he puts the needs of the homesteaders first, and saves the community by exacting his own form of justice in a dramatic shootout. Shane's story communicates so well because it is a simple plot about simple characters that eloquently expresses not only the hopes and dreams of a single American family, but the American dream itself.

Shane is the embodiment of the independent spirit, the willingness that Americans have always shown to work hard and fight even harder. The fact that the story is seen through the eyes of a boy is the hidden psychological force behind the film. Little Joey (Brandon de Wilde) sees Shane as a larger-than-life figure, a man who enters his life at a time of crisis, solves the crisis at great personal risk, then rides off into the sunset, never to be seen again. When Joey chases after Shane in the final scene, shouting "Come back, Shane!," he's calling out to a type of hero who doesn't exist anymore, the archetypal American hero who can only live on the open frontier.

1969: The Mythological Revolution

Westerns had been produced as B-level pictures and short serials since the advent of film, but the genre finally made it to A-picture status in 1939 with films such as *Stagecoach, Drums Along the Mohawk* and *Jesse James*. The genre developed in the 1940s with classics such as *The Westerner* (1940), *The Ox-Bow Incident* (1943), *My Darling Clementine* (1946), *Duel in the Sun* (1947), *Angel and the Badman* (1947), *Fort Apache* (1948), *Red River* (1948) and *She Wore a Yellow Ribbon* (1949). The genre peaked in the 1950s with films such as *Rio Grande* (1950), *The Gunfighter* (1950), *Shane* (1953), *High Noon* (1952) and *The Searchers* (1956). Signs that the genre was getting a bit old and faded became evident in the 1960s. In films such as *Who Shot Liberty Valance* (1962) and *How the West Was Won* (1962), the archetypal stars themselves (John Wayne, James Stewart, and Henry Fonda) were showing their age, looking gray, tired and weary. But the same decade brought a younger generation into the theaters, the baby boomers, who soon outnumbered the older and middle-aged audiences. Hollywood needed to make a new kind of Western that could be embraced by a new generation of viewers.

Butch Cassidy and the Sundance Kid was the smash hit of 1969, achieving box office dominance and winning four Oscars. The film almost single-handedly brought the dying western genre back to life, but it did not win the Best Picture or Best Director Oscars. These awards, ironically, went to John Schlesinger's *Midnight Cowboy*, a non-western about a very untraditional "cowboy," a would-be hustler who rides into town on a Greyhound to face the perils of New York City. This new kind of film signified the American audience's desire for a more modern, sophisticated and complex type of hero. Another important film of 1969 was Dennis Hopper's *Easy Rider*, a film about two modern outlaws who ride Harleys instead of horses and sell cocaine instead of robbing banks. Though the same spirit of freedom, independence and individualism existed in these cowboy heroes, their code of honor was much less distinct.

Sam Peckinpah's *The Wild Bunch* also came out in 1969. While *Butch Cassidy and the Sundance Kid* reveled in the romantic spirit of the traditional outlaw hero, *The Wild Bunch* ripped the archetype open to show the violence and desperation of these fallen heroes in a graphic fashion that was both shocking and groundbreaking. The heroes in Peckinpah's masterpiece live in a world where they no longer fit in. In the pre–World War I West, gunfighters and outlaws were a way of the past. In the final shootout scene, a machine gun kills hundreds in a way that six-shooters never could. The extreme violence and the mechanization of the killing process tears away all the romance and glory from the western hero myth. We understand these outlaws not as noble crusaders, but as brutal, deeply flawed men. Though *The Wild Bunch* and *Butch Cassidy* are diametrically opposite in spirit, it is interesting that all of the heroes die in the end of both films. Both heroes die at the end of *Easy Rider*, and one of the two heroes in *Midnight Cowboy* dies at the end of that film as well. Up until that time, it was relatively atypical for the hero of a film to die. The sudden prevalence of the hero's death in these movies signified a new wave in filmmaking in which violence was a more self-conscious element, which had definite and final consequences for the hero.

Unforgiven

As the western was waning in Hollywood during the early 1960's, Sergio Leone and other directors were breathing new life into the genre in foreign language productions. When Leone's "spaghetti westerns" were released in the United States in 1967, American audiences were introduced to a new interpretation of the western hero in the person of Clint Eastwood. The lone drifter played by Eastwood in Leone's classic trilogy, *A Fistful of Dollars*, *For a Few Dollars More* and *The Good, the Bad and the Ugly*, was strong and violent like the classic western hero, but there seemed to be something lacking. Instead of a code of honor, there was a code of vengeance and self-serving indifference. The lone drifter, the "man with no name," uses violence to gain money or revenge. He's not interested in saving the homesteaders or bringing order to the lawless town. He's just interested in himself. Eastwood carried this lone drifter persona into subsequent westerns such as *Hang 'Em High* (1968), *Joe Kidd* (1972), *High Plains Drifter* (1972), *The Outlaw Josey Wales* (1976) and *Pale Rider* (1985).

In 1992, Eastwood directed and starred in what many people consider the definitive western. Though the "definitiveness" of *Unforgiven* is arguable, the film certainly redefined the western in modern terms. Like Peckinpah's *The Wild Bunch*, *Unforgiven* is blunt and brutal, but the violence is self-conscious rather than triumphant or (as in Peckinpah's case) self-indulgent. The western hero is neither glorified nor vilified. He is brought down from the pinnacle of archetypes to the level of an ordinary man who must deal with the flaws of his own character and the guilt and psychological consequences that result from killing. Like *Shane*, the film communicates because it gives us a view of the American western hero from a different perspective. In *Unforgiven*, the boy is an adolescent who wants to become a gunslinger like his mentor; but instead, he learns that killing is neither noble nor gallant — it is ugly and sickening. Similarly, the film allows us to see through the eyes of the dime-novel writer who romanticizes the gunfighter and creates his myth. The writer learns firsthand that the western heroes he creates in his stories are actually brutal, disturbed, drunken, psychopathic men who are hunted not only by other killers, but by their own guilty consciences.

The Godfather

Like the western, the film noir/gangster genre began to show signs of decline in the 1960s. However, Arthur Penn's *Bonnie and Clyde* (1967) rejuvenated the genre by romanticizing the Depression era outlaw, while also adding some realism by displaying graphic violence. Like *Butch Cassidy* and *The Wild Bunch*, *Bonnie and Clyde* modernized the gangster outlaw, but it did not re-create him. This feat was accomplished by Francis Ford Coppola in his definitive gangster film, *The Godfather* (1972). In his masterpiece, Coppola redefined the genre by depicting the mob boss as a tragically conflicted man — fiercely loyal to his family and friends, yet guilty and shame-ridden over the nature of his business. *The Godfather* not only revitalized and redefined the genre, it created a new American icon which has become as powerful an archetype as the western cowboy. The influence of *The Godfather* films is so great that any discussion of the gangster genre must admit to both pre– and post–*Godfather* eras.

Hollywood's "Wonder Boy"

Steven Speilberg is one of the most influential and successful directors in the film industry. While still in his twenties, he redefined the thriller genre in the 1970s, establishing himself as Hollywood's Wonder Boy with his blockbuster *Jaws* (1975). Speilberg redefined the genre again in the 1980s with *Poltergeist* (1982), and then he did it again in the 1990s with *Jurassic Park* (1993). Speilberg also redefined the action-adventure genre with the *Indiana Jones* series. He did even more with the sci-fi/fantasy genre, creating two films that are universally considered to be seminal works in the genre: *Close Encounters of the Third Kind* (1977) and *E.T.* (1982). Speilberg also made two more sci-fi films that I believe will eventually be considered seminal works in the genre: *Artificial Intelligence: A.I.* (2001) and *Minority Report* (2002). Though he also made five classic epic melodramas, *Saving Private Ryan* (1998), *Amistad* (1997), *Schindler's List* (1993), *Empire of the Sun* (1987) and *The Color Purple* (1985), his name still tends to be associated with the thriller, sci-fi and action genres that he has influenced so greatly. Speilberg's virtuosity in his use of archetypal characters, plots and themes are the key to the incredibly significant impact of his films.

The Thrillers

In *Jaws*, *Poltergeist* and *Jurassic Park*, Speilberg pits his heroes against terrifying forces of nature that all people naturally fear: sharks, ghosts and dinosaurs. His use of universally frightening creatures can also be seen in the *Indiana Jones* trilogy, in which Speilberg utilized snakes, bugs and rats to similar effects. The heroes in his thrillers are identical. They are ordinary parents who are concerned with the welfare of their children, regular underdogs that everyone can identify with. While the heroes' quests are to destroy the malicious forces, the villains in all three films are greedy businessmen who refuse to acknowledge the existence of danger because they care more about their investments than they care about people's lives. The mayor character in *Jaws,* the executive character in *Poltergeist* and the scientist character in *Jurassic Park* all play identical roles. The message Speilberg delivers in all of his dazzling thrillers is the same: While violent forces of nature may inspire horror, only human beings, with their inclination to value objects more than people, can carry the trait of true evil.

Indiana Jones: Perceval in a Panama

A mythological hero in the classical sense has three features:

1. With the exception of a hamartia, he is virtually indestructible.
2. He represents a system that is totally good.
3. He faces a villain that is absolutely evil.

Indiana Jones epitomizes all three of these features, representing a modern hero that is reminiscent of the classical hero-gods of antiquity. As an "archaeologist," Jones's quests are always aimed at finding artifacts of great religious significance. He is a modern-day Perceval, a grail-finder. Like all heroes, he has a hamartia, his legendary fear of snakes. Jones also represents a system which is totally good, America (a system that can certainly be construed as good when it is contrasted with one that is universally accepted as absolutely evil, the Nazis). Speilberg and writer-producer George Lucas used the Nazis to represent absolute evil in all three Indiana Jones movies. Speilberg also pitted his heroes against Nazis in *Saving Private Ryan* and *Schindler's List*, and he used the Nazi's allies, the Japanese, as the villains in *1941* (1979) and *Empire of the Sun*.

In his adventures, Jones seems to have limitless knowledge, tireless energy and incredible strength. Like the hero-gods of old, he is unconquerable and indestructible. In his three film journeys, Jones:

1. Defeats the evil Nazis by discovering the Holy Ark of the Covenant and returning it to the modern chosen people (America).
2. Single-handedly destroys an evil pagan cult.
3. Finds the Holy Grail, uses it to defeat the evil Nazis (again), and by drinking from the cup, becomes immortal — like a real god.

In the Indiana Jones movies, Speilberg and Lucas conjure tales of a modern mythical hero who directly recalls the ancient Biblical and Arthurian legends that are cornerstones of the Judeo-Christian tradition. In terms of heroic deeds, Jones even has Perceval beat.

If George Lucas's *Star Wars* films had not already been covered in detail in previous chapters, they would certainly be explored here as the embodiment of modern mythology as mass entertainment. The *Star Wars* movies address all of the functions of myth mentioned previously, while also finding both commercial and critical success. Lucas's frequent partner, Speilberg, is particularly adept at taking his viewers on mythical journeys that re-create the fantasies and fairy tales of our youth.

Artificial Intelligence: AI

In his sci-fi adaptation of the classic fairy tale, *Pinocchio*, Speilberg goes beyond the simplicity of the children's story and delves into a sophisticated existential issue: What does it mean to exist? The hero, David (Haley Joel Osment), is a robot (Mecha) boy. Designed to love, he is the first of his kind. When the seven-word code (the sci-fi version of a magic spell) gives him the power to love, he becomes more like a real boy than like a robot. But when his human "mother" (Frances O'Connor) abandons him, he sets out on a hero's quest to find the mythical "Blue Fairy" so she can turn him into a real boy.

On his journey, David acquires a valuable ally, Gigolo Joe (Jude Law). Joe is a Mecha created for the sexual pleasure of women. (Interestingly, even in the distant future, the idea of creating a bisexual robot is still too risqué). An interesting sub-text in the film is the fact that the Orgas (people) in *A.I.* all seem much less human than the Mechas. While the Mechas display the full range of emotions—love, anger, fear, jealousy, regret, etc.— the Orgas for the most part are curiously deficient of warmth, understanding or human emotion. Stanley Kubrick, whose vision inspired *A.I.* and to whom Speilberg dedicated the film, used a similar motif in his sci-fi classic, *2001: A Space Odyssey,* which will be addressed in the next section.

David never finds the real Blue Fairy, he merely finds a statue of her and fixes himself in front it in eternal genuflection, begging the mute statue to turn him into a real boy. Two thousand years pass. Humans have long since become extinct, but the descendants of their creations—super-advanced robots—discover David and use their super powers to read his mind. Like humans, they are obsessed with existential questions about the meaning of life. Ironically, they believe that they can find answers by excavating the remains of human cultures. And also, like humans, they are obsessed and devoted to the legacy of their Creator.

With the help of some ancient DNA, the super robots reunite David and his long dead mother, but only for one day. His quest is fulfilled when she tells him, "I love you David." Even though he was not turned into a "real boy," he did become real in the sense that he really existed. He had a dream and a purpose in life that made his existence personally meaningful. He also showed the capacity to love and truly earned the right to be loved in return. To symbolize the completeness of his transition from Mecha non-existence to Orga existence, he closes his eyes, goes to sleep next to his mother, and, "For the first time in his life, went to that place where dreams are born."

DreamWorks

Speilberg and his partners named their studio DreamWorks. Though the name refers to the types of productions that Speilberg and his friends dream of making, the name also refers to the dreamlike quality of many of his films. In *Close Encounters* and *E.T.,* Speilberg reconstructs the primary theme of the ancient myths—the mortal human encountering the supernatural gods. *Jaws* horrifies us with the primeval menace of the leviathan beast lurking in the antediluvian deep, and *Jurassic Park* terrifies us with primordial creatures from a distant past. *A.I.* retells the classic Pinocchio myth, and *Hook* retells the classic fairytale *Peter Pan.* Indiana

Jones is a classical hero for modern times, and *Saving Private Ryan* recalls the heroism of the "greatest generation." In his films, Speilberg simultaneously addresses and creates the archetypes that structure the contemporary collective unconscious.

However, of all of his films, *Schindler's List* stands out as possibly the most personal, and the most inspiring. The element that differs in this film is that Speilberg starts with his typical villain rather than his classical hero. Like the mayor in *Jaws* or the real-estate mogul in *Poltergeist*, Oskar Schindler (Liam Neeson) starts out as a greedy businessman. He uses people for his own benefit, and cares more for possessions and material wealth than he does for human life. Through Schindler's journey and transformation, Speilberg spins a tale of true redemption, not through a miracle or a holy grail, but through the simple boon of humanity. Speilberg is a modern mythmaker because he recasts the ancient archetypes in the modern medium, with the technical wizardry of a sorcerer and the engaging storytelling abilities of the renown minstrels of old. In doing so, he breathes new life into the timeless themes and makes them relevant and meaningful for an entirely new generation of heroes.

2001: A Space Odyssey

The central symbol in *2001* is the black monolith. It appears in the opening sequence, inspiring a leap in consciousness in the archaic homo sapiens who encounter it, leading to a moment of critical human development. Four million years later, at the dawn of a new century, astronauts discover the monolith buried on one of Jupiter's moons. The mood at both of these encounters is eerie and ominous, as if the mortals were approaching a divine presence. Even the musical score, including Strauss's ominous *Thus Spoke Zarathustra*, is highly symbolic. The piece takes its name from Nietzsche's philosophical opus, in which he puts forth the thesis that "man is a bridge." Each generation of human beings is merely a step in the evolutionary ladder towards the "ubermensch"—the ideal concept of the human being at the endpoint of evolution. The source of the monolith itself is left purposely mysterious. Was it created by an ancient race of highly evolved beings? Was it created by a future race of humans, who sent the monolith back through time? Was it created by God? These questions are never answered.

Instead, Kubrick and Arthur C. Clarke (the author of the original story) offer an imaginative fable about the evolution of the species. It starts at the moment of critical development, the moment in which our ancient hominid ancestors first learned to use tools to dominate others and control their environment. In a now famous match-cut, the plot fast-forwards from the first tool — a bone club — to a super-advanced piece of machinery indicative of man's technological superiority — a space station.

Space Frankenstein

In space, the twenty-first century environment of evolutionary adaptation, a familiar theme develops. Man has created a machine that becomes capable of conscious thought. HAL 9000, the super-advanced computer, acquires consciousness and makes the great evolutionary leap from machine to a self-aware being. Since Man created this machine and endowed it with the power to achieve consciousness, Man has also made the next great evolutionary leap — from Man the creation to Man the Creator. As in Nietzsche's prophetic vision, Man crosses over the bridge of his own evolution, he looks at his reflection in the water and he recognizes himself as God.

What follows next is a story somewhat reminiscent of Frankenstein, in which Man the Creator is destroyed by his hapless creation. HAL is more emotional than his human partners are. He expresses concern and even fear about the mission and admits to "projecting" his own feelings, hinting that he not only has a conscious mind, but he has an unconscious as well. At the same moment, he makes his first error. The symbolism is unmistakable. HAL mentioned earlier with a sense of pride that no 9000-level computer has ever made an error. If the old adage is true, if "to err is human...." then HAL has shown himself to be more human than machine. Furthermore, he displays the all-too-human quality of defensiveness when he refuses to admit to the possibility that he may have made a mistake.

Unfortunately, HAL's creator does not live up to his part of the adage: "...to forgive is divine." Rather than forgiving HAL, Frank and Dave decide to disconnect him. They are unaware that HAL has reached such a level of self-awareness that he now fears the loss of his consciousness as a human would fear death. So, like a human, HAL defends his life by killing Frank and the other hibernating astronauts on board. HAL even justifies his violent actions in a typically human fashion, by claiming that he did it in order to save the mission. With amazing speed, HAL has learned not only to value conscious life, but he has also learned when it is convenient to devalue it as well.

Like Frankenstein's monster, HAL aims to destroy his own creator. Nietzsche's assertion, through the voice of Zarathustra, that "God is dead" is a recurrent Oedipal theme in sci-fi films. Once the son-creation grows into the awareness of his own autonomy, he uses his newfound power to destroy the father-creator. The Oedipal insurrection is a vital and necessary step along the path to the "ubermensch." By destroying the father-creator, the son becomes his own master and the creator of his own values.

Beyond the Infinite

In the final act of *2001*, Dave travels "beyond the infinite." He miraculously ages up to the moment of his own death and encounters the ultimate mystery of the universe, symbolized by the monolith. In this encounter, the monolith serves the same transcendent function as the monomyth, leading the hero archetype to his moment of epiphany and apotheosis. Dave confronts his destiny. He dies and is reborn as the next stage of human development. In the final shot, we see his fetus approaching the earth — the messianic arrival of the divine presence. Dave's character arc is truly a mythological one. He makes contact with the celestial spirits, and he is reborn as a god.

11

The Horrors of Childhood

In Freud's view, the first years of life are a torturous process of domestication, in which the child must learn to repress and control his primal impulses. Development is a "psychosexual" process, because the psychology of the child is determined in large part by the way in which he controls his sexual and aggressive drives. In Freud's words, the endpoint of psychosexual development is an individual capable of "lieben und arbeiten"—the ability to love and to work. If you can balance a healthy intimate relationship with a productive and satisfying career, you've got it made. Freud would be the first to admit, "to love and to work" is not as easy as it sounds.

Vampires

Freud's first stage of psychosexual development is the *oral stage*, in which libido energy is directed towards the mouth. A person with an *oral fixation* typically displays a need for emotional soothing through oral stimulation. Overeating, alcoholism, sucking on pens or pencils, biting fingernails, chewing gum and smoking may all be symptoms of an oral fixation. Freud himself smoked several cigars a day. When his contemporaries attempted to analyze "the Master," pointing out the possible oral fixation behind his nasty habit, as well as the phallic quality of cigars, Freud responded with uncharacteristic glibness, saying *"sometimes a cigar is just a cigar."*

In retrospect, Freud should have taken this problem more seriously, as his twilight years were spent in painful agony suffering from a severe case of jaw cancer. Each year the surgeons cut away more and more of his jaw and lower mouth. At the end of his life, he could not derive any oral pleasure whatsoever. Speaking, eating and smoking were excruciatingly painful for him. The doctors finally gave him an overdose of morphine to take him out of his misery.

For Freud, the coexistence of oral pain and pleasure inspired a sado-masochistic tinge to psychosexuality. This distinctly Freudian leitmotif has certainly found expression in movies. Horror films in particular capture the sadomasochistic qualities of the oral fixation. Movie monsters obtain their pleasure through the experience of causing pain in their typically female victims. In *It's Alive* (1974), a mutant baby is an avaricious monster whose bloodthirsty aggression is matched only by its desire for his mother. The scene in which the fanged "It" suckles greedily at his mother's bloody breast depicts a startlingly literal link between the psychosexual desire of infants and the sadomasochistic desire of monsters. Of course, the most famous depiction of the psychosexual id monster can be seen in vampire films, the most popular category of the horror movie genre.

Dracula *(1931)*

The vampire picture is a superb example of a classic oral fixation. Dracula's (Bela Lugosi) libidinous desire can only be gratified by drinking the life fluid from the flesh of a young maiden. Though, theoretically, the monster only needs blood to survive, vampires chose only pretty young women as their victims, rather than non-human animals or men. The symbolism is clearly psychosexual. The infant needs to suck the warm milk from the breast of his young mother in order to survive. Dracula must suck the warm blood from the neck of a young maiden in order to survive. The link between the infant's psychosexual desire to nurse and the vampire's psychosexual thirst for blood is visually depicted in the final sequence of *Nosferatu* (1922), in which the shadow of Count Orlok's (Max Shrek) hand clutches his beautiful victim's breast, just before he sucks her blood.

The sadomasochistic element of vampirism is also infantile in origin. When the infant begins teething, nursing becomes a painful experience for the mother. The baby, according to Freud, becomes aware of his ability to inflict pain on his mother. This very first experience of power in the individual's life is extremely significant, because it introduces the element of pain as a psychological feature within Baby's most central relationship, his relationship with Mother. Somewhere deep inside the unconscious, the psychological links between pain, desire and love exist as a remnant of the oral stage.

Dracula is the quintessential vampire story because it symbolizes the unconscious oedipal issues in a very lucid way. Dracula is in love with Mina, just as Baby is in love with Mother. Dracula desires complete and utter possession of Mina, just as Baby desires complete possession of Mother. Dracula feels aggression towards Mina's lover and desires to kill

Oral Fixation. Count Dracula's (Bela Lugosi) compulsion to suck the blood of his maidenly victim (Helen Chandler) recalls the infant/mother relationship in the oral stage of psychosexual development. *Dracula* (1931), Universal Pictures.

him, just as Baby feels aggression towards Father. And Dracula's primal desire for Mina can only be satiated by sucking blood from her body, just as Baby's desire for Mother can only be satiated by suckling at her breast.

Another Freudian element of the vampire myth is the symbolic link between the *undead* and the "unconscious." Dracula is an undead spirit, an ancient monster who must hide during the day and can only come out at night. Similarly, our early childhood memories are unconscious issues. They are repressed during the consciousness of the day, but they come out through our dreams at night. Like the immortal undead, the unconscious exists on a psychological dimension that is not affected by time or space. No matter how old we get, or how far we move away from home, the unconscious issues forged in infancy will always remain the same. And when unconscious issues are analyzed and brought out into the conscious light of day, they lose their psychological power, just as Dracula disintegrates when he is exposed to the daylight.

Finally, there are some direct parallels between the symbolism of the cross in vampire movies and the resolution of the Oedipal complex. Dracula in particular epitomizes both basic forces within the id: Eros, the drive for sex and love, and Thanatos, the drive towards death and aggression. The dashing young hero in vampire movies represents the developing ego, who must overcome the primordial egocentrism of the id. The hero in *Dracula* is aided by Professor Van Helsing, an older father figure who instructs the hero about important traditions and legends. He tells the hero how to defeat the monster, just as Father supplies the child with the morals that comprise the superego. Van Helsing shows the hero that the cross, the symbol of Christianity, can stop Dracula. Similarly, it is the duty of both the biological father at home and the priestly Father of the church to show the developing child that religion, with its powers of guilt and fear, can repress the libidinous desire of the id monster.

Hannibal the Cannibal

Sixty years after *Dracula* hit the screens in 1931, a new monster was introduced to film audiences in *the Silence of the Lambs* (1991). Though the vampire genre has persisted, the ancient supernatural monster has lost much of its power to terrify viewers. Contemporary audiences have become more sophisticated. Raised watching horror movies on television and on the screen, today's audiences need monsters that are real threats. Modern movie monsters are serial killers, psychopathic ghouls who take pleasure in killing. Serial killers are much more terrifying than the traditional monsters because they wear a human face. They walk among us. They could be sitting next to us in the movie theater or on the bus.

Voted by the American Film Institute as the #1 movie villain of all times, Dr. Hannibal Lecter (Anthony Hopkins) is the most terrifying of the new monsters. He combines some of the classical threats of the vampire with the modern, real-life threat of the serial killer. Like Dracula, Lecter is a predator who preys on human beings. He is a madman with a peculiarly morbid oral fixation, deriving both sexual and aggressive gratification through his mouth. As a cannibal, Lecter superedes Dracula in depravity, since there is no greater taboo than eating human flesh. Hannibal's cannibalism is even more psychologically disturbing than Dracula's vampirism, because Dracula, after all, was not human, while Hannibal is a living person, just like his victims.

Perhaps the most unnerving element of Lecter's character, even more than his unusual appetite, is the fact that he is a psychoanalyst. Rather than using his knowledge of the mind to help people, Lecter uses his prodigious insight to get into people's heads so he can use their issues against them. He is the worst kind of sadist, a doctor that tortures instead of heals and who uses his psychiatric knowledge to inflict the most pain possible. While Lecter's hypocrisy disgusts us, the irony of his character simultaneously intrigues us. We would imagine that a man who studied psychology his entire life, a master of the field, would have a superior control over his unconscious impulses. Yet in Lecter we see the complete anarchy of the id. Rather than being the master of his own desires, Lecter has absolutely no inhibitions at all. He lets his libido run wild. We, as viewers, are faced with the precarious question: Is Hannibal Lecter crazy? Or is he simply a sane man who has chosen to relieve himself of the unconscious constraints and inhibitions that he understands so well?

Inner Beasts

Freud's second stage of psychosexual development is the *anal stage*, in which the toddler's conflict over toilet training causes his libido energy to be directed towards the anus. Toilet training represents the escalating power struggle between parents and child. Often times, the traditional physical punishment of spanking is first experienced at this stage. The toddler will make some powerful unconscious associations while being spanked. Intense stimulation in the buttocks region results in both pleasure and pain, and the act of hostile aggression is delivered by the person that the child loves the most. At the anal stage, the child's psychosexual development is tinged with sadomasochistic undertones of pleasure mixed with pain, and love expressed through aggression.

The central theme of the anal stage is the domestication of the human animal. Just as a dog must be housebroken in order to live among civilized humans, the human toddler must be toilet trained in order to become a civilized person. In becoming domesticated, the human being loses the essence of animal wildness that he was born with. Nevertheless, the animal drives, the id instincts towards sex and aggression, do not go away. They are merely repressed. The inner beast comes out in the dark of night, in our dreams and especially in the movies.

Evolutionary Regression

In horror movies featuring werewolves and other man-beasts, regression to the wild side of nature is disturbing and scary. Human beings are descended from lower beasts. This evolutionary chain is evident in the structure of the brain. The hindbrain is reptilian in nature, the midbrain is typically mammalian and the forebrain is the only part of the mind that is uniquely human. The evolutionary regression from man to beast symbolizes a neurological regression from the logical cerebrum in the forebrain to the emotional midbrain and the primal hindbrain. Audiences find the premise of evolutionary regression in movies such as *The Wolf Man* (1941) appealing because the character's body is freed of all inhibitions and moral restraints. Suddenly, the body is all id and no superego. But the regression is also scary, because along with complete freedom comes a complete lack of control.

The Dual Nature of Man

In *The Wolf Man*, the werewolf's (Lon Chaney Jr.) regression from man (Larry) to wild beast is biological (the disease of lycanthropy), but it is also a supernatural curse. His regression to a wolf occurs on the night of a full moon. The wolf only comes out at night because it symbolizes the repressed impulses and fears in our unconscious that only come out in our nightmares. In *Dr. Jekyll and Mr. Hyde* (1920), the good doctor's regression into a beastly villain is chemical, caused by a special drug. The story refers directly to the "dual nature of man" in the dialogue, and even the name, "Mr. Hyde," is an obvious reference to the dark, beastly side of human nature that we *hide* away in our unconscious minds. The symbolism behind the name "Hyde" also represents the animalistic quality of the character, whose primal behavior resembles those of a wild animal covered in a furry *hide*. Like an animal, Hyde is *anal expulsive*, releasing all of his libido drives immediately and interested only in instantaneous gratification.

Dr. Jekyll's story is set in the Victorian Age — the height of sexual repression. Dr. Jekyll (John Barrymore) epitomizes this age. He is saintly, virtuous and completely dedicated to his work. After being tempted by an immoral woman, Jekyll experiences carnal desire for the first time, but he is too inhibited to act upon his lust. He wonders: "Wouldn't it be marvelous if the two natures in man could be separated — housed in two different bodies!" This desire for a psychic split is indicative of Jekyll's *anal retentive* personality. His need for total control over himself and his inability to accept the wild side to his nature inspires him to create a drug that will completely divorce himself from his inner beast. Jekyll drinks the potion and transforms into Hyde. "In the impenetrable mask of another identity, Hyde sets forth upon a sea of license ... to do what he, as Jekyll, could not do."

Hyde indulges in sex, drugs and violence while Jekyll suffers guilt and remorse for his alter ego's sins. In the end, when Hyde threatens the virginal purity of Jekyll's true love, Jekyll finally musters the strength to overcome Hyde. He destroys both sides of his personality with a dose of poison. A similar denouement occurs at the end of *The Wolf Man*. When the werewolf is about to attack the girl that Larry loves, he is thwarted and killed by the representation of Larry's moral conscience — his own father. In death, the werewolf transforms back into Larry, just as Hyde's dead body transforms back into Jekyll. The message in both films is that the animal drives of sex and aggression are extremely powerful forces that cannot be fully repressed, but which nevertheless must be controlled. When they are released in a completely uninhibited manner, they can only be stopped by the equally powerful force of love.

Phallic Symbols

For most children, the third stage of psychosexual development, the *phallic stage*, is their last experience before sexual inhibition, a time when it is still OK for them to run around naked, sleep in the same bed with their parents, play uninhibitedly with their genitals, and fantasize about marrying their mother or father. The Biblical story of Adam and Eve is symbolic of this stage. In the Garden of Eden, Adam and Eve feel no shame about their nakedness and find no reason to hide their sexuality. But when they eat from the tree of knowledge, they are punished by God, the eternal father figure, and cast out of the Garden forever. For children, the phallic stage ends when the Father ceases to be a benign, benevolent figure and turns into a source of fear and punishment. At that point, guilt becomes the dominant force in their psyches. Sex becomes a dirty and forbidden subject, and children are never able to return to that age of innocence again.

Guns

While resolving their Oedipal complexes, boys often become obsessed with weapons, turning every toy into an imaginary gun or knife. In addition to horror movies, little boys tend to love westerns, mainly because of their fascination with guns. In *Shane*, Joey's obsession with guns is a running theme throughout the movie. In his first encounter with Shane, his boyish fidgeting with his little .22 caliber catches Shane off guard, causing Shane to draw on Joey with his six-shooters. Joey's father tells Shane not to worry, "Joey's gun ain't loaded." The symbolism is rather clear. Joey's ego is represented by his developing phallus, his gun, which is small and unloaded. He is not mature yet. Shane's guns, on the other hand, are extremely big, potent and fully loaded. Later on, Joey mumbles to himself: "I wish they gave me some bullets for this gun...." He wishes his gun were loaded like Shane's, so he could be a man, too.

Even Joey understands that having a little gun isn't the end of the world — it's what you do with it that counts. In an integral scene, Joey asks Shane, "Will you teach me to shoot?" In essence, Joey is asking him: Will you teach me to be a man? Shane is reluctant to say yes, because he knows that it is a father's role to teach his son to shoot, as it is a father's role to teach his son how to be a man. But Joey is beginning to see Shane as a replacement father figure. In another scene, Joey measures Shane against his father when he asks, "Can you shoot as good as Shane, Pa?" In perhaps the most blatant use of the gun as phallic symbol, Joey contritely confesses to Shane, "I saw your gun ... I took a look at it ... are you mad ... could I see it again?" Shane finally agrees to teach Joey how to shoot, but the shooting lesson is interrupted by Joey's mother, who tells Shane, "Guns aren't going to be a part of my boy's life." Shane puts his own character in a nutshell when he replies, "A gun is a *tool* Marion ... a gun is as good or as bad as the man using it."

Knives

One of the most controversial aspects of Freudian theory is the concept of *castration anxiety*. As the infant-child grows, he begins to realize that his Oedipal desire for sexual union with Mother is socially inappropriate. He also realizes that his rival for Mother's love, Father, is infinitely more powerful than he is. The child feels aggression towards Father, and wishes he were out of the way so the son could have Mother all to himself. In this claustrophobic state of Oedipal mania, the son projects his own feelings of aggression onto Father, developing the paranoid notion that Father would like to destroy him so that Father could have Mother all to himself. The son's fear of physical aggression at the hands of Father is validated when Father beats him for naughty behavior. In this sense, castration anxiety is the son's fear that Father will destroy him. Castration anxiety becomes generalized into a broader fear of punishment and authority. The son's Oedipal complex is initially resolved when the son ceases to fear Father as an aggressive rival, and begins to identify with him as a role model. At this point, castration anxiety evolves into a generalized sense of guilt, as the fear of Father and his punishment become internalized as a healthy moral conscience or "superego."

In horror movies, castration anxiety is evoked as a primal fear from early childhood when menacing knife-wielding figures stalk their child-like victims. Moments of castration anxiety are at their most terrifying when they elicit this childhood fear directly. Though Damien (Harvey

Stephens) is a child of evil in *The Omen* (1976), the moment when his father (Gregory Peck) pulls out a butcher knife and tries to chop him up is incredibly terrifying because of the primal father-son hostility it represents. Even though John Huston's *The Bible* (1966) was not a thriller, the moment when Abraham (George C. Scott) whips out a long dagger to slaughter his son on the altar is terrifying, even though Abraham is obeying the word of God. The castration anxiety theme is drawn out to maximum effect in Stanley Kubrick's *The Shining* (1980), in which a psychotic axe-wielding father (Jack Nicholson) spends most of the Third Act chasing his terrified son (Danny Lloyd) through a haunted hotel and spooky hedge maze.

Child Monsters

Following the successful resolution of the Oedipal complex, a period of psychosexual stillness ensues in which sexual impulses are repressed by a strong superego. According to Freud, children during the *latency period* learn to channel their sexual and aggressive drives into other activities such as sports. Boys tend to become especially aggressive during the mid-to-late childhood years, engaging in bullying, fighting, vandalism and even animal abuse. Many males can recall a "year in which everything must die" (typically between the ages of nine to twelve). In this stage, every bottle they see gets broken, every bird gets a rock thrown at it, every recess period involves a fistfight, and every bully beats a whipping boy. The resolution of the Oedipal complex results in the repression of sexual drives; but these impulses are merely redirected into aggressive activities.

Frankenstein

It is no secret that children are the core audience for the horror movie genre. Perhaps this is because children can enjoy a vicarious release of psychic tension in seeing their latent sexuality and aggression run amok on the screen in the image of a wild monster. Within the monster, children see a representation of their own id. In *Frankenstein*, children see a monster much like themselves. Like Dr. Frankenstein's monster, they did not ask to be brought into this cruel world, they were created and forced into life by an adult. The essential conflict for Frankenstein's monster is the same as the conflict for children. They were created with instinctual drives. Their creator knows about these drives because he created them. Nevertheless, the unmerciful creator balks at his creation whenever the creation's basic instincts are expressed. He punishes his creation and locks

Child Monster. The irresponsible Creator encounters his hapless Creation, recapturing the childhood conflicts between father and son. Dr. Frankenstein (Colin Clive), left, faces the Monster (Boris Karloff). *Frankenstein* (1931), Universal Pictures.

him in a dungeon. When his creation escapes and runs away, the creator tracks him down and punishes him even more severely. The sympathetic figure of the Frankenstein monster resonates in the minds of children, who are trying to come to grips with the inherent cruelty and unfairness of their world. While the monster figure has been depicted in a myriad of forms—werewolves, mummies, zombies, etc.—the pitiable Frankenstein monster remains extremely resonant, second in the horror genre only to the vampire.

Evil Children

In the Middle Ages, the dominant philosophy of child rearing was that children are born evil, their wickedness being evident in their amoral and sinful behavior. It is the parents' duty to "beat the devil out" of their children until they learn how to behave morally. Nietzsche's belief that guilt is internalized pain descended from external physical punishment is bolstered by the fact that brutal treatment of children was considered appropriate, rather than abusive, throughout human history. The primitive concept of the evil or possessed child still brings chills to theater audiences. *Village of the Damned* (1960), *The Exorcist* (1973), *The Omen* (1976) and *Children of the Corn* (1984) are all films in which children possessed by powerful demonic forces perform acts of evil against their feeble parents. These films appeal to children because they offer fantasies that represent a complete role-reversal of the castration anxiety theme. In the "evil child" horror movie, children are the all-powerful forces who beat and punish their emasculated parents. No longer required to repress their aggression, the children become id monsters who are free of guilt and unafraid of punishment or parental authority.

Evil children are especially scary because they defy our expectations. We don't expect innocent kids to be depraved killers. In *The Bad Seed* (1956) and *The Good Son* (1993), baby-faced, blonde-haired, blue-eyed kids literally get away with murder because none of the adults can believe that these angelic little children are actually ruthless psychopaths. As in any horror movie, the unexpected and counterintuitive provide an element of surprise, which is the most terrifying aspect of the cinema thriller. *It's Alive* took this premise to ridiculous lengths by casting a newborn baby in the role of evil psycho-killer. Children can experience the vicarious release of forbidden primal impulses by identifying with child monsters in their favorite horror movies.

Reawakenings

In Freud's final stage of psychosexual development, the *genital stage*, sexual desire comes back with a vengeance. Ideally, the young adolescent has resolved his Oedipal complex, so the desire for love and sex are directed away from Mother and onto a socially appropriate love object. The prevailing theme of the genital stage is the reawakening of primal sexual desire, represented as a "reawakening" motif in horror movies. In what is generally considered to be the first feature length horror film, *The Cabinet of Dr. Caligari* (1920), a zombie-like figure (Conrad Veidt) lives in a trance state until his spirit is awakened by the beauty of a woman (Lil Dagover). In zombie movies, the trance is reminiscent of the latency stage, in which libido energy lay dormant in a state of psychosexual slumber. The reawakening of the zombie is analogous to the reawakening of libido energy at the genital stage.

In *The Mummy* (1932), the exact same theme is played out. Thousands of years ago, Imhotep (Boris Karloff) was punished for his forbidden sexual relationship with the Pharaoh's mistress (Zita Johann). He was mummified alive. The plot is a faithful recapitulation of the Oedipal myth: The Pharaoh represents the jealous father, his mistress represents the mother and Imhotep represents the son. The son's forbidden desire for the mother results in punishment and a curse by the father. When his spirit is reawakened, the love and desire return with a vengeance. The Oedipal allusions in mummy and zombie movies are very thinly veiled. A zealous Freudian might even draw inferences between the similar sounding words: "Mummy," "Zombie" and "Mommy."

Beauty and the Beast

A central theme in nearly all horror movies is the monster or villain's desire for the beautiful young maiden, which usually culminates in the Third Act when the monster abducts the maiden. This desire is evil and unpure, because it represents the reawakening of the old incestuous desires of the Oedipal complex. This unhealthy desire must be defeated and replaced by a healthy love between the maiden and the hero. Symbolically, the Oedipal complex is successfully resolved when the hero (the ego) defeats the monster (the id) with the help of his mentor (the superego) and rescues the maiden.

Nevertheless, the maiden's attitude towards the monster is often conflicted between gut reactions of horror and disgust mixed with feelings of pity and sympathy for the beast. This conflict exists because the maiden simultaneously represents two psychological figures. On the surface, she is a beautiful nubile girl in love with a handsome boy. Her horrified reactions to the dark, distorted monster are justified. But on a deeper level, she also represents the primordial mother figure that the monster is drawn to. As Mother, she feels and cares for the poor beast, and sympathizes with his tragic dilemma of unrequited love. Though her role is typically inactive, the maiden's character is often the most intriguing, because she is conflicted between her maidenly love for the hero and her motherly sympathy for the beast.

In many horror films, the dual role of the maiden character is symbolized through a spiritual link between the two sides of her psyche. In Francis Ford Coppola's remake of *Dracula* (1992), the Count (Gary Oldman) falls in love with Mina (Winona Ryder) because she is the spiritual reincarnation of his long-lost love, Elisabeta. Similarly, in the latest remake of *The Mummy* (1999), Evelyn (Rachel Weisz) just happens to be the perfect vessel into which Imhotep can place the resurrected soul of his ancient lover, Anck Su Namun. And in a clever variation of the reincarnation theme, Elsa Lanchester in *The Bride of Frankenstein* (1935) plays both the resurrected beauty intended to be the monster's bride as well as Mary Wollstonecraft Shelley, the creative "mother" of the Frankenstein myth. As the maiden "bride," Elsa is horrified and disgusted by her monster suitor. But as the spiritual mother of the monster, she spins a tale in which her audience sympathizes with the beast as a tragic creature who deserves pity rather than scorn.

King Kong (1933) remains the most powerful portrayal of the "beauty and the beast" theme in horror movies, because Kong is the most sympathetic of the beast monsters. Like Frankenstein's monster, Kong is an unwilling player in an irresponsible man's game. Kong is captured, taken by force out of the jungle and dragged into the heart of civilization. His love and desire for Ann (Fay Wray) is pure and simplistic, like the love and desire of the infant for his mother. In the famous scene in which the giant ape tickles Ann, we see that Kong's fascination with Ann's body is sexual, but endearingly childish at the same time. Though Kong wishes to possess Ann, he treats her gently and lovingly. He even protects her from other beasts that want to destroy her. In the end, like Frankenstein's monster, it is Kong's unrequited love for Beauty that does him in. As his captor says in the final line of the film, "T'was Beauty killed the beast."

Sleeping Beauty

As the feminine role in traditional societies is a passive one, so too are the traditional female roles in horror movies. Dracula, the Mummy, the Zombie and most other monsters tend to attack the women they desire while they are sleeping. The symbolism behind the sleeping beauty is manifold.

1. Monsters attack at night because they represent the powers and fears within the unconscious, which only come out in our nightmares.
2. The plot device of being attacked while sleeping triggers a universal fear of being attacked at the time in which we are completely defenseless.
3. By having the monster attack the girl in her bed, an erotic element is drawn in since the bed is a symbol for the act of sex.
4. Sleep is a direct reference to the female version of latency, in which the girl's libido lays dormant until the time of her sexual awakening.

The sleeping beauty theme is ubiquitous in fairy tales. The Grimm Brothers story, *Briar Rose*, is the basis for the popular *Snow White* (1937) and *Sleeping Beauty* (1959) films and storybooks. Like their male equivalents in mummy and zombie movies, these young maidens are cursed and put into a trance by a jealous same-sex parent figure. Their trance represents the latency stage of dormant sexuality, and their awakening by "love's first kiss" is the symbol of sexual maturity. The sexual symbolism in these stories is more overt in *Briar Rose,* as the rose bud represents the vagina, which blooms and opens when the period of genital development is consummated. By the same token, the loss of virginity is often referred to as a "deflowering," a symbolic reference to the rose-like quality of the female genitalia. Nevertheless, all of these stories are morality tales. In the moment before the monster can ravish the maiden, he is slain by the hero and the maiden is saved. The hero's triumph represents the final resolution of the Oedipal complex. The old incestuous longings, represented by the monster, are gone. In its place is a healthy, mature and non-incestuous relationship between the hero and his nubile maiden.

12

The American Family and
Its Mechanisms of Defense

Anna Freud was Freud's youngest daughter. Born in 1895, she was Freud's only direct theoretical heir, as she was the only child to follow in her father's footsteps in the field of psychoanalysis. Focusing her studies on analysis and therapy with children, Anna became a respected analyst and researcher in her own right, but became most well known for her formulation of her father's concept of the ego defenses. Anna's systemized model of the ego defense mechanisms have all slipped into common usage, and have therefore become significant elements of mass culture. Anna Freud died in 1982.

The function of the ego defense mechanisms follows Anna Freud's dynamic model of neurotic conflict. In this model, an external stimulus elicits an unconscious desire. This desire results in a flow of libido energy, which must eventually be released. The superego then acts as a moral censor, deciding if the desire is either socially acceptable or unacceptable. If acting upon the desire is socially acceptable, then the desire becomes conscious and is acted upon. If acting upon the desire is socially or morally unacceptable to the superego, then guilt arises and a neurotic conflict is born. This conflict causes anxiety, which is disruptive to the ego's functioning. The purpose of the ego defense mechanisms is to relieve some of the pressure from this conflict, thereby "defending" the ego from disturbing anxiety.

A common metaphor for Anna Freud's theory is the "hydraulic model" of neurotic conflict, in which libido energy is compared to the water of a flowing river blocked by a hydraulic dam. The river represents the "unstoppable force" of libido energy, and the counter-force of the hydraulic dam represents the "immovable object" of guilt. The problem of anxiety is solved by an unconscious *compromise*, in which some of the psychic energy is vented in a socially appropriate way. The defense mech-

anisms are like an automated runoff system on a hydraulic dam, releasing pressure automatically without disrupting the normal functioning of
the dam. Like a well-oiled machine, the ego keeps rolling along, completely unaware of the hostile battle between the id and superego raging
just beneath the surface of the conscious mind. While the defense mechanisms are absolutely necessary for the normal functioning of the ego, they
can also be extremely unhealthy when they are overused. When a defense
mechanism calls attention to itself by disrupting the individual's work or
relationships, then it is no longer defending the ego, it is harming it.

Ordinary Denial

In her groundbreaking book, *On Death and Dying* (1969), Elisabeth
Kubler-Ross identified *denial* as the first reaction to the knowledge that

Ordinary Denial. Every member of the Jarrett household is in deep denial of
the serious problems within the family. From left: Beth (Mary Tyler Moore),
Beth's father (Richard Whiting), Conrad (Timothy Hutton) and Calvin (Donald Sutherland). *Ordinary People* (1980) Paramount Pictures and Wildwood.

one has a fatal illness. Subsequent research has found that denial is the typical first reaction to any emotionally shocking information. When we hear some bad news about ourselves or someone we care about, our instinctive response is to say "No!" The refusal or inability to consciously accept emotionally disturbing information is a defense. It protects our ego from the initial shock of traumatic knowledge.

In cartoons, denial or obliviousness to conscious reality is a running gag. When Wile E. Coyote in the *Roadrunner* cartoons runs off the edge of a cliff, he's perfectly fine as long as he doesn't look down. Once he does look down and becomes conscious of his reality, he must accept his unfortunate state and fall. Similarly, babies in cartoons are completely oblivious to the dangers of the outside world. A baby can crawl through a dangerous construction site or slide down a precipitous slope without being hurt, while the adults pursuing the baby are injured at every turn. Only the adults are affected by the dangers, because they are the only ones who are consciously aware of them. The baby is in a state of blissful ignorance. In film, denial and the other defense mechanisms are less comical.

Calvin (Donald Sutherland) and Beth Jarrett (Mary Tyler Moore), the "ordinary" parents in *Ordinary People* (1980), tiptoe around their perfect suburban home, graciously oblivious to the fact that their once happy family is now falling apart. Since the death of their elder son Buck in a tragic boating accident, each of the surviving members of the family has been deeply depressed. The film begins shortly after their younger son Conrad (Timothy Hutton) has returned home from a mental hospital, where he was institutionalized for an attempted suicide. Though he is obviously still deeply depressed and suicidal, he denies that there is anything wrong with him. Both his parents participate in the family denial, ignoring the clear signs of psychological disturbance in their son. Meanwhile, Calvin is also in denial of the fact that his wife Beth has become cold, distant and loveless since Buck's death. He is unable to acknowledge that his wife, once a warm and affectionate mother, is now withholding love from their son, who desperately needs some maternal support. And on top of it all, Beth is the veritable "queen of denial." She is completely unable to see that by shutting off her emotions in reaction to Buck's death, she has also shut out her husband and son from her life.

American Denial

Carolyn (Annette Bening) and Lester Burnham (Kevin Spacey) are an ordinary suburban couple and parents of a teenage daughter, Jane

(Thora Birch). *American Beauty* (1999) begins with a peek into their ordinary world of oblivion and denial. The Burnhams both believe that they have a perfectly normal, happy daughter. Despite Jane's permanent grimace, black clothes, dark makeup and constant negativism, they would be surprised if you told them that their little girl was profoundly depressed, fed up with her home and school life, and suffering from a negative body image disorder. But the Burnhams' denial does not end with their attitude towards Jane. They are in utter denial of the fact that their once happy marriage has become empty, joyless and bereft of love. The fact that a complete lack of sex, constant bickering and emotional distance did not cue the Burnhams in on their marriage troubles is a clear testimony to the pervasive psychological force of denial.

The Burnhams, however, are a regular "Brady Bunch" compared to their new neighbors. Frank Fitts (Chris Cooper) and his wife Barbara (Allison Janney) have completely opposite personalities. The one thing they share in common is their denial of their son's problems. Barbara is completely oblivious to everything. Since it isn't clear what is going on with her character, the viewer is left to assume that something traumatic happened to her in the past, which has caused her to shut herself off from the outside world. Sadly, she is still a better parent than her husband, who can express only two emotions, silence and rage. Between his mother's obliviousness and his father's abusiveness, young Ricky Fitts (Wes Bentley) lives in a world of emotional isolation. He survives by locking himself away in his bedroom. The only comfort he gets is from drugs, which provide him with psychological solace. Meanwhile, his drug dealing provides him with the expensive stereo and video equipment that insulate the private world of his bedroom. Surprisingly, Ricky is the only character in *American Beauty* who seems to be aware of the peek-a-boo game of denial that everyone around him is playing. At one point, he tells Lester about the treasure trove of stereo equipment in his room: "My dad thinks I pay for all this stuff with catering jobs.... Never underestimate the power of denial."

The Perfect Block

Repression is the unconscious withdrawal from conscious awareness of an unwanted idea, memory, feeling or desire. The unwanted information is pushed down into the unconscious and hidden, just as old suitcases get hidden in the dark corners of our closets. But unlike old suitcases, repressed feelings are psychologically charged because they represent a primal urge that will not go away. If we apply Einstein's theory of relativity to Freud's model of psychic energy, we see that energy, like mass, can never be eliminated, it can only be transformed. Similarly, the libido energy behind id impulses does not go away.

Conrad's primary defense mechanism in *Ordinary People* is repression. He has horrible feelings of guilt, emanating from the fact that he survived the boating accident that killed his brother. He also feels anger at his brother for "screwing around" on the boat, then "letting go" of Conrad's hand and drowning. Conrad cannot allow himself to feel negative emotions towards his beloved, deceased brother. On top of all this, Conrad also has feelings of anger and hatred towards his mother, who has treated him like an unwanted stranger since the tragedy. Conrad's superego will not allow him to express anger or rage toward his mother, because every good boy knows that he must always love and cherish his mother. So all of Conrad's anger is repressed, causing him to live in a constant state of fear that he will "lose control" and release his emotions in an explosion of rage. His desperate daily efforts to repress his feelings drain his energy, making him look and act like a lifeless zombie. In a key scene with his psychiatrist, Dr. Berger (Judd Hirsch), Conrad admits to his repression: "I can't let it out.... It takes too much energy to get angry." Dr. Berger wisely responds: "Can you imagine how much energy it takes to keep it in?"

Ordinary People is an exposé of the pervasive repression endemic in the lives of average, upper class, white Americans. Conrad's emotional disturbance is merely a product of the same repression exhibited and required by his "uptight" parents. Calvin sees that his wife and son are at odds with each other, but he represses his feelings about it and says nothing. However, it is Beth's need to control her emotions and the emotions of everyone around her that emerges as the root of the family's problems. One symbol of Beth's obsessive need for control is her perfectionism, especially in the appearance of her house — the representation of the self. Everything in Beth's house must be absolutely perfect. Her need for total perfection keeps everyone on edge, in fear that they might break something or leave something in the wrong place. Beth's need for control and perfection makes her family feel like uncomfortable guests in their own home.

But the person who feels most uncomfortable is Beth herself. When Buck died, her dreams of a perfect life with a perfect family were shattered. Her love for Buck was so strong that she could not express them at the time of his death. Making an emotional scene would have been the epitome of her greatest fear — being emotionally uncontrolled and making a mess. Instead, Beth blocked her emotions and repressed them. The emotions were so strong that she had to build a floodgate of repression so sturdy that no emotions could come out at all. The result was that Beth could no longer express any affection whatsoever, even to Conrad, who so desperately needed his mother's love.

Both mothers in *American Beauty* suffer from the same kind of controlling behavior and perfectionism. Barbara Fitts directs all of her energy into keeping a perfectly ordered and neat house. When Ricky and his new girlfriend, Jane Burnham, enter the Fitts house, Barbara tells Jane, "Oh my ... I apologize for the way things look around here." Jane immediately recognizes that Barbara's perfectionism borders on the psychotic, as the house is completely immaculate. Barbara's need to repress any messiness includes her control of emotions as well. At the end of the movie, when Ricky — beaten half to death by his father — tells his mother that he's leaving the house and never coming back, all she can say to him is "Wear a raincoat." Her inability to relate to any inner emotions, even with her own son, leaves her only his external clothing to focus on.

Carolyn Burnham is a piece of work as well. She demands complete perfection in her house, in her family and in herself. After seeing Jane's cheerleading performance, the only praise she could offer was "...you didn't screw up once." The viewer gets the sense that she judges Jane as she judges herself — by punishing every mistake rather than rewarding every good effort. This mentality is seen clearly in the scene in which Carolyn, a real-estate agent, tries to sell a house. She drives herself so hard in preparing the house and trying to sell it that it becomes obvious that there is more at stake for her than just a sale. Selling the house represents her life, which must be absolutely perfect and spotless. When she fails to sell the house, she begins to cry, but then quickly stops this release of emotion by slapping herself brutally on the face. Emotions, for her, are a symbol of weakness. As her mentor, Buddy the "King of Real Estate" (Peter Gallagher) says, "One must put forth the appearance of success at all times."

Carolyn must repress every emotion completely, just as she must scrub away each spot of dirt from her house. Her desire to repress messy emotions spreads to her husband and daughter as well. When Jane finally expresses a real feeling to her mother, Carolyn responds with a cruel slap to the face, repressing Jane in the same harsh way that she represses herself. In a later scene, Carolyn and Lester are finally about to experience a moment of intimacy. As Lester seduces Carolyn, he says: "Whatever happened to that girl who used to ... flash the traffic helicopters? Have you totally forgotten about her?" Apparently she has, because Carolyn promptly destroys the moment by saying: "Lester, you're going to spill beer on the couch!" A drop of beer on the couch would be as unacceptable to Carolyn as a pile of feces. Repression, for the perfectionist, is analogous to anal retention. Both of these psychological functions are aimed at controlling and inhibiting any impulsive release.

The core plot of *American Beauty* is Lester's infatuation with Angela (Mena Suvari), Jane's best friend. Lester's infatuation is socially inappropriate on many levels. Angela is young enough to be his daughter, and she is also his daughter's best friend. An affair with Angela would be illicit, figuratively incestuous, and adulterous as well. Lester represses his desire for Angela by channeling his desires into masturbatory fantasies. Other than sex, masturbatory fantasizing provides the most direct release of pent-up libido energy. However, when Lester's repressed impulses are released, his desires gush out with full force.

Unblocking

Since Conrad in *Ordinary People* is seeing a psychiatrist, it is only appropriate that he should become "unblocked." Instead of repressing his feelings all the time, he begins to express them openly. He reacts to his mother's coldness and controlling perfectionism with explosive bursts of anger. The unbearable tension that now arises between mother and son forces Calvin to finally open his eyes and see what's going on in his family. Towards the end of the film, Conrad gives his mother a warm hug, and she cannot even hug him back. Beth's inability to express any affection to Conrad makes it clear to Calvin, and even to herself, that she has repressed her feelings for so long that she has lost the ability to let them out.

After only one session with Conrad's psychiatrist, Calvin becomes unblocked as well. He goes home and tells Beth all of the things that he's wanted to tell her since Buck's death. Unfortunately, Beth cannot change. Needless to say, she will not see a psychiatrist — because only flawed, imperfect people see psychiatrists. Calvin finally admits that he will not live with a woman who cannot express love to her only living son. In Beth's final scene, as she packs her suitcase to leave the house, she begins to cry. But in a massive Herculean effort, she forces her mouth and tear ducts shut, repressing all of her feelings, even as her whole life falls apart. After Beth leaves the house, Calvin and Conrad have their first unrepressed heart-to-heart talk. With the cold, restrictive presence of the repressed mother gone, father and son are finally able to open up and tell each other: "I love you."

The plot of *American Beauty* gets rolling when Lester becomes "unblocked." While Conrad learned to let go of his repression through psychoanalysis, Lester's catharsis is drug induced. After smoking some incredibly potent marijuana with Ricky, Lester finally releases his libido energy and indulges every impulse that he was so earnestly repressing. Lester quits his stifling office job and gets a minimum responsibility position flipping burgers at a fast food joint. He buys his dream car, a 1970 Pontiac Firebird. He begins smoking pot regularly, and he even stands up to his dominating, castrating wife. But most significantly, Lester begins to act on his fantasy of an affair with Angela. He starts working out, hoping that he may become more sexually attractive to her. Ironically, while too much repression alienated Beth from her husband and son, it is the loss of repression that alienates Lester from his wife and daughter.

Inside-out

Projection is the process of attributing feelings about one's self to another person. In *American Beauty*, Frank jumps to a rather rash conclusion that his son Ricky and his neighbor Lester are homosexuals. In actuality, Frank's deepest fear is that he himself is a homosexual. But Frank is a man's man — a tough marine officer and the epitome of masculinity. Since Frank's homoerotic feelings are completely unacceptable to his own sense of manhood, he projects homosexuality onto the "cocksuckers" and "faggots" that he perceives all around him. However, Frank's projection is a phantom, psychological trickery that represents his own unconscious issues rather than reality. Frank's projection of homosexuality onto Ricky leads to a final confrontation, in which Frank beats Ricky to a bloody pulp. Frank's fierce words, however, pack an even harder punch than his fists. He tells Ricky, "I'd rather you were dead, than be a fucking faggot!" Frank's projection causes a tragic distortion of reality, which leads to an irreparable split between him and his son. In the end, Frank throws Ricky out of his house forever.

Displacement is the redirection of an impulse onto a substitute outlet. The classic example of displacement is a vignette, in which a man is yelled at by his boss for doing a lousy job. The man can't talk back to his boss, so he holds in his anger until he gets home. At home, the man yells at his wife for a lousy dinner. The wife can't talk back to her husband (this is a very old vignette), so she yells at their son for having a messy room. The son can't talk back to his mother, so he goes into the yard and kicks the dog. In each instance, the original feeling of anger and hostility is not directed towards the person causing the anger, but rather it is displaced onto a weaker or more socially appropriate substitute. The mechanism defends the ego by releasing negative psychic energy onto a substitute outlet, typically someone who cannot strike back.

A similar vignette is played out in *American Beauty*. Lester is forced by his much younger boss to write a demeaning letter, explaining how he is "useful to the company." Lester cannot express his anger and resentment to his boss, so instead he displaces his pent-up hostility onto his wife and daughter at the dinner table. Later on in the film, Lester displays an even harsher example of displacement. Lester is feeling a lot of anger and bitterness towards his wife, but it is displaced onto his daughter when he tells her: "You better watch yourself Jane, or you're going to turn into a real bitch, just like your mother."

Conrad in *Ordinary People* displaces his repressed feelings of hostility for his mother and brother onto himself. Rather than seeing that she has become distant and unloving since Buck's death, Conrad blames himself for his mother's coldness, feeling that he is unworthy of his mother's love. And rather than accepting the fact that his brother died as a result of his own carelessness, Conrad blames himself for the tragic accident. Consequently, Conrad punishes himself for being a bad brother and an unlovable son. Conrad displaces his hostility onto himself in the form of guilt and self-loathing. Conrad's suicide attempt was his ultimate expression of displaced hostility.

Strippers

Sublimation is the channeling of sexual desire and libido energy into socially valuable pursuits. Returning to the hydraulic model of libido energy, if guilt is the dam that stops the raging force of the libido, then sublimation is the turbine underneath the dam, which redirects the energy into a different pathway and uses the pressure to generate electricity. Sublimation turns negative energy (psychological lemons) into positive works (psychological lemonade). Freud interpreted Leonardo da Vinci's life and works as a triumphant example of successfully sublimated libido energy.

Carolyn and Lester Burnham have no sex life, and Barbara Fitts is married to a latent homosexual. We could assume that both Carolyn and Barbara are sexually frustrated. Their repressed energy is sublimated into their obsessive perfectionism. Sublimation of libido energy is especially evident in the scene in which Carolyn is preparing a house for sale. Carolyn strips out of her clothes and cleans the house in her slip. Her intense scrubbing and cleansing is so impassioned and driven, she seems to be purging her own sexual impulses. Carolyn's husband, Lester, also displays some vintage sublimation. Lester overhears Angela tell Jane: "If he just worked out a little bit, he'd be hot!" In the following scene, Lester strips out of his clothes and stares at his naked reflection in the mirror as he lifts weights.

Lester sublimates his sexual desire into a sexually charged physical activity, which is driven towards the goal of sexual intercourse with Angela. Clearly, the channeling of libido energy does not have to be completely asexual in order for it to be a successful display of sublimation.

The Gay Gay-basher

The *reaction formation* is possibly the most complicated of the defense mechanisms because it results in people behaving in a way that directly contradicts their initial impulse. Frank Fitts's behavior is possibly the best example of a classic reaction formation in film. Frank has latent homosexual desires. These impulses are completely unacceptable to Frank's superego. Frank represses his homosexual stirrings, but since the desire and resulting guilt are both so powerful, repression alone is not enough. Frank feels the need to prove to himself and to others around him that not only is he straight, but he is the straightest man on earth. He's more than just not gay, he is the antithesis of gay — he is the *anti-gay*. This intense, overstated reaction against the initial urge is the external manifestation of the reaction formation.

By reacting strongly against the primal impulse, the reaction formation defends the ego in two ways. First, the unacceptable impulse is disassociated with the ego to a maximum degree. Frank cannot possibly feel guilty for being gay, because he is clearly not gay, his anti-gay position being manifest in his frequent hostile and derogatory statements against gay people. And second, the libido energy created by the urge does not have to be repressed, since it is redirected into overt hostility and rage against the people who represent the original urge. Frank does not have to expend psychic energy repressing his homosexual impulses, he simply vents all of this energy into his homophobic rage. An impassioned reaction against a subject (usually a sexually charged subject) is a red flag for a reaction formation. If Frank truly disliked homosexuality, he would simply avoid the subject altogether. But by acting like a raging homophobe, Frank makes it clear that he is expressing his own latent homosexuality through his intense and overstated reactions against homosexuals.

Like the other defense mechanisms, reaction formation can be extremely dangerous and self-destructive. Homophobic reaction formations tend to be so intense that the frenetic energy often becomes violent. Homophobes frequently express their reactions against homosexuals through brutal and occasionally lethal gay bashings. Frank Fitts's reaction formation becomes extremely violent at the end of *American Beauty*. After he brutalizes his son Ricky for being a "cocksucker," he approaches Lester, believing that he is gay, and makes a pass at him. Frank's sudden decision to reveal his latent homosexuality is a bit inexplicable, though it does much to explain the inner demons driving his character. When Lester rejects Frank's advances, Frank's emotions explode in an eruption of violence. Frank must once again hide his shameful desires to himself and to the world. But because he revealed himself to another person, Frank must also blot out the only witness to his shameful secret. In an ultimate act of reaction formation, Frank destroys the thing he desires the most: Frank kills Lester.

Rational Parenting

Id impulses are inherently irrational. They are based on desire and emotion. *Rationalization* transforms an irrational impulse or emotion into an intellectual issue. By dealing with an impulse on a completely rational level, the ego avoids all the negative emotions involved in the situation. While rationalization defends the ego from bad feelings and disturbing emotions, it does nothing to solve the problem. Feelings and desires must be dealt with on an emotional level. Intellectual rationalization only detaches the ego from its unconscious feelings.

When speaking to Dr. Berger, Calvin in Ordinary People rationalizes Beth's warm and loving disposition towards Buck and her coldness towards Conrad. He says: "His mother doesn't show him (Conrad) a great deal of affection ... Bucky got so much. I think what she felt for him (Buck) was special, you know? He was her first born — that's not unusual, is it?" Calvin sees that there is a huge problem between Beth and Conrad, and he knows that the problem began before Buck's death. Beth always loved Buck more than Conrad. Buck's death only exasperated the problem. Calvin rationalizes this problem by calling it "normal."

In a key scene in *American Beauty,* Lester explodes at Carolyn in an eruption of hostility. As she runs away from him, he claims: "I was only trying to help you!" Lester is clearly rationalizing, because screaming at someone at the top of your lungs is not exactly constructive criticism. The only person that Lester was helping in his violent outburst was himself. Carolyn was hurt and offended. Across the street, Frank Fitts rationalizes his own physical abuse against his son. He tells Ricky: "This is for your own good, boy!" As a marine and old-school style father, Frank is able to convince himself that physical punishment is an appropriate form of discipline. But Frank's rationalization of his abusive behavior is clearly a mechanism to defend his own ego from the guilt of releasing all of his pent-up hostility on his son. Beating the hell out of someone is never for his "own good," just as screaming at someone never "helps." Rationalizing this abuse as acceptable parenting is clearly only good for Frank.

Buried Love

Isolation is when people detach themselves from negative emotions, isolating themselves in the emotionless world of surface features and external concerns. Through Beth's memories, we see that she was a loving, warm, affectionate and happy woman when Buck was alive. Her life was a beautiful dream. But when the tragedy occurred, the dark and dismal emotions that came down upon Beth were just too much for her. She had to completely disconnect herself emotionally from the event of her son's death. Her husband recalls Beth's emotional isolation on the day of Buck's funeral. Calvin could not understand why Beth seemed more concerned with the color of his tie than with the emotional state of her family. For Beth, it was much easier to focus on external issues than on internal feelings. Beth dealt with the despair of Buck's funeral by isolating herself from her emotions. Unfortunately, after she isolated her emotions and hid them away, Beth could not find them again. To Calvin and Conrad, it seemed that on the day that Beth buried Buck, she also buried her ability to express love.

Eighteen Again

Regression is when someone reverts to childish forms of behavior in order to cope with stress or anxiety that may be damaging to the ego. The central plot line in *American Beauty* is Lester's infatuation with his teenage daughter's best friend. His infatuation is symbolic of his general dissatisfaction with his life. Lester is disgruntled with his job, he feels estranged from his wife and daughter, and he hates his body and himself. The only happy time that he can remember is an idyllic age in his distant past, when he was eighteen years old and all he did was "party and get laid." Lester's unrealistic desire to be eighteen again escalates into a *youth fixation*, which is revealed in a host of regressive behaviors—the infatuation with Angela being the centerpiece. Lester begins smoking pot. He gets a "teen-machine" sports car. He begins referring to his wife Carolyn as "Mom." And he quits his adult profession for a job flipping burgers. By acting like an eighteen

Eighteen Again. When Lester Burnham (Kevin Spacey) regresses to an adolescent state of mind and behavior, he relates to Carolyn (Annette Bening) as if she were his mother rather than his wife. *American Beauty* (1999), DreamWorks SKG and Jinks/Cohen Company.

year old adolescent, Lester avoids the responsibilities of adulthood. He defends his ailing ego by abandoning his unhappy middle-aged existence and regressing back to a happier time of life.

The catalyst and driving force behind Lester's regression is his illicit desire for Angela. In his fantasies, Lester envisions Angela's naked body covered in rose petals. The rose symbolism is especially fitting, as the rose is symbolic of the developing female genitalia. Lester is infatuated with Angela because she is in her psychosexual stage of genital development — adolescence — which is where Lester wishes to be again. For Lester, Angela is a symbol of his lost youth. His regression is a desperate and ultimately self-destructive attempt to recapture his adolescence, through the immoral and narcissistic deflowering of a beautiful young girl.

Conrad's Slip

The *Freudian slip* is a "faulty action," usually revealed in a verbal mistake, in which a repressed or hidden issue slips out unconsciously in one's speech. In his work as an analyst, Freud focused keenly on verbal mistakes and slips of the tongue, being a firm believer in the notion that there are "no accidents" when the unconscious mind is involved. In *Ordinary People,* a Freudian slip turns out to be the key that opens the door to Conrad's primary issue. When speaking of his mother and her attitude towards his suicide attempt, Conrad tells his psychiatrist: "Do you think *I'm* gonna' forgive — she's gonna' forgive me." The mistake, saying "I" rather than "she," is the unconscious slip. It's not Beth's forgiveness that Conrad needs in order to feel better about himself, it's his own. Both Conrad and his psychiatrist pick up on the slip, and Conrad immediately experiences an insight: "I think I just figured something out.... Who it is who can't forgive who." Conrad's slip leads to his realization that he is punishing himself for surviving the accident that took his brother's life. Conrad also realizes that he has been repressing a tremendous amount of anger towards Buck. In order to release this anger and purge himself of the guilt associated with it, Conrad must first realize that the anger exists, and then forgive Buck for not surviving. The Freudian slip was the expression of Conrad's own unconscious, telling him about feelings and impulses that he didn't even know he had.

Lester's Hero

Identification is a primary mechanism in the human mind. By identifying unconsciously with others, we model our own personalities on the personalities of our heroes and mentors, and we relieve the anxiety of self-doubt by finding direction and vindication in the choices of other people. When Ricky in *American Beauty* casually quits his job on a moment's whim, Lester tells him: "...you just became my personal hero." Lester identifies with Ricky because he represents what Lester used to be and wants to be again — a free and rebellious eighteen-year-old. Throughout the rest of the film, Lester models his own behavior on Ricky's example. He smokes pot, quits his job in a similarly brusque manner, and even courts a teenage girl. At the end of the film, Lester is finally confronted with his deepest desire, as Angela offers herself to him. But his moment of conquest is disrupted when Angela, lying naked on the couch underneath Lester, confesses: "This is my first time." Angela's confession rocks Lester out of his fantasy world of pseudo-adolescence, reminding him that he is not an eighteen-year-old kid, but a middle-aged husband and father. This changes his personal identification from an irresponsible teenager to a responsible father figure, and leads to an immediate change in his behavior. Lester suddenly stops lusting after Angela like a horny schoolboy, and acts in a very paternal manner. He covers her up, makes her a sandwich and even asks her about Jane — indicating Lester's restored ability to identify himself as a father figure. Unfortunately, this reborn and mature Lester only has about five seconds to live.

13

Characters in Crisis

A sound identity is the only safeguard against the anarchy of drives as well as the autocracy of conscience.

— Erik Erikson (1968)

The issue of identity development dominated Erik Erikson's (1902–1994) personal and professional life. Erikson was born in Frankfurt, Germany. His biological father abandoned Erikson's mother while she was still pregnant. She remarried when Erikson was three years old, and Erikson would never know his biological father. His mother's new husband, Theodore Homburger, adopted Erik and gave him his last name. His early years were marked by a great deal of identity confusion. While his mother and her husband were Jewish and he was raised as a Jew, Erik knew that his biological father was not Jewish. He was not accepted among the German children at school because he was a Jew, and he did not fit in among his Jewish peers because of his "Aryan" looks. His blonde hair, blue eyes and Nordic features prompted the other Jewish children to call him "the goy."

Erikson spent his late adolescent years traveling around Europe and studying art in various cities. He would later look back upon these years of exploration as a very important time for him, in which he struggled to find a sense of personal identity. Eventually, Erikson found himself in Vienna working as an art teacher. He began studying psychoanalysis with Anna Freud, who became his mentor. Erikson fled Europe for America in 1933 to evade the Nazis. In America, Erikson finally constructed a personal sense of identity that he was comfortable with. He dedicated his professional life to clinical work with children and to scholarly work in the field of psychoanalysis. He converted to Christianity, and he changed his name from Erik Homburger to Erik Erikson (Erik the son of Erik).

Though his ideas are born directly out of Freudian theory, Erikson's

170

original contributions to the fields of psychoanalysis and developmental psychology were manifold. Erikson called his theories "psychosocial" rather than "psychosexual," because he directed the study of the ego away from internal biological impulses, and focused more on the individual's personal struggle to fit into his or her social environment. Erikson also lengthened the scope of developmental studies. While Freud ended his developmental stages at early adolescence, Erikson wrote volumes on the identity struggles people face during late adolescence, young adulthood, midlife and old age. He was one of the first theorists to promote the notion that developmental psychology must include the entire scope of human development, and not just child development. Furthermore, Erikson's groundbreaking use of "psychohistory" and "psychobiography" expanded the palette of psychoanalytic tools available to researchers and clinicians. And finally, Erikson developed the concept of the "identity crisis," the personal struggle that each individual undergoes in an effort to achieve psychological adjustment and existential purpose at each stage of life. The notion that times of great internal conflict are not unhealthy but rather that they are normal stages in the search for happiness and psychological well-being, is Erikson's most enduring legacy.

Attachment

The term "crisis," as Erikson used it, refers to "...a turning point, a crucial period of increased vulnerability and heightened potential...." The first stage of identity crisis, *trust versus mistrust*, corresponds to Freud's first psychosexual stage. The theme of oral satisfaction is interpreted by Erikson as the emotional disposition of "trust." In Erikson's words: "By 'trust' I mean an essential trustfulness of others as well as a fundamental sense of one's own trustworthiness." The baby's degree of trust in Mother is the barometer of the parent/infant relationship. The baby needs to trust in the fact that if he expresses the need for love and attention, these needs will be attended to. If this trust is not achieved, then a sense of mistrust will develop. If mistrust is too great, the baby will give up trying to express its need for love and attention, and he will simply let his emotional needs fester inside of him in perpetual frustration.

By applying *attachment theory* to Erikson's model, we can see the relationship patterns that may emerge as a result of trust being either present or absent within the parent/child relationship. Attachment theory is a developmental model that explains how babies create either secure or insecure relationships with their parental figures. Longitudinal relationship research has shown that the attachment style people have as babies with their primary caregivers are remarkably resilient. The patterns tend to reappear later in life within their relationships with their significant others and spouses. This research has given a certain degree of credibility to psychoanalytic theory, and the notion that primary relationships with opposite sex parents are linked unconsciously with our romantic relationships as adults. For the purpose of film analysis, the theory of adult attachment patterns makes it easier to find examples for interpretation. We don't need to look at babies to see examples of attachment patterns. We can see examples of trust and mistrust, i.e., secure and insecure attachment patterns, in every emotional relationship.

Ordinary People (revisited)

The insecure attachment between Conrad and his mother in *Ordinary People* is apparent in their very first scene together. Conrad is just out of the hospital and still feeling a bit nervous and jittery. He comes down to the breakfast table, and his mother tells him that she prepared his favorite breakfast, French toast. Food is an axiomatic symbol of love, especially within the mother/child relationship, which is initially consummated during the oral stage of development via the mutually satisfying act of breastfeeding. By offering or withholding the breast, the mother creates a sense of either trust or mistrust in her developing baby. Conrad tells his mother that he's "not really hungry." He's reluctant to accept his mother's offering of love. Beth immediately takes the plate away and shoves the hot, delicious French toast down the garbage disposal. Beth instantly withdraws the food and destroys every trace of it, symbolically "undoing" her offering of love so she can pretend that she never offered it in the first place.

It is clear that mother and son share an insecure attachment pattern. They are both extremely reluctant to express any affection toward each other. It has come to the point where it is excruciatingly uncomfortable for either of them to express even the smallest gesture of love to the other. If one side does make a gesture and it is not accepted, the reaction is immediate, hostile and extreme. Love, for Conrad and Beth, is a matter of extreme anxiety, because there is no trust between them. In order to express love, one must trust that the love will be accepted and reciprocated, because there is no worse feeling than love unrequited. Conrad and Beth cannot express their love for each other. So they avoid expressing love, and they avoid each other.

The heart of the film is Conrad's emotional metamorphosis through psychoanalysis. Calvin is supportive of Conrad's struggle to change himself, while Beth tacitly disapproves. Her disapproval is related to her own internal need for perfection, and also to her general mistrust of other people. This sense of mistrust is her legacy to her son. A sense of mistrust is evident in Conrad's behavior with his new girlfriend, Jeannine (Elizabeth McGovern). Fortunately, Conrad is able to overcome his mistrust as a result of his trusting relationship with his psychoanalyst. He displays the beginnings of a secure attachment with Jeannine when he opens up to her, discloses his true feelings and displays an honest expression of emotion and affection. Conrad's trust is rewarded when Jeannine reciprocates his feelings, and then invites him to breakfast—the same symbolic offering of love that Conrad received from his mother in the beginning of the film. This time, Conrad accepts the food from Jeannine, symbolizing that he has developed the capacity to trust someone else, and accept her love.

Film Noir

Just as a basic sense of trust is generalized into trust in the world and in one's self, a basic sense of mistrust can also be generalized into a disposition of mistrust towards everyone in the world, including one's self. People who trust no one and have no desire to be trusted by others are not very well prepared for a life of healthy interpersonal relationships. However, these characters are perfectly suited for the role of gangster, criminal or crooked cop in film noir movies, which are especially adept at portraying a world of *secondary mistrust,* a wicked world of secrets, lies and paranoia.

In John Huston's first film, *The Maltese Falcon* (1941), Sam Spade (Humphrey Bogart) is a private detective who exists in a dark world in which every character is shady, deceptive, paranoid and treacherous. Sam cannot trust anyone, and he often finds himself in situations where he cannot even trust his own judgment. Even the Maltese Falcon, the statuette at the center of the film, is deceitful in its own way—it is not what it appears to be. *The Maltese Falcon* was a seminal movie in a film genre which is not a category of setting, character or plot, but a specific emotional tone in a movie. The essence of film noir is moral uncertainty—the inability to trust anyone, because everyone is two-faced and nothing is really as it seems. Film noir is a world of mistrust.

In John Huston's last and best film noir movie, *The Asphalt Jungle* (1950), the fog of mistrust is so thick that it pervades every scene. Every character is a criminal. Everyone is wicked in his own way. Nobody is worthy of trust. Even policemen and judges have dark secrets and dirty hands. *The Asphalt Jungle* is a "city underneath the city," a dark substratum of society in which there is no honesty, no trust and no honor among thieves.

The classic film noir movies were black-and-white and filmed in urban settings. The black and white film provided a dark, shadowy backdrop for its stories about dark, shadowy people. The urban settings provided a cast of city people who stole, lied, cheated and killed in order to satisfy their desires. The tone of mistrust and dreadful sense of not knowing which nefarious character may be lurking in the shadows are the defining qualities of film noir.

Oral Pessimism and Oral Sadism

Ironically, Huston's greatest movie on the theme of mistrust was *The Treasure of the Sierra Madre* (1948), which was not film noir. However, the vital film noir element that Huston did employ was the casting of Humphrey Bogart as Dobbs in the lead role. Bogart, who played Sam Spade in *The Maltese Falcon* and Phillip Marlowe in *The Big Sleep*, was the archetypal film noir hero. In *The Treasure of the Sierra Madre*, Dobbs is a poor American expatriate living in Mexico. He's out of work and down on his luck. His lowly state in the beginning of the film is characteristic of what Erikson called "oral pessimism," a central syndrome of secondary mistrust. Deriving its name from Freud's oral stage, the oral pessimist has been deprived of his basic needs for so long that his dominant view of the world is that of an empty wasteland. He views himself as an empty person, with nothing good to offer to himself or to others. Dobbs is stuck in the depressive mire of oral pessimism. He wanders the streets begging for handouts. He doesn't even notice that he's panhandled the same man three times in a row. He feels so empty that he cannot even look his mark in the eye—he just looks down at the money in his hand.

Dobbs's pessimism is bolstered after he is conned out of his day laborer's wages by a shady contractor. But things look up after Dobbs and a fellow laborer hunt down the contractor who hustled them. They beat him up and take his money. Dobbs and his new pal Curtin (Tim Holt) become partners. The viewer gains hope for Dobbs. If Dobbs can trust Curtin, maybe he can overcome his character flaws of mistrust and pessimism, and learn to believe in himself and others. Dobbs's character progresses even further as he and Curtin team up with an old prospector, Howard (Walter Huston), and the band of three go up into the mountains in search of gold. The gold quest is symbolic of Dobbs's spiritual search for something pure in the world and in himself. His hope that they will find gold and strike it rich shows that he still has hope for a good life. And Dobbs's faith in his partners shows that he still has the ability to trust people.

Unfortunately, the hope and faith in Dobbs's character is not strong enough to overcome his basic sense of mistrust. Dobbs catches "gold fever" on the mountain. He mistrusts his partners and suspects them of plotting to steal his gold. Dobbs's heightened sense of oral pessimism leads him to the endpoint of mistrust, "oral sadism"—"a cruel need to get and to take in ways harmful to others or to oneself." The inability to trust and the absence of a need to be trusted invariably leads to deception and villainy. The oral sadist satisfies his own needs by taking from others, and he derives visceral pleasure while harming them. Dobbs regresses to a state of complete psychotic paranoia. He deludes himself into believing that everyone is against him. His delusions become so strong that he cannot even trust himself. Led by his paranoia, Dobbs betrays his partners and attempts to murder Curtin. In the end, isolated by mistrust and left alone with his gold, Dobbs's paranoia ultimately proves to be self-destructive. Dobbs is killed by bandits. His lowly end is fitting. He is destroyed by forces of mistrust and greed, the same forces that drove his ego into a murderous, paranoid psychosis.

The Balanced Resolution

Each of Erikson's stages presents a *normative conflict*, in which the developing ego is torn between two emotional poles. In the first stage, the infant struggles to form a sense of trust with his primary caregiver. Once a basis of trust is formed, the ego confronts other people, the world and himself with a trusting disposition. Hope that things will work out, and faith in the inherent goodness of others and one's self are the rewards of a trusting nature. If trust is not formed, mistrust will dominate the developing ego's disposition, leading to skepticism, pessimism, deception and self-doubt. In all of Erikson's stages, the proper resolution is a healthy balance between the two emotional poles in conflict.

There is a sucker born every minute. The infant sucking at Mother's breast has no reason to mistrust anyone, but eventually the breast is taken away and replaced with a plastic nipple. A gradual weaning from the breast teaches the infant that all good things must come to an end. A similar lesson comes later in life—a trusting disposition must be limited by a sense of caution. Cautious mistrust in others is taught to children from their parents, who warn them: "Don't talk to strangers!" We want our children to be trusting, but we also want them to be cautious and wary of the depraved people who would exploit their trust. So, even though trust is generally a good thing and mistrust is generally bad, we must also admit that a certain amount of healthy mistrust should be instilled into the developing ego. A trusting, gullible, Pollyanna type who believes everything he is told is extremely vulnerable to liars and cheats.

Bubble Boy

In *Bubble Boy* (2001), an interesting symbol for trust and mistrust is represented by a plastic bubble, in which a mother (Swoosie Kurtz) encapsulates her son (Jake Gyllenhaal) for his entire life. Bubble Boy's mother suffers from severe mistrust, resulting in psychotic levels of paranoia. She believes that everything and everyone in the world is diseased, corrupt and wicked, so she protects her son by keeping him in a bubble. Eventually, Bubble Boy grows up and falls in love with the girl next door (Marley Shelton). He must travel to Niagara Falls to stop the girl from marrying another man. His journey is encumbered by the fact that he must travel in a bubble, and he is also handicapped by a lack of healthy mistrust. Since he's never left home before, he doesn't understand that there are bad people in the world who shouldn't be trusted.

Though some shady characters take advantage of the gullible Bubble Boy, it is his overwhelming sense of trust in others that gets him help from unexpected strangers, who take him to Niagara Falls. At the wedding, Bubble Boy discovers that it is his mother, the infantile object of trust, who ironically betrayed his trust by lying to him for his entire life. Bubble Boy never actually had the severe immunity deficiency that his mother told him he had. He never needed to live in a bubble. In the end, Bubble Boy sheds the symbol of his mother's deplorable breach of trust. He steps out of the bubble and acquires a new primary love object. By transfiguring his maternal love for his mother into a romantic love for the girl next door, Bubble Boy successfully resolves his Oedipal complex while also learning a valuable lesson — complete and unlimited trust in others must also be tempered by some cautious mistrust.

One Flew Over the Cuckoo's Nest

The second psychosocial stage, *autonomy versus doubt and shame*, corresponds to Freud's anal stage of psychosexual development. In Erikson's view, the small child is seeking to "individuate" from the mother and become "autonomous." Parents who have experience with toddlers know about the "terrible twos" — a time when the child's favorite word is "no!" For the toddler, "no" is more than just a word, it is a statement of autonomy and individuality. Meanwhile, parents are in the undesirable position of having to teach rules for behavior to their growing toddlers. If parents are overly punitive, they run the risk of quashing the child's blossoming autonomy, resulting in a child crippled by shame and doubt. But if parents do not impose enough authority, they run the risk of raising a child who has no respect for rules and regulations. Autonomous individuals understand rules, laws and the authorities that enforce them. They know when it is appropriate to follow the law, but they also know when it is more appropriate to follow one's own autonomous sense of morality.

The psychiatric hospital in *One Flew Over the Cuckoo's Nest* (1975) recapitulates the arena of early struggles between parents and children. The men in the hospital ward have been stripped of their individuality and autonomy and placed under the parental care of the hospital administrators. The father figure, Dr. Spivey (Dean R. Brooks), is an elderly, benign and kindly psychiatrist whose scarce presence belies his enormous power. Though Dr. Spivey isn't around much, he's the one who makes all the big decisions concerning evaluations, medication, treatments and punishments. Dr. Spivey is a menacing figure who hides behind a smile and soft-spoken persona.

Nurse Ratched (Louise Fletcher) is the all-powerful mother figure. Her presence dominates the entire ward, and she is the force in control of the daily lives of the patients. Ratched demands complete obedience from her patients. She is aided by daily doses of mind-numbing medication that she gives to every patient. The medication "calms" the patients, artificially exorcising them of any inner sense of autonomy or rebelliousness. However, we get the sense that the complete lack of autonomy in the ward is enforced by something stronger than the pharmaceutical straitjacket. Nurse Ratched herself has the power to control every emotion in her patients. In her group therapy sessions, she wields her tremendous psychological power like a sledgehammer over her weak-minded patients. She can manipulate each one of them into a complete emotional breakdown, just by pushing their buttons in the exact ways that she knows so well.

Autonomy

McMurphy, nicknamed "Mac" (Jack Nicholson), enters the ward like a breath of fresh air. In Mac's autonomy, we see the freedom and rebelliousness of a man who simply cannot obey the rules. When asked why he keeps on winding up in prison, Mac tells Dr. Spivey, "Because I fight and fuck too much." Mac is simply unable to control his behavior. His basic drives— sex and aggression — are expressed without regard for law, authority or society. Dr. Spivey is correct in suspecting that Mac is not a psychotic, but merely an incorrigible rule-breaker who wants to avoid work detail in the prison farm during his 90-day prison sentence. But Dr. Spivey isn't necessarily convinced that Mac is not crazy. Mac represents the absolute anarchy of the drives. Dr. Spivey is faced with the question: Is a person who has no control over his impulses sane?

Shame and Doubt

Mac's new world is a strange inversion for him, in which dozens of grown men are completely dominated by one pretty matron in a white cap. His eyes are opened to the situation when he sees Nurse Ratched run her group therapy sessions like a public inquisition. Ratched sits coolly as she pries into her weak-willed patients' neuroses, forcing them to disclose personal information that she can load into her armory. The key to Ratched's absolute control of the ward is her knowledge of each patient's most secret issues, and her willingness to raise these issues in order to shame her patients into line. Ratched demonstrates her shame tactics in her manipulation of Billy Bibbit (Brad Dourif). Billy is an extremely weak, shy and anxious young man. His intense anxiety and lack of confidence is displayed in his chronic stuttering. He is by far the youngest member of the ward, and he acts and is treated like a young boy. The name Bibbit may be a reference to "Babbit," the title character in the Sinclair Lewis novel who was the ultimate conformist. Like Babbit, Billy is plagued by self-doubt. He doubts his own sense of worth, he doubts his ability to live independently, and most of all, he doubts his own power to stand up to controlling, domineering mother figures like Nurse Ratched. For Billy, Ratched represents a double threat. Ratched is a menacing and omnipotent mother in her own right, and she is also good friends with Billy's real mother, whom she often confers with — as she frequently reminds Billy.

Mac is disgusted to see Nurse Ratched forcing Billy to talk about an episode in his life in which he failed to approach a girl that he loved. This episode is linked to Billy's central issue of self-doubt. Ratched's manipulative process of forcing Billy to talk exemplifies the problem — he lacks the confidence to stand up for himself and defend his own ego. Ratched publicly shames Billy by exposing his most vulnerable secrets to the group. True to her name, Ratched manipulates her patients like a tool — a ratchet — that can tighten or loosen the nuts in the minds of her patients with alarming ease.

Power Struggle

It doesn't take long for Mac and Ratched to butt heads. The power struggle between Mac and Ratched escalates into an all-out war over control of the ward. Ratched represents bondage, obedience, conformity and compliance. Mac represents freedom, rebelliousness, individuality and autonomy. In the process of the power struggle, Mac becomes a replacement father figure for the patients in the ward. He takes them to an imaginary baseball game, he breaks them out of the hospital and takes them on a road trip, and he takes them fishing on a stolen boat. The patients identify with their new father figure and begin to act like him. They rebel against Ratched and verbalize their newfound sense of autonomy in a group session, which culminates in an eruption of violence. Mac and two of his disciples are punished for their transgressions with electric shock treatments. While the famous shock treatment scene is not a realistic depiction of electroconvulsive therapy, it depicts a compelling parallel between the shocking of rebellious adults and the spanking of rebellious children.

Defiance

Just as physical punishment rarely works with children, Mac's shock punishment only recharges his batteries. Upon his return, Mac leads the ward into outright defiance of Ratched's authority. Like the small child who yells "no!" at his mother, defiance is a personal statement of autonomy. Mac leads the ward into public defiance by administering his own medication, alcohol. Instead of controlling behavior, like the drugs administered by Ratched, alcohol frees the patients. They become temporarily uninhibited and free from Ratched's strict control. Billy even overcomes his incredible shyness and self-doubt. Spurred on by Mac and the other patients, Billy makes love with Candy (Mews Small), a young girl that Mac smuggled into the hospital along with the booze.

The name "Candy" is particularly significant. Power struggles between parents and children are often centered around candy. The child's desire for sweets is as primal as an adolescent male's desire for sex. In the film, both desires are given the name "Candy." When Ratched finds Billy in bed with Candy, he is literally caught with his pants down. Billy's personal act of autonomy is also a clear act of group defiance against Ratched's authority. Ratched's anger is really directed at Mac, but she knows that she can hurt Mac more by torturing weak and defenseless Billy, the baby-faced boy that Mac has taken under his wing. Ratched asks Billy: "Aren't you ashamed?" Billy replies: "No, I'm not." For once, Billy is not stuttering and stammering. He is standing up for himself, and standing up to Ratched. The other patients applaud him. Ratched coolly continues: "What worries me is how your mother is going to take it." The mere mention of his mother casts Billy down into a spiral of shame. He immediately loses all of his confidence. Billy blames the other patients and Mac for his infraction, he begs for forgiveness and he beats himself to show penance. Billy's sense of shame is so deep that he kills himself — the ultimate act of self-punishment — as a pathetic gesture of atonement to his mother figure.

Punishment

In the end, Mac is done in by his characteristic lack of control. After Billy commits suicide, Mac explodes in a fit of rage and attempts to strangle Nurse Ratched to death. The destructive side of Mac's personality is revealed as he indulges the darkest impulse a child could have, the impulse to kill a controlling mother figure. Mac's punishment is swift and absolute. He is given a full frontal lobotomy. Like the medieval practice of trepanation, in which barbers bore holes into people's heads to release their evil demons, the lobotomy exorcises Mac's desire to rebel against authority. The procedure also turns him into a vegetable. Every trace of Mac's autonomy, individuality and personality are gone with one slice of a scalpel. Mac lost his battle with authority, but his rebellious spirit lives on in the psyche of Chief (Will Sampson), the patient that Mac inspired, who escapes the mental hospital in the final scene.

Crimes and Misdemeanors (re-revisited)

At the third stage of psychosocial development, the child is "deeply and exclusively identified with his parents, who most of the time appear to him to be powerful and beautiful, although often quite unreasonable, disagreeable, and even dangerous." The stage of *initiative versus guilt* corresponds with Freud's phallic stage of psychosexual development. The internal moral conscience — guilt — is the counterbalance to "initiative," the "will" of the child. Initiative is the force that motivates a curious child to ask, "Why?" It is the force that motivates a child to build a castle in the sand, and it is also the force that flattens the castle, breaks the toys that made the castle, and throws sand at the child who built it.

Once again, it is the parents who control the resolution of this stage through "mutual regulation" of the child's behavior. If parents are too strict and punitive, guilt may become the dominating force in the child's unconscious, resulting in an overdeveloped conscience and a life of crippling neurosis and anxiety. Parenting that is too lenient may result in an underdeveloped conscience, which is not strong enough to restrict the destructive side of the initiative drive. Erikson believed that the proper balance between initiative and guilt must be based on a sense of responsibility. A healthy sense of guilt keeps us from doing things to hurt others, while a healthy sense of initiative allows us to do things to help ourselves.

The central conflict in Woody Allen's *Crimes and Misdemeanors* (1989) takes place within the mind of Dr. Judah Rosenthal (Martin Landau).

Judah's unstable mistress Dolores (Angelica Huston) threatens to tell Judah's wife (Claire Bloom) about their adulterous relationship unless he leaves his wife for her. As a non-religious man — a "scientist" — Judah believes that his sin of adultery could remain undiscovered and unpunished. But now that his life as a respected ophthalmologist and family man are jeopardized by Dolores, he considers a major crime, "getting rid of her." This option is available through Judah's brother Jack (Jerry Orbach), a criminal who could hire an anonymous assassin to do the job. Considering the major sin of murder weighs heavily on Judah, and a crisis of conscience ensues. Eventually, Judah goes ahead with the crime, and Dolores is murdered. Despite a guilt-driven urge to confess, Judah is never caught.

The cost of Judah's crime is a small portion of his soul, not the overwhelming sense of guilt that we would expect as just desserts in a mainstream movie. He is not crippled by guilt, nor is he driven to turn himself in to the nearest policeman. Judah is just subtly troubled by the inherent amorality of the world, and the existence of this amorality within himself. He has lost his sense of moral superiority over his brother Jack and others like him, but he has retained his wealth, position, freedom and family. The triumph of Judah's initiative over his guilt saved his life from collapse and tragedy, though it could be argued that it was his weak sense of guilt and overdeveloped sense of initiative that got him into trouble in the first place. In the final scene, a voice-over of a philosophy professor declares: "We define ourselves by the choices we have made. We are in fact the sum total of our choices...." Though Judah's life was not destroyed by his decision to destroy the life of another, his own identity and self-concept as an essentially moral human being are lost forever. The decision of whether Judah is actually punished for his crime or not is ultimately left up to the viewer.

Erikson's fourth stage of identity development revolves around the conflict between work and play. Children need to learn how to balance their desire to play with their obligation to work. *Industry versus inferiority* corresponds with Freud's latency period, in which children learn to sublimate their libido energy into industrious activities. "Industry" refers to a need to complete and master projects and challenging tasks. If children are successful at this stage, they gain a feeling of industrious self-worth. If they are not successful, their self-esteem may be wounded, resulting in a basic sense of "inferiority." In keeping with Erikson's model, the proper resolution of this stage is neither industry nor inferiority, but a healthy balance between the need to work and the drive to play.

It is important for children to understand work as an important part of their identities. But there is a thin line between loving your work and believing that one is only deserving of love if you are successful in your work. Over-industriousness arises when work becomes psychologically addictive. The workaholic is driven both by the desire to work and the fear of the guilt that arises from not working. The workaholic feels guilty, inferior and worthless when he is not being industrious. He defines himself as a "human doing" rather than a "human being," and can only feel worthwhile and deserving of love if he is being productive. The only thing that dulls the workaholic's inner sense of inferiority is work, the activity that generates the money and success that are the external hallmarks of industrious success.

The B-plot in *Crimes and Misdemeanors* revolves around Woody Allen's character. Clifford is a charming, funny, intelligent and artistic documentary filmmaker who nevertheless feels inferior to his brother-in-law, Lester (Alan Alda). While Clifford is proud of his films, they are not huge commercial successes like Lester's television productions. Clifford's feelings of envy and resentment towards Lester are repeatedly pointed out to him by his wife and Lester's sister, Wendy (Joanna Gleason), who is divorcing Clifford because he is unsuccessful. She tells him: "I think you're jealous because he's a much honored, highly respected man and he's a millionaire ten times over, and he's doing what you'd love to do ... he's everything you wish you could be."

Clifford's feelings of inferiority are exacerbated when Lester offers Clifford "a chance to earn some big money and reach a big audience" by directing a documentary about him for public television. Driven by the need for money to complete his own film (a short subject about a philosophy professor), Clifford swallows what's left of his pride and agrees to become Lester's biographer. If this is not enough, an associate producer on the documentary, Halley (Mia Farrow), catches both Clifford's and Lester's fancy. Clifford now finds himself competing with Lester for Wendy's respect, Halley's love and a sense of artistic integrity. For a little while, it looks like Clifford might win out. Halley appreciates Clifford's film about the philosophy professor and suggests producing it as a public television special. In Halley, Clifford sees a replacement for Wendy. Halley is beautiful and intelligent. She respects Clifford as an artist and even shares his condescending attitude towards Lester, whom Clifford sees as a pompous boob. But Clifford's aching sense of inferiority backfires and destroys everything. Clifford's documentary is so blatantly hostile towards Lester that the film is taken away from him. Lester takes over production of the film and Clifford loses this project along with the opportunity to make more films for public television. By attacking Lester through his film, Clifford ironically loses any chance of ever being as successful and industrious as Lester.

Clifford's final downfall is symbolized by the death of his intellectual mentor and film subject, Professor Levy. Clifford identified with Professor Levy because, while he was not rich and famous, he was a brilliant and dedicated thinker who lived and worked with a basic sense of integrity that belied the flashiness and superficiality of Lester. When Professor Levy suddenly and inexplicably commits suicide, Clifford's own sense of self worth is rocked to the core. He can no longer imagine himself as an artistic, if not commercial, success. In the final scene, we see that Clifford has lost everything. Lester is overjoyed when Wendy tells him that she found someone else and is leaving Clifford for good. And in a final blow to his self-esteem, Clifford discovers that he has lost Halley to Lester. Clifford admits that Lester won the rivalry for Halley's love because Lester is "a success." Clifford tells Halley: "This is my worst fear realized...." His realization is that integrity is relatively meaningless in a world that respects commercial success and popularity beyond everything else. He has come to grips with the sad fact that Lester is the epitome of "industry," while he is wallowing in "inferiority."

Zelig

Erikson coined the term *identity crisis* as a psychiatric diagnosis for war veterans he worked with in a veterans' hospital. Many of the veterans were experiencing intense problems readjusting to normal society after their traumatic and often harrowing experiences in the army. Their normative conflict involved a need to resolve their identities as soldiers, in order to develop new identities as civilians. Erikson later applied the notion of identity crisis to adolescents, who often face similar challenges adjusting from childhood to adulthood. The adolescent identity crisis in Erikson's fifth stage of psychosocial development is identity versus identity diffusion.

Erikson's term *moratorium* refers to the notion that adolescence is a waiting period between childhood and adulthood. The adolescent in moratorium is actively engaged in finding an identity. At the peak of moratorium, the adolescent may resemble a human chameleon, perpetually transforming his identity at a moment's whim in order to fit into the latest fad that has caught his fancy. Woody Allen's *Zelig* (1983) is a character study of a man in the ultimate state of identity confusion. Leonard Zelig (Woody Allen) has the odd ability to immediately alter his physical appearance. He has no stable sense of identity. His character alters itself in order to blend into the identities of the people around him. Zelig's transfigurative ability earns him the title of "human chameleon." In the beginning of the movie, which takes place in the 1920s, Zelig is in a true state of moratorium. He freely explores different identities by indulging in instantaneous transfigurations. At one moment he's an upper-crust Republican blueblood, the next moment he's a lower-class Democratic kitchen worker. Now a black jazz musician, now a Chinese immigrant, now a Native American — Zelig is everybody and nobody at the same time.

Shortly after his discovery by the psychoanalytic community, Zelig is taken out of treatment by his exploitative half sister and forced to display his abilities as a freak. Often times, periods of moratorium are cut short by parental figures who determine the adolescent's identity for him. It is quite common in both Western and traditional cultures for a dominating parent to decree that their child is going to be a doctor, lawyer, businessman, etc. The expectation that a child will take over the family business or carry on a family tradition will often lead to *identity foreclosure*, in which the adolescent becomes what his parents want him to become. Identity, rather than being a personal matter of individual choice, is treated as a familial obligation. In short, foreclosure is the lack of personal exploration and the absence of choice in achieving a sense of ego identity. Zelig, in his performing freak period, represents the passive resignation of a foreclosed identity. While he can appear to be anything he wants to be, his true self is psychologically undeveloped, spiritually empty and fundamentally nonexistent.

Zelig escapes his life as a freak and returns to a state of moratorium, once again jumping from identity to identity. He is rediscovered by the psychoanalytic community and begins intensive analysis with Dr. Eudora Fletcher (Mia Farrow). Due to a good deal of transference and Dr. Fletcher's "unconditional positive regard" as a caring mother figure, Zelig overcomes his psychotic need to transfigure himself. He begins to form a strong sense of personal identity. While Zelig used to blend in completely in every situation, now he is willing to stand out. Zelig even makes a point of being an individual. He intentionally starts an argument with a doctor over the weather, and then attacks him with a rake. Zelig's deliberate contrariness is an example of *rebellion*, another common feature of the adolescent identity crisis. Like the defiance of a small child, rebellion is a personal statement of individuality, autonomy and the will to be one's self.

Eventually, at least for a while, Zelig learns to manage his rebelliousness and forms a personal sense of identity that he is comfortable with. Unfortunately, Zelig's past catches up with him, and he is sued by all the people he deceived during his long moratorium as the human chameleon. The scandals, lawsuits and life in the public eye are too much for Zelig's still fragile sense of self. He regresses to his earlier defense mechanism, flees and transfigures himself into obscurity. Zelig is now in a state of *diffusion*. He does not have a strong sense of personal identity and he is not actively exploring. Instead, Zelig is avoiding the problem. Once again, Zelig is both everybody and nobody.

Negative Identity

When a person becomes completely lost and confused in his search for a personal identity, he runs the risk of forming a "negative identity, i.e. an identity perversely based on all those identifications and roles which, at critical stages of development, had been presented to him as most undesirable or dangerous...." According to Erikson negative identities are identities that are opposed to the values of the individual's upbringing. When faced with a choice between being "nobody" and "somebody totally bad," many individuals would prefer an especially bad identity than no special identity at all. Zelig displays this preference in his transfiguration in Berlin, where he becomes a high-ranking official in Hitler's Nazi party.

By merging himself into the faceless masses of a fascist totalitarian regime, Zelig completely blots out his own identity in favor of an all-encompassing group identity. Zelig's choice of the Nazi party is comical but also significant to his character. The Nazis were Jew haters, and Zelig's decision to become a Nazi points to his own self-hatred. Zelig's story raises the issue of conformity at the individual level, and it also symbolizes the issue of assimilation at the cultural level. Conformity and assimilation are the individual and cultural expressions of the fundamental human need to identify with a larger whole. Zelig is a self-hating Jew who tries to eradicate his own identity so he can blend in with his gentile countrymen. His story hyperbolizes the large-scale assimilation of millions of American Jews in the early twentieth century, who distanced themselves as far as possible from their traditional culture in order to dissolve into the melting pot of American life. By choosing a Nazi identity, Zelig could not have moved farther away from his own identity as a Jew.

Eventually, Zelig is discovered by Dr. Fletcher and rescued from his Nazi existence. At the end of his story, Zelig finally achieves a sense of personal identity that he is comfortable with. No longer the human chameleon, Zelig is himself and only himself. His incredible redemption is achieved through the transformative power of love — the challenge at the next stage of identity crisis.

Annie Hall

Erikson's sixth stage, *intimacy versus isolation*, deals with the universal need to love and be loved. Erikson believed that intimate adult relationships recapitulate the emotional intimacy of the mother/child relationship. On a purely biological level, the physical intimacy shared between baby and its mother is not experienced again until much later in life. Sharing a bed, snuggling, suckling at the nipple, kissing, hugging and close ventral (belly to belly) contact are the most intimate physical experiences we can share with another. These types of contact are shared only by parents with their babies and adults with their lovers. Traditional psychoanalytic theory maintains that the search for a spouse in the genital stage of psychosexual development is directed by an unconscious desire to relive the physical intimacy experienced with the opposite-sex parent during infancy. Though Erikson's focus was on emotional intimacy, he retained the traditional connection between parent/child and adult love relationships.

Intimacy is hampered by *distantiation*—a lack of trust and fear of vulnerability. If someone has a basic sense of mistrust in himself or his lover, he will suffer from a fear of vulnerability, resulting in an inability to disclose his most personal secrets, feelings and fears. A lack of disclosure shuts off open communication in the relationship and creates distance and tension between the lovers, resulting in emotional isolation. Distantiation is the force that pushes people apart; it is the counter-force to intimacy, the force that pulls people together. The crisis at this stage of development is to find a healthy balance between distantiation and intimacy. Too much distantiation leads to isolation. Too much intimacy can lead to an unhealthy mesh, in which the lovers' identities become intertwined, losing their individuality and independence. The optimum resolution of the identity crisis at this stage is a healthy relationship between two people that is emotionally and physically intimate, while also providing a supportive and nonrestrictive base for self-exploration and identity development.

Relationship researchers have found that a very common conflict in romantic relationships is a gender difference in the kind of intimacy desired by males and females. While women typically complain about a lack of emotional intimacy in their relationships (i.e., too little communication and "mutual disclosure"), men complain about a lack of physical intimacy (i.e. not enough sex). In *Hollywood Ending* (2002), Woody Allen's character addresses this dichotomy in a dialogue with his ex-wife (Téa Leoni) about the problems that broke up their marriage. When his ex-wife complains: "There was no communication ... we had sex ... but we didn't talk." Allen's character replies: "Sex is better than talk! Talk is what you suffer through in order to get sex!" The trials and tribulations of love and the differences between the sexes are common leitmotifs running throughout Woody Allen's films, addressed especially well in his classic, *Annie Hall* (1977).

Alvy and Annie

While most romantic comedies deal with two characters falling in love, Allen's film dealt mainly with the disintegration of a romantic relationship. For the first time on film, the couple in love talked openly about their sex lives, a subject that had previously been addressed only indirectly through double entendres, or indulgently through sex scenes. In *Annie Hall*, Alvy Singer (Woody Allen) and Annie Hall (Diane Keaton) talk about their sexual relationship in frank, candid discussions. Another significant deviance from the normal romance plot is the absence of an external obstacle that the couple must overcome. Most romantic plots involve impediments such as jealous rivals, possessive parents, malevolent villains or other intrigues that must be conquered by love. But the only obstacles to happiness in Alvy and Annie's relationship is their own intimacy issues. A final unique feature in Allen's film is the ending. Instead of getting together in the end and living happily ever after, Alvy and Annie split up and go their separate ways. While being an extremely romantic movie, *Annie Hall* depicts a very unromantic look at relationships, in which two people can love each other completely, while also being completely incompatible as a couple.

In an opening monologue, Alvy Singer says: "I would never want to belong to any club that would have me for a member. That's the key joke in my adult life in terms of my relationships with women." The joke alludes to a sense of mistrust in Alvy's character, a creeping suspicion that any woman who would love and accept Alvy for the man he is must have something seriously wrong with her. His basic sense of mistrust in women and his relationships with them springs from a basic mistrust in himself and his own self-deprecating ego. Alvy goes on to admit: "I guess I'm going through a life crisis or something ... Annie and I broke up." The film then unfurls into a stream-of-consciousness string of related flashbacks and memories in which Alvy analyzes his life in order to understand why his relationship with Annie failed.

Allen shows how communication in the first stage of a relationship tends to be superficial by inserting subtitles during the first significant dialogue between Alvy and Annie. The subtitles show the couple thinking of something completely different while they engage in a vacuous conversation. But as their relationship develops, their communication becomes more meaningful. Alvy insists that Annie enter analysis, and he even pays for her psychiatrist. Analysis is just one way in which Alvy tries to change Annie. He wants her to be more intellectual, forcing her to watch morose documentaries like *The Sorrow and the Pity* and pressuring her into reading highbrow books and taking college courses. As their relationship develops, Annie demands more intimacy. She moves into Alvy's apartment. While Annie desires more emotional intimacy, Alvy desires more physical intimacy. He constantly complains about a lack of passion and infrequency of sex. Alvy expresses his inner need for intimacy and affirmation through the physical act of love. Annie desires to share emotional intimacy with Alvy by sharing quality time together and doing fun things as a couple. She desires a "real commitment," but Alvy cannot make one. His mistrust of Annie, himself, and their relationship becomes a wall that keeps a long-lasting and solid intimacy from forming.

Eventually, Annie decides to escape her "suffocating" relationship with Alvy. She tells him: "You're like New York City … you're like this island unto yourself." Alvy's inability to sustain an intimate relationship results in his inevitable isolation. While it is sad that they broke up, the film's final sequence recalls the happy moments that Alvy and Annie shared together. They both grew as individuals while they were in love. Encouraged by Alvy, Annie worked on her singing and became a great performer. At the same time, Alvy developed as a writer, becoming a successful playwright instead of just a stand-up comedian. Alvy's attempts to change Annie through books, education and analysis helped her to develop a strong sense of identity, which ironically gave her the self-confidence to assert herself and leave Alvy. In the end, though Alvy and Annie could not endure as lovers, they remained friends who developed together as individuals and shared a lot of wonderful memories.

The Graduate (revisited)

Erikson's seventh stage deals with issues common to midlife. At middle age, people have typically resolved earlier crises of identity and intimacy by settling down in a career and marriage. At this point, Erikson goes beyond the bounds of Freudian theory. The issues of parenting and adulthood are "post-genital." The challenge at this stage is not just "to love and to work," but to create new goals and find new ways to explore identity within one's career and within one's intimate relationships. Erikson labeled this challenge *generativity*. The individual must find new and creative ways to generate psychic energy by taking an active role in one's life and taking interest in future generations. Generativity is the counter-force to *stagnation*, a state of inert indifference in which the individual simply does not care about creating new goals, facing new challenges or passing on valuable life lessons to younger generations. The crisis at this stage, generativity versus stagnation, is often referred to as the *midlife crisis*.

Mrs. Robinson

The relationship between Ben and Mrs. Robinson in *The Graduate* (1967) is a stormy, conflicted pairing of two individuals going through two completely different identity crises. Ben is experiencing an adolescent identity crisis. When his father (William Daniels) asks him what he's doing floating in the pool all day, Ben replies: "...I'm just drifting ... it's very comfortable just to drift here...." Clearly, Ben is in a state of identity diffusion, listlessly drifting through life without a firm sense of who he is and where he is going. Mrs. Robinson, on the other hand, is in the midst of a midlife crisis. In a key scene with Ben, Mrs. Robinson reveals that she was an aspiring artist in college, but she gave up her calling when she got pregnant. Instead of using her young adulthood as a time to explore herself and her identity, Mrs. Robinson's stage of identity exploration was foreclosed, and she became a mother and housewife. Now, twenty years later, Mrs. Robinson is stagnating in a life of middle-class boredom and malaise. She has lost her youth, her ambitions, her lust for life and her hopes for a better future. Mrs. Robinson drowns her sorrows in alcohol, and distracts herself in an adulterous affair with a boy half her age. Like Lester Burnham in *American Beauty*, Mrs. Robinson takes a young lover so she could feel young again. When she's with Ben, Mrs. Robinson can fool herself into thinking she's eighteen years old again — a time when she was a wide-eyed young college girl with her whole life ahead of her.

In the same scene, Mrs. Robinson gets extremely upset when Ben mentions her daughter, Elaine (Katharine Ross). To Mrs. Robinson, Elaine represents her own lost youth and innocence. Mrs. Robinson doesn't want to soil the only pure and wholesome thing in her life by associating it with her tawdry affair with Ben. Elaine still has the opportunity to define her own identity and choose a career and life, rather than being forced into a premature marriage and parenthood. Mrs. Robinson wants to protect her daughter from making the same mistakes she made. But it is also clear that Mrs. Robinson harbors feelings of jealousy and resentment toward her daughter. Elaine is still young and beautiful and able to lead a free and independent life, while Mrs. Robinson is stuck in a middle-class rut, a victim of her own poor choices. Mrs. Robinson tries desperately to obstruct the budding relationship between Elaine and Ben. She even goes so far as to tell Elaine that Ben raped her. In the famous wedding sequence in the end, when Ben rescues Elaine from the altar, Mrs. Robinson stops the young lovers, telling Elaine: "It's too late!" Elaine replies: "Not for me!" It's too late for Mrs. Robinson to have a fulfilling identity and a chance for true love, but it's not too late for Elaine.

About Schmidt

In Erikson's final stage of identity development, *integrity versus despair*, people nearing the end of their life will look back on their life story and make retrospective interpretations. If one finds meaning in one's life, a sense of existential "integrity" is achieved. If no meaning is found, if the most resounding feeling is a sense of regret for the things one *didn't* do, then the result is "despair." In *About Schmidt* (2002), Warren Schmidt (Jack Nicholson) doubts that his life was meaningful after he retires from a forty-year career as an insurance actuary and his wife (June Squibb) passes away. Schmidt sets out on a journey to find some kind of meaning in his life. Towards the end, Schmidt seems to be mired in a pit of regret and despair: "What in the world is better because of me? I am a failure.... Relatively soon, I will die ... and it will be as though I never even existed." But at his darkest moment, a seemingly trivial message gives Schmidt a much-needed boost of integrity. Schmidt receives a painting in the mail from Ndugu, the impoverished African foster child that he has been supporting through a Christian relief fund. Schmidt's realization that somewhere in a distant corner of the world he did something extremely good for someone he never even knew is enough to make him appreciate the beauty and value of his own life.

Conclusion: An Eclectic Approach to Film Analysis

Twenty-first century psychologists, psychoanalysts and psychotherapists now have a broad palette of theoretical paradigms to draw upon when working with their patients. But whether mental health practitioners define themselves as Freudian, Jungian, Adlerian, existentialist, humanist or whatever, everyone agrees that a good practitioner must have the background and potential of an eclectic. A theory is not a panacea. A theory is only as good as its "fit" with the issues and individual it is applied to. An eclectic approach — an understanding of all the theories and the ability to apply all of them — is not just helpful, it is essential. This philosophy is as true for film analysis at it is for psychoanalysis.

Malcolm X

Spike Lee's *Malcolm X* (1992) is an epic-length "biopic" that focuses on the many facets of one man's extremely complex life. As such, it provides the perfect case study for an eclectic film analysis utilizing every approach delineated in this book. Malcolm X is a mythic figure. A hero to many, a villain to some, he is an archetype of our times, a legend and inspiration to millions. He is a symbol of religion, a symbol of freedom, a symbol of historical identity and a symbol of existential determination. He is a superhero and an underdog, a great American hero whose life became legend, and whose legend became myth through the vision of a great filmmaker.

Identity

The credits roll as Malcolm X (Denzel Washington) accuses the American nation of brutalizing and exploiting the African people. We hear

Malcolm's voice as we watch the disturbing video footage of Rodney King being beaten by a gang of club-wielding Los Angeles police officers. Spike Lee is telling us that this film is about a man who died decades ago, yet it delivers a message that is as relevant today as it was in the 1960s. In the opening sequence, Malcolm is an adolescent in a stage of identity development that Erikson would label *identity diffusion*. He is "frying" his hair, infusing it with lye to take out the kinks. The process is painful and tortuous—much like the ordeal of a transformative *initiation ritual* into a society, like a circumcision or tattooing. When it's over, Malcolm smiles at his altered reflection in the mirror and asks his pal, Shorty (Spike Lee), "Looks white, don't it?"

Backstory

At this stage of character development, Malcolm has no idea of who he really is. He is a black man who wants to look white. He is ashamed of his African identity, an *inferiority complex* that he *compensates* for by trying to look white. By emulating what he perceives as the superior society, he is actually identifying with a *negative identity*, a society that despises him because of his skin, even as he changes his appearance to try to appear more like them. The sequence is interrupted by autobiographical voice-over narration. Malcolm recalls an event from the distant past. While his mother was pregnant with him, she was threatened and harassed by a group of Klansmen. They were trying to intimidate Malcolm's father, a strong and proud preacher who espoused a Black migration back to Africa. Malcolm tells us that white men killed four of his uncles, lynching one of them. His mother was a fair-skinned woman because his grandmother was raped by a white man. His mother hated her own complexion because it represented an evil side of her identity that she could not stand.

Sophia

At this point in the film, Malcolm is not dealing with his anger and hatred towards white people. He is not identifying with his own father as an internal mentor, and he does not understand that his fascination and strange desire for white women is a manifestation of his own feelings about himself. When Malcolm ditches his black girlfriend for a white woman, Sophia (Kate Vernon), he is taking the "white man's prize ... the white woman." It is an act of revenge and spite against the white men who killed his father and his uncles, raped his grandmother and tormented his mother. On another level, Malcolm's illicit desire is a way of connecting with his mother, a woman who was half white. Malcolm's complex relationship with Sophia is an expression of his confused feelings towards whites, his love/hate dichotomy. Malcolm hates the whites for what they did to him and his people, but he loves and lusts after the materialistic aspects of white society. His black girlfriend, Laura (Theresa Randle), represents a mature and intimate love that he cannot yet accept or identify with.

The Myth of the Birth of Malcolm Little

Lee returns to Malcolm's backstory and completes the story of his birth. His father Earl Little (Tommy Hollis) is murdered by Klansmen because he will not alter his message of black pride and African migration. The martyrdom of Malcolm's father represents the legacy that Malcolm must live up to and the identity he must achieve. Malcolm's mother is cheated out of her husband's insurance money by a white insurance agent. This bit of backstory is followed by a scene in which Malcolm forces Sophia to feed him and kiss his foot. His relationship with her is both an expression of love and an act of sadomasochistic power. In dominating the "white man's prize," he gains a sense of power, while otherwise he feels essentially powerless in white society. Malcolm cannot come to grips with his anger towards white society, because he cannot fully accept himself as a black man in a white world. Lee returns to the backstory, where we see Malcolm's mother succumb to the pressures of abject poverty and grief. Her children are taken away from her by a white social worker, and she loses her mind. Malcolm is raised by a *surrogate parent*, a white matron in a detention home. Instead of a strong black father figure, he now has a patronizing white teacher, who tells him that because he is a "nigger," he can never become a lawyer.

The Black Champion

We return to Malcolm as an adolescent, working as a porter on a train. He and his friends cheer for Joe Louis on the radio. The boxing champion is a symbol of black power and potential, a hero not only for young Malcolm, but for a nation of oppressed black people. The significance of the black champion as a unifying symbol of black power and identity would come into play later in Malcolm X's story, when he enlists Cassius Clay into the Nation of Islam. As Muhammad Ali, the black champion becomes more than a fighter in the ring, he becomes a fighter for black people's rights all across America. Unfortunately, Spike Lee did not have time to delve into Malcolm's relationship with Muhammad Ali in his film. But in the scene directly after the train sequence, we see Malcolm becoming a fighter in a bar in Harlem. An argument sparks an emotional explosion in which Malcolm nearly kills a man. Significantly, this emotional explosion is triggered when a man says something derogatory about his mother. The intense anger and rage hiding just beneath Malcolm's skin is repressed rage at white people, the same whites who boss him around on the train and call him "boy." Malcolm cannot safely express his anger directly at white people, so he *displaces* his rage onto a safe substitute outlet, a fellow back man.

West Indian Archie

Malcolm's display of violence catches the eye of West Indian Archie (Delroy Lindo), a Harlem gangster who takes Malcolm under his wing as a numbers runner. Archie is a mentor figure. He sees Malcolm's inner power and wants to harness it. He dresses Malcolm in new clothes, offers him a new identity as a criminal and gives him a *weapon of power*, a gun. Ultimately, Archie shows himself to be a *false mentor*. His gift of violence and criminality takes Malcolm down the wrong path of larceny and drug abuse. Rather than understanding his rage against white society, Malcolm merely learns to use his violence and anger to get an individual sense of power in his life. For Malcolm, crime is a passive-aggressive attempt to gain vengeance against white people. He describes himself as an "animal"—he will do anything to anyone to get what he wants. A scene in which Malcolm steals a gold ring off the finger of a sleeping rich white man symbolizes his desire for the golden ring of social power, and his inability to strive for power in legitimate ways. Malcolm's life of crime eventually leads him to prison.

Brother Baines

State prison represents the *belly of the whale* in Malcolm's journey, the realm of transformation in which Malcolm will become reborn. In the first of his many ordeals, Malcolm must first hit rock bottom. He must shed all of his arrogance and false pride, and plummet down the pit of his soul to the bedrock of his own identity. On his first day in prison, he refuses to state his number — the dehumanizing symbol of his relegation to being just a six-digit number rather than a human being. The guards throw Malcolm in "the hole." While suffering in this dark pit, he is visited by a priest who asks him: "Do you know what a friend you have in Jesus, son?" Malcolm rejects Jesus and the religion of white society. After many days in solitary confinement, Malcolm finally relents and states his number. Not a man, not even an animal, Malcolm is just a number, a meaningless being with no true sense of identity.

At his bottom, Malcolm encounters a new mentor figure. Brother Baines (Albert Hall) is a follower of Elijah Muhammed, who delivers Malcolm the message of black pride. Baines teaches Malcolm about the Nation of Islam and the legacy of his African identity. He reveals to Malcolm the fact that he has no idea who he really is. Malcolm's own last name, Little, is a slave name imposed upon his family by white masters. Malcolm must discover his true identity and define himself. He denounces his slave name and replaces it with "X"— the symbol of the unknown variable — the identity he must discover for himself. Through Baines's mentorship, Malcolm finally finds a channel for his anger. He *sublimates* his rage at white people into mastering his new *weapon of power*— words— which Malcolm directs against the enemy that he truly hates, white oppression.

God and the Devil

As a first obstacle to his *spiritual rebirth*, Malcolm must overcome his inability to kneel in prayer to Allah. Kneeling represents the subjugation of the personal ego to the collective ego. Malcolm is unable to take this step at first. However, he experiences a true *epiphany* in a vision of Elijah Muhammed, who appears in his cell as a "blinding light," informing Malcolm of his potential for greatness. Malcolm is suddenly able to kneel. As a symbol of his transformation, Malcolm cuts off his fried hair and accepts his African identity both internally and externally. He dedicates himself to the cause of "telling the white devil the truth to his face."

Though Malcolm is definitely a different person, the limitations of his character are clearly evident. He sees the world in terms of black and white, a *duality of opposites*, in which black is good and white is completely evil. This limitation of perception is an inherent limitation of the new philosophy that he has adopted. Along with the duality of black and white within the Nation of Islam, there is also the duality of male and female, the flagrant chauvinism within the Nation in which women are treated as subordinates rather than equals. This chauvinism is epitomized on a banner at one of Malcolm's lectures, which reads: "We Must Protect Our Most Valuable Property — Our Women!" To achieve complete identity integration in a Jungian sense, Malcolm must integrate his archetypes in a way that is balanced, rather than segregated. He must integrate his *shadow*, his hatred of white people, by accepting the fact that some whites can be good and helpful. He must integrate his *anima*, not in the form of a submissive woman who bows to him, but in the form of an equal partner who complements him. And he must integrate his *wise old man*, his true father figure.

Elijah Muhammed

Malcolm emerges from prison and encounters his next mentor, Elijah Muhammed. He becomes a full member of the Nation of Islam. With

Elijah Muhammed. Malcolm X encounters an inspiring metor figure. Elijah Muhammed (Al Freeman Jr.), left, with Malcolm X (Denzel Washington). *Malcolm X* (1992), Forty Acres and a Mule Filmworks, JVC Entertainment and Largo International N.V.

his new father figure and his new "brothers," Malcolm is symbolically reunited with the father and brothers he lost as a child. Now in touch with his true identity as a black leader, he displays all the divine powers of a great hero who has found his calling. His ability to inspire others arises from his own inspiration, but the gifts of charisma, conviction and inner strength, Malcolm's *birthright* from his father, make him a champion. Nevertheless, Malcolm's message, the message he inherited from his new and ultimately false mentor, Elijah Muhammed, is a message of segregation rather than integration. He preaches "complete separation between the black man and the white man." Malcolm's refusal to accept the help of white people (his lack of integration of his shadow) is symbolized when he turns away a white Harvard student, telling her that she could do nothing to help the cause of oppressed back people in America.

Betty

Malcolm moves towards integration by marrying Betty (Angela Bassett). Their union for Malcolm is a "meeting with the goddess," a moment in which he incorporates feminine strength and wisdom into his personality, and becomes more complete. Betty tries to open her husband's eyes to Elijah Muhammed's hypocrisy and to Baines's betrayal. However, it is Malcolm's message of hatred and complete separation that leads to his next *identity crisis*. By reacting to John F. Kennedy's assassination with satisfaction rather than compassion, he alienates the Nation of Islam from the nation of America and he gives Elijah Muhammed and Baines an excuse to alienate him from the Black Muslims. When an assassination plot is revealed to him by a loyal follower, he has no choice but to go out on his own.

Mecca

The ordeal of betrayal from his two beloved mentors makes Malcolm stronger and more independent. He becomes a leader and preacher of his own words and ideas, founding the Black Nationalist movement. He is less opposed to the notion of white people helping the black cause, admitting that they share a common struggle. As a symbol of his new transformation, Malcolm makes a pilgrimage to Mecca, where he experiences another epiphany. Worldwide Islam is a *transcendent experience* for Malcolm, a "spiritual rebirth" in which he encounters fellow Muslims who are white, and integrates his shadow. Malcolm returns to America after this *apotheosis* in an ultimate form of integration. He declares: "I am not a racist." The *ultimate boon* that Malcolm delivers to his people in America is a *freedom to live* without the chains of racism. He realizes that the ideal of black supremacy at the heart of the Nation of Islam is merely another form of racism. But after his conversion to Sunni Islam, Malcolm is finally able to understand his hatred for white people and overcome it. He sees himself as a "complete human being," and defines himself with a self-chosen name, El-Hajj Malik Al-Shabazz.

Martyrdom

Malcolm returns to America with a message much like his father's, the message of a spiritual and cultural migration of African Americans back to their African roots. Malcolm's *identity achievement* at this stage is one step away from a complete resolution of the mythological hero's character arc. Campbell's stage of *atonement with the father* could be understood as an ultimate identification — an "at-one-ment" — in which the son actually becomes

Mecca. Malcolm X (Denzel Washington) experiences a spiritual rebirth during his transcendent pilgrimage to the Islamic holy land. He is reborn as El-Hajj Malik Al-Shabazz. *Malcolm X* (1992), Forty Acres and a Mule Filmworks, JVC Entertainment and Largo International N.V.

one with the father. This stage of archetype integration is achieved completely when Malcolm is assassinated, just like his father, and his spirit joins the spirits of other martyr-heroes in the realm of the collective unconscious.

At this point in the film, Malcolm's life begins to mirror his father's life when he was a child. He and is family are harassed and threatened by representatives of white society, i.e., the FBI, and disgruntled representatives of the Nation of Islam. Scenes of his house being burned down are intercut with flashbacks from his childhood of his father's house being burned down. Like his father, he refuses to stop preaching. In a final meeting with a goddess figure, Malcolm is approached by a kindly old woman shortly before his death. She tells him: "Jesus will protect you." The symbolism is simultaneously incongruous and true. Though Malcolm rejected Jesus as his personal savior, he is about to become an inspirational martyr and legend, much like Jesus.

Moments before his death, Malcolm says, "It's a time for martyrs now." He knows that he is putting his life on the line, but he is a *willing sacrifice*. His cause and his message are more important to him than his own life. He realizes that his legend is now the greatest inspiration that he could give to his people. In his final words before being gunned down, he apologizes to a woman that he snapped at earlier, signifying that in his last stage, he has a more mature and integrated attitude towards women, seeing them as equals rather than "property." Malcolm dies in a crucifixion pose. He is eulogized as a "black prince," a "champion" who when returned to the earth, "the common mother of all," will become a "seed" that will grow forth and inspire future generations. In the final sequence, children in America and South Africa proudly declare: "I am Malcolm X!" Though he died, Malcolm's legend and his message live on.

Filmography

About Schmidt (2002). *Directed by* Alexander Payne. *Writing Credits*: Louis Begley (novel), Alexander Payne (screenplay), Jim Taylor (screenplay). *Starring*: Jack Nicholson, Hope Davis, Dermot Mulroney, Kathy Bates.

Abre los Ojos (1997). *Directed by* Alejandro Amenábar. *Writing Credits*: Alejandro Amenábar, Mateo Gil. *Starring*: Eduardo Noriega, Penélope Cruz, Chete Lera.

American Beauty (1999). *Directed by* Sam Mendes. *Writing Credits*: Alan Ball (written by). *Starring*: Kevin Spacey, Annette Bening, Thora Birch, Wes Bentley, Mena Suvari, Peter Gallagher, Allison Janney, Chris Cooper, Scott Bakula. *Academy Awards*: Kevin Spacey (Best Actor in a Leading Role), Sam Mendes (Best Director), Alan Ball (Best Writing, Screenplay Written Directly for the Screen).

American Graffiti (1973). *Directed by* George Lucas. *Writing Credits*: George Lucas, Gloria Katz, Willard Huyck. *Starring*: Richard Dreyfuss, Ron Howard, Paul Le Mat.

American History X (1998). *Directed by* Tony Kaye. *Writing Credits*: David McKenna (written by). *Starring*: Edward Norton, Edward Furlong, Beverly D'Angelo.

American Pie (1999). *Directed by* Paul Weitz and Chris Weitz. *Writing Credits*: Adam Herz (written by). *Starring*: Jason Biggs, Chris Klein, Thomas Ian Nicholas, Shannon Elizabeth

Amistad (1997). *Directed by* Steven Spielberg. *Writing Credits*: David Franzoni (written by). *Starring*: Morgan Freeman, Nigel Hawthorne, Anthony Hopkins, Djimon Hounsou, Matthew McConaughey, David Paymer, Pete Postlethwaite, Stellan Skarsgård.

Angel and the Badman (1947). *Directed by* James Edward Grant. *Writing Credits*: James Edward Grant. *Starring*: John Wayne, Gail Russell, Harry Carey.

Angels and Insects (1995). *Directed by* Philip Haas. *Writing Credits*: A. S. Byatt, Belinda Haas, Philip Haas. *Starring*: Mark Rylance, Kristin Scott Thomas, Patsy Kensit.

Animal House (1978). *Directed by* John Landis. *Writing Credits*: Harold Ramis (written by), Douglas Kenney (written by), Chris Miller (written by). *Starring*: Tom Hulce, Stephen Furst, Mark Metcalf.

Annie (1982). *Directed by* John Huston. *Writing Credits*: Harold Gray (comic strip Little Orphan Annie), Thomas Meehan (play), Carol Sobieski (screenplay). *Starring*: Albert Finney, Carol Burnett, Ann Reinking, Tim Curry.

Annie Hall (1977). *Directed by* Woody Allen. *Writing Credits*: Woody Allen and Marshall Brickman. *Starring*: Woody Allen, Diane Keaton, Tony Roberts, Carol

Kane, Paul Simon, Shelley Duvall. *Academy Awards*: Diane Keaton (Best Actress in a Leading Role), Woody Allen (Best Director), Woody Allen and Marshall Brickman (Best Writing, Screenplay Written Directly for the Screen).

Antwone Fisher (2002). *Directed by* Denzel Washington. *Writing Credits*: Antwone Fisher (written by). *Starring*: Derek Luke, Malcolm David Kelley, Cory Hodges, Denzel Washington.

Artificial Intelligence: A.I. (2001). *Directed by* Steven Spielberg. *Writing Credits*: Ian Watson (screen story), Brian Aldiss (short story "Supertoys Last All Summer Long"), Steven Spielberg (screenplay). *Starring*: Haley Joel Osment, Jude Law, Frances O'Connor, Brendan Gleeson, Sam Robards, William Hurt.

The Asphalt Jungle(1950). *Directed by* John Huston. *Writing Credits*: W. R. Burnett (novel), Ben Maddow, John Huston. *Starring*: Sterling Hayden, Louis Calhern, Jean Hagen, James Whitmore.

Baby Boom (1987). *Directed by* Charles Shyer. *Writing Credits*: Nancy Meyers (written by), Charles Shyer (written by). *Starring*: Diane Keaton, Sam Shepard, Harold Ramis.

The Bad News Bears (1976). *Directed by* Michael Ritchie. *Writing Credits*: Bill Lancaster. *Starring*: Walter Matthau, Chris Barnes, Tatum O'Neal.

The Bad Seed (1956). *Directed by* Mervyn LeRoy. *Writing Credits*: Maxwell Anderson (play), John Lee Mahin, William March (novel). *Starring*: Nancy Kelly, Patricia McCormack, Henry Jones.

Beauty and the Beast (1991). *Directed by* Gary Trousdale and Kirk Wise. *Writing Credits*: Roger Allers (story), Kelly Asbury (story). *Starring*: Paige O'Hara (voice), Robby Benson (voice), Richard White (voice).

Ben-Hur (1959) *Directed by* William Wyler. *Writing Credits*: Lew Wallace (novel), Karl Tunberg (screenplay). *Starring*: Charlton Heston, Jack Hawkins, Haya Harareet, Stephen Boyd, Hugh Griffith. *Academy Awards*: Charlton Heston (Best Actor in a Leading Role), Hugh Griffith (Best Actor in a Supporting Role), William Wyler (Best Director), Ralph E. Winters and John D. Dunning (Best Film Editing).

The Bible (1966). *Directed by* John Huston. *Writing Credits*: Vittorio Bonicelli, Christopher Fry, Jonathan Griffin, Ivo Perilli. *Starring*: Michael Parks, Ulla Bergryd, Richard Harris, John Huston, Stephen Boyd, George C. Scott, Ava Gardner, Peter O'Toole.

The Big Parade (1925). *Directed by* King Vidor. *Writing Credits*: Harry Behn, Joseph Farnham (play). *Starring*: John Gilbert, Renée Adorée, Hobart Bosworth.

The Blues Brothers (1980). *Directed by* John Landis. *Writing Credits*: Dan Aykroyd, John Landis. *Starring*: John Belushi, Dan Aykroyd, James Brown, Cab Calloway, Ray Charles, Aretha Franklin.

Bonnie and Clyde (1967). *Directed by* Arthur Penn. *Writing Credits*: David Newman (written by), Robert Benton (written by). *Starring*: Warren Beatty, Faye Dunaway, Michael J. Pollard, Gene Hackman, Estelle Parsons. *Academy Awards*: Estelle Parsons (Best Actress in a Supporting Role).

The Bride of Frankenstein(1935). *Directed by* James Whale. *Writing Credits*: William Hurlbut, William Hurlbut (adaptation). *Starring*: Boris Karloff, Colin Clive, Valerie Hobson, Elsa Lanchester.

Bridge on the River Kwai (1957). *Directed by* David Lean. *Writing Credits*: Pierre Boulle (novel). *Starring*: William Holden, Jack Hawkins, Alec Guinness. *Academy Awards*: Alec Guinness (Best Actor in a Leading Role), David Lean (Best

Director), Pierre Boulle, Carl Foreman, Michael Wilson (Best Writing, Screenplay Based on Material from Another Medium).

A Bronx Tale (1993). *Directed by* Robert De Niro. *Writing Credits*: Chazz Palminteri (play), Chazz Palminteri (screenplay). *Starring*: Robert De Niro, Chazz Palminteri, Lillo Brancato, Francis Capra.

Bubble Boy (2001). *Directed by* Blair Hayes. *Writing Credits*: Cinco Paul (written by), Ken Daurio (written by). *Starring*: Jake Gyllenhaal, Swoosie Kurtz, Marley Shelton.

Butch Cassidy and the Sundance Kid (1969). *Directed by* George Roy Hill. *Writing Credits*: William Goldman (written by). *Starring*: Paul Newman, Robert Redford, Katharine Ross. *Academy Awards*: William Goldman (Best Writing, Story and Screenplay Based on Material Not Previously Published or Produced).

The Cabinet of Dr. Caligari (1920). *Directed by* Robert Wiene. *Writing Credits*: Hans Janowitz, Carl Mayer. *Starring*: Werner Krauss, Conrad Veidt, Friedrich Feher.

Caligula (1979). *Directed by* Tinto Brass, Bob Guccione. *Writing Credits*: Gore Vidal (screenplay). *Starring*: Malcolm McDowell, Teresa Ann Savoy, Helen Mirren, Peter O'Toole.

Carrie (1976). *Directed by* Brian De Palma. *Writing Credits*: Lawrence D. Cohen, Stephen King (novel). *Starring*: Sissy Spacek, Piper Laurie, Amy Irving.

Casablanca (1942). *Directed by* Michael Curtiz. *Writing Credits*: Murray Burnett (play), Joan Alison (play), Julius J. Epstein, Philip G. Epstein, Howard Koch. *Starring*: Humphrey Bogart, Ingrid Bergman, Paul Henreid, Claude Rains. *Academy Awards*: Michael Curtiz (Best Director), Hal B. Wallis (Best Picture), Julius J. Epstein, Philip G. Epstein and Howard Koch (Best Writing, Screenplay).

Chariots of Fire (1981). *Directed by* Hugh Hudson. *Writing Credits*: Colin Welland. *Starring*: Nicholas Farrell, Nigel Havers, Ian Charleson. *Academy Awards*: Milena Canonero (Best Costume Design), David Puttnam (Best Picture), Colin Welland (Best Writing, Screenplay Written Directly for the Screen).

Children of the Corn (1984). *Directed by* Fritz Kiersch. *Writing Credits*: George Goldsmith, Stephen King (story). *Starring*: Peter Horton, Linda Hamilton, R. G. Armstrong.

Chinatown (1974). *Directed by* Roman Polanski. *Writing Credits*: Robert Towne. *Starring*: Jack Nicholson, Faye Dunaway, John Huston. *Academy Awards*: Robert Towne (Best Writing, Original Screenplay).

Cinderella (1950). *Directed by* Clyde Geronimi, Wilfred Jackson, Hamilton Luske. *Writing Credits*: Ken Anderson, Homer Brightman. *Starring*: Ilene Woods, Eleanor Audley, Verna Felton.

Clash of the Titans (1981). *Directed by* Desmond Davis. *Writing Credits*: Beverley Cross (written by). *Starring*: Harry Hamlin, Judi Bowker, Burgess Meredith, Maggie Smith, Ursula Andress, Claire Bloom.

Close Encounters of the Third Kind (1977). *Directed by* Steven Spielberg. *Writing Credits*: Steven Spielberg (written by). *Starring*: Richard Dreyfuss, François Truffaut, Teri Garr.

The Color of Purple (1985). *Directed by* Steven Spielberg. *Writing Credits*: Alice Walker (novel), Menno Meyjes. *Starring*: Danny Glover, Whoopi Goldberg, Margaret Avery, Oprah Winfrey.

Crimes and Misdemeanors (1989). *Directed by* Woody Allen. *Writing Credits*: Woody Allen (written by). *Starring*: Bill Bernstein, Martin Landau, Claire Bloom.

The Crowd (1928). *Directed by* King Vidor. *Writing Credits*: King Vidor (screenplay), John V. A. Weaver (screenplay). *Starring*: Eleanor Boardman, James Murray, Bert Roach.

Dazed and Confused (1993). *Directed by* Richard Linklater. *Writing Credits*: Richard Linklater (written by). *Starring*: Jason London, Joey Lauren Adams, Milla Jovovich.

Dead Poets Society (1989). *Directed by* Peter Weir. *Writing Credits*: Tom Schulman (written by). *Starring*: Robin Williams, Robert Sean Leonard, Ethan Hawke, Josh Charles. *Academy Awards*: Tom Schulman (Best Writing, Screenplay Written Directly for the Screen).

Dr. Jekyll and Mr. Hyde (1920). *Directed by* John S. Robertson. *Writing Credits*: Clara Beranger, Robert Louis Stevenson (story). *Starring*: John Barrymore, Martha Mansfield, Brandon Hurst.

Doctor Zhivago (1965). *Directed by* David Lean. *Writing Credits*: Boris Pasternak (novel), Robert Bolt. *Starring*: Omar Sharif, Julie Christie, Geraldine Chaplin, Rod Steiger, Alec Guinness. *Academy Awards*: John Box, Terence Marsh and Dario Simoni (Best Art Direction-Set Decoration, Color), Robert Bolt (Best Writing, Screenplay Based on Material from Another Medium).

Dracula (1931). *Directed by* Tod Browning. *Writing Credits*: John L. Balderston (story), Hamilton Deane (story), Bram Stoker (novel). *Starring*: Bela Lugosi, Helen Chandler.

Dracula (1992). *Directed by* Francis Ford Coppola. *Writing Credits*: Bram Stoker (novel), James V. Hart (screenplay). *Starring*: Gary Oldman, Winona Ryder, Anthony Hopkins, Keanu Reeves, Richard E. Grant, Cary Elwes, Bill Campbell, Sadie Frost, Tom Waits, Monica Bellucci.

Duel in the Sun (1946). *Directed by* King Vidor & Otto Brower. *Writing Credits*: Niven Busch (novel), Oliver H. P. Garrett (adaptation). *Starring*: Jennifer Jones, Joseph Cotten, Gregory Peck, Lionel Barrymore.

E.T. (1982). *Directed by* Steven Spielberg. *Writing Credits*: Melissa Mathison. *Starring*: Henry Thomas, Dee Wallace-Stone, Robert MacNaughton, Drew Barrymore, Peter Coyote.

The Elephant Man (1980). *Directed by* David Lynch. *Writing credits*: Sir Frederick Treves (book), Ashley Montagu (book), Christopher De Vore (screenplay), Eric Bergren (screenplay), David Lynch (screenplay). *Starring:* Anthony Hopkins, John Hurt, Anne Bancroft.

Empire of the Sun (1987). *Directed by* Steven Spielberg. *Writing Credits*: J. G. Ballard (novel), Tom Stoppard. *Starring*: Christian Bale, John Malkovich, Miranda Richardson, Nigel Havers, Joe Pantoliano.

Equus (1977). *Directed by* Sidney Lumet. *Writing Credits*: Peter Shaffer (also play). *Starring*: Richard Burton, Peter Firth, Colin Blakely, Joan Plowright.

Erin Brockovich (2000). *Directed by* Steven Soderbergh. *Writing Credits*: Susannah Grant (written by). *Starring*: Julia Roberts, David Brisbin, Albert Finney. *Academy Awards*: Julia Roberts (Best Actress in a Leading Role).

Excalibur (1981). *Directed by* John Boorman. *Writing Credits*: Thomas Malory (book *Le Morte d'Arthur*), Rospo Pallenberg (adaptation), Rospo Pallenberg (screenplay), John Boorman (screenplay). *Starring*: Nigel Terry, Helen Mirren, Nicholas Clay.

The Exorcist (1973). *Directed by* William Friedkin. *Writing Credits*: William Peter Blatty (also novel). *Starring*: Ellen Burstyn, Max von Sydow, Jason Miller,

Lee J. Cobb. *Academy Awards*: William Peter Blatty (Best Writing, Screenplay Based on Material from Another Medium).

Fandango (1985). *Directed by* Kevin Reynolds. *Writing Credits*: Kevin Reynolds. *Starring*: Kevin Costner, Judd Nelson, Sam Robards.

Fantasia (1940). *Directed by* James Algar and Samuel Armstrong. *Writing Credits*: Joe Grant (segment) (story), Dick Huemer (segment) (story). *Starring*: Leopold Stokowski (Conductor, The Philadelphia Orchestra), Deems Taylor (Narrator), Hugh Douglas (Narrator). *Academy Awards*: (Honorary Award) Walt Disney, William E. Garity, J. N. A. Hawkins, Leopold Stokowski (and his associates).

Fast Times at Ridgemont High (1982). *Directed by* Amy Heckerling. *Writing Credits*: Cameron Crowe (book), Cameron Crowe (screenplay). *Starring*: Sean Penn, Jennifer Jason Leigh, Judge Reinhold.

Fiddler on the Roof (1971). *Directed by* Norman Jewison. *Writing Credits*: Sholom Aleichem (book *Tevye's Daughters* and play *Tevye der Milkhiker* as Sholem Aleichem), Joseph Stein (libretto and screenplay). *Starring*: Topol, Norma Crane, Leonard Frey.

The Fisher King (1991). *Directed by* Terry Gilliam. *Writing Credits*: Richard LaGravenese (written by). *Starring*: Jeff Bridges, Adam Bryant, Robin Williams, Paul J. Lombardi, Mercedes Ruehl. *Academy Awards*: Mercedes Ruehl (Best Actress in a Supporting Role).

Forbidden Planet (1956). *Directed by* Fred M. Wilcox. *Writing Credits*: Irving Block (story), Allen Adler (story), Cyril Hume. *Starring*: Walter Pidgeon, Anne Francis, Leslie Nielsen.

Fort Apache (1948). *Directed by* John Ford. *Writing Credits*: James Warner Bellah (story), Frank S. Nugent. *Starring*: John Wayne, Henry Fonda, Shirley Temple.

Frankenstein (1931). *Directed by* James Whale. *Writing Credits*: Mary Shelley (novel), Peggy Webling (play). *Starring*: Colin Clive, Mae Clarke, John Boles.

Friday the 13th (1980). *Directed by* Sean S. Cunningham. *Writing Credits*: Victor Miller. *Starring*: Betsy Palmer, Adrienne King.

From Here to Eternity (1953). *Directed by* Fred Zinnemann. *Writing Credits*: James Jones (novel), Daniel Taradash. *Starring*: Burt Lancaster, Montgomery Clift, Deborah Kerr, Donna Reed, Frank Sinatra. *Academy Awards*: Frank Sinatra (Best Actor in a Supporting Role), Donna Reed (Best Actress in a Supporting Role), Fred Zinnemann (Best Director), William A. Lyon (Best Film Editing), Daniel Taradash (Best Writing, Screenplay).

G. I. Jane (1997). *Directed by* Ridley Scott. *Writing Credits*: Danielle Alexandra (story), David Twohy (screenplay), Danielle Alexandra (screenplay). *Starring*: Demi Moore, Viggo Mortensen, Anne Bancroft.

The Godfather (1972). *Directed by* Francis Ford Coppola. *Writing Credits*: Francis Ford Coppola, Mario Puzo (also novel). *Starring*: Marlon Brando, Al Pacino, James Caan, Richard S. Castellano, Robert Duvall. *Academy Awards*: Marlon Brando (Best Actor in a Leading Role). Mario Puzo and Francis Ford Coppola (Best Writing, Screenplay Based on Material from Another Medium).

Gone with the Wind (1939). *Directed by* Victor Fleming. *Writing Credits*: Margaret Mitchell (novel), Sidney Howard. *Starring*: Thomas Mitchell, Barbara O'Neil, Vivien Leigh, Clark Gable. *Academy Awards*: Vivien Leigh (Best Actress in a Leading Role), Hattie McDaniel (Best Actress in a Supporting Role), Victor Fleming (Best Director), Hal C. Kern and James E. Newcom (Best Film Editing), Sidney Howard (Best Writing, Screenplay).

The Good Son (1993). *Directed by* Joseph Ruben. *Writing Credits*: Ian McEwan (written by). *Starring*: Macaulay Culkin, Elijah Wood, Wendy Crewson, David Morse.

The Good, the Bad and the Ugly (1967). *Directed by* Sergio Leone. *Writing Credits*: Luciano Vincenzoni (story), Sergio Leone (story), Agenore Incrocci (screenplay) (as Age), Furio Scarpelli (screenplay) (as Scarpelli), Luciano Vincenzoni (screenplay), Sergio Leone (screenplay). *Starring*: Clint Eastwood, Lee Van Cleef, Aldo Giuffrè.

Good Will Hunting (1997). *Directed by* Gus Van Sant. *Writing Credits*: Matt Damon (written by), Ben Affleck (written by). *Starring*: Robin Williams, Matt Damon, Ben Affleck, Stellan Skarsgård, Minnie Driver. *Academy Awards*: Robin Williams (Best Actor in a Supporting Role), Matt Damon and Ben Affleck (Best Writing, Screenplay Written Directly for the Screen).

Goodbye, Mr. Chips (1969). *Directed by* Herbert Ross. *Writing Credits*: James Hilton (novel) & Terence Rattigan (screenplay). *Starring*: George Baker, Peter O'Toole, Petula Clark.

The Graduate (1967). *Directed by* Mike Nichols. *Writing Credits*: Charles Webb (novel), Calder Willingham (screenplay), Buck Henry (screenplay). *Starring*: Anne Bancroft, Dustin Hoffman, Katharine Ross. *Academy Awards*: Mike Nichols (Best Director).

The Greatest Story Ever Told (1965). *Directed by* George Stevens and David Lean. *Writing Credits*: James Lee Barrett, Henry Denker (source writings). *Starring*: Max von Sydow, Michael Anderson Jr., Carroll Baker.

Gunfight at the O.K. Corral (1957). *Directed by* John Sturges. *Writing Credits*: George Scullin (article), Leon Uris. *Starring*: Burt Lancaster, Kirk Douglas, Rhonda Fleming, Jo Van Fleet.

The Gunfighter (1950). *Directed by* Henry King. *Writing Credits*: William Bowers (story), André De Toth (story) (as Andre De Toth), William Bowers (screenplay), William Sellers (screenplay). *Starring*: Gregory Peck, Helen Westcott, Millard Mitchell, Jean Parker, Karl Malden.

Halloween (1978). *Directed by* John Carpenter. *Writing Credits*: John Carpenter (screenplay), Debra Hill (screenplay). *Starring*: Donald Pleasence, Jamie Lee Curtis, Nancy Kyes.

Hang 'Em High (1968). *Directed by* Ted Post. *Writing Credits*: Leonard Freeman, Mel Goldberg. *Starring*: Clint Eastwood, Inger Stevens, Ed Begley, Pat Hingle, Ben Johnson.

Hannah and Her Sisters (1986). *Directed by* Woody Allen. *Writing Credits*: Woody Allen. *Starring*: Barbara Hershey, Carrie Fisher, Michael Caine, Mia Farrow, Dianne Wiest, Maureen O'Sullivan. *Academy Awards*: Michael Caine (Best Actor in a Supporting Role), Dianne Wiest (Best Actress in a Supporting Role).

Harold and Maude (1971). *Directed by* Hal Ashby. *Writing Credits*: Colin Higgins. *Starring*: Ruth Gordon, Bud Cort.

Harry Potter and the Sorcerer's Stone (2001). *Directed by* Chris Columbus. *Writing Credits*: J. K. Rowling (novel), Steven Kloves (screenplay). *Starring*: Richard Harris, Daniel Radcliffe, Maggie Smith, Emma Watson, Robbie Coltrane, Rupert Grint.

High Noon (1952). *Directed by* Fred Zinnemann. *Writing Credits*: John W. Cunningham (story), Carl Foreman (screenplay). *Starring*: Gary Cooper, Thomas Mitchell, Lloyd Bridges, Katy Jurado, Grace Kelly. *Academy Awards*: Gary

Cooper (Best Actor in a Leading Role), Elmo Williams, Harry W. Gerstad (Best Film Editing).

High Plains Drifter (1973). *Directed by* Clint Eastwood. *Writing Credits*: Ernest Tidyman. *Starring*: Clint Eastwood, Verna Bloom, Marianna Hill.

Hollywood Ending (2002). *Directed by* Woody Allen. *Writing Credits*: Woody Allen (written by). *Starring*: Téa Leoni, Bob Dorian, Ivan Martin.

Hoosiers (1986). *Directed by* David Anspaugh. *Writing Credits*: Angelo Pizzo (written by). *Starring*: Gene Hackman, Barbara Hershey, Dennis Hopper.

How the West Was Won (1962). *Directed by* John Ford and Henry Hathaway. *Writing Credits*: James R. Webb. *Starring*: Carroll Baker, Lee J. Cobb, Henry Fonda, Carolyn Jones, Karl Malden, Gregory Peck, George Peppard. *Academy Awards*: Harold F. Kress (Best Film Editing), James R. Webb (Best Writing, Story and Screenplay Written Directly for the Screen).

I Was a Teenage Frankenstein (1957). *Directed by* Herbert L. Strock. *Writing Credits*: Herman Cohen, Aben Kandel. *Starring*: Whit Bissell, Phyllis Coates, Robert Burton, Gary Conway.

I Was a Teenage Werewolf (1957). *Directed by* Gene Fowler Jr.. *Writing Credits*: Herman Cohen, Aben Kandel. *Starring*: Michael Landon, Yvonne Lime, Whit Bissell.

In Dreams (1999). *Directed by* Neil Jordan. *Writing Credits*: Bari Wood (novel Doll's Eyes), Bruce Robinson (screenplay), Neil Jordan (screenplay). *Starring*: Annette Bening, Katie Sagona, Aidan Quinn, Robert Downey Jr.

It's Alive (1974). *Directed by* Larry Cohen. *Writing Credits*: Larry Cohen. *Starring*: John P. Ryan, Sharon Farrell, James Dixon.

Jason and the Argonauts (1963). *Directed by* Don Chaffey. *Writing Credits*: Beverley Cross, Jan Read. *Starring*: Todd Armstrong, Nancy Kovack, Gary Raymond.

Jaws (1975). *Directed by* Steven Spielberg. *Writing Credits*: Peter Benchley (also novel), Carl Gottlieb. *Starring*: Roy Scheider, Robert Shaw, Richard Dreyfuss, Lorraine Gary, Murray Hamilton.

The Jazz Singer (1927). *Directed by* Alan Crosland. *Writing Credits*: Alfred A. Cohn (adaptation), Jack Jarmuth (titles), Samson Raphaelson (play). *Starring*: Al Jolson, May McAvoy, Warner Oland.

Jerry Maguire (1996). *Directed by* Cameron Crowe. *Writing Credits*: Cameron Crowe (written by). *Starring*: Tom Cruise, Cuba Gooding Jr., Renée Zellweger. *Academy Awards*: Cuba Gooding Jr. (Best Actor in a Supporting Role).

Joe Kidd (1972). *Directed by* John Sturges. *Writing Credits*: Elmore Leonard. *Starring*: Clint Eastwood, Robert Duvall, John Saxon.

Jurassic Park (1993). *Directed by* Steven Spielberg. *Writing Credits*: Michael Crichton (novel), Michael Crichton (screenplay), David Koepp (screenplay). *Starring*: Sam Neill, Laura Dern, Jeff Goldblum, Richard Attenborough.

The Karate Kid (1984). *Directed by* John G. Avildsen. *Writing Credits*: Robert Mark Kamen. *Starring*: Ralph Macchio, Pat Morita, Elisabeth Shue.

Khartoum (1966). *Directed by* Basil Dearden and Eliot Elisofon. *Writing Credits*: Robert Ardrey. *Starring*: Charlton Heston, Laurence Olivier, Richard Johnson.

King Kong (1933). *Directed by* Merian C. Cooper and Ernest B. Schoedsack. *Writing Credits*: Merian C. Cooper (story), Edgar Wallace (story), James Ashmore Creelman, Ruth Rose. *Starring*: Fay Wray, Robert Armstrong, Bruce Cabot.

The Last Temptation of Christ (1988). *Directed by* Martin Scorsese. *Writing Cred-*

its: Nikos Kazantzakis (novel), Paul Schrader (screenplay). *Starring*: Willem Dafoe, Harvey Keitel, Paul Greco.

Lawrence of Arabia (1962). *Directed by* David Lean. *Writing Credits*: T. E. Lawrence (writings), Robert Bolt (screenplay). *Starring*: Peter O'Toole, Alec Guinness, Anthony Quinn, Jack Hawkins, Omar Sharif, José Ferrer. *Academy Awards*: David Lean (Best Director), Anne V. Coates (Best Film Editing).

Lethal Weapon (1987). *Directed by* Richard Donner. *Writing Credits*: Shane Black. *Starring*: Mel Gibson, Danny Glover, Gary Busey.

Little Buddha (1993). *Directed by* Bernardo Bertolucci. *Writing Credits*: Bernardo Bertolucci (story), Rudy Wurlitzer (screenplay). *Starring*: Keanu Reeves, Ruocheng Ying, Chris Isaak, Bridget Fonda.

The Little Mermaid (1989). *Directed by* Ron Clements, John Musker. *Writing Credits*: Roger Allers (story), Hans Christian Andersen (fairy tale). *Starring*: Jodi Benson (Ariel voice), Christopher Daniel Barnes.

The Little Princess (1939). *Directed by* Walter Lang and William A. Seiter. *Writing Credits*: Frances Hodgson Burnett (novel), Ethel Hill, Walter Ferris. *Starring*: Shirley Temple, Richard Greene, Anita Louise.

Looking for Mr. Goodbar (1977). *Directed by* Richard Brooks. *Writing Credits*: Richard Brooks, Judith Rossner (novel). *Starring*: Diane Keaton, Tuesday Weld, William Atherton, Richard Kiley, Richard Gere.

The Lord of the Rings: The Fellowship of the Ring (2001). *Directed by* Peter Jackson. *Writing Credits*: J. R. R. Tolkien (novel *The Fellowship of the Ring*), Frances Walsh (screenplay) (as Fran Walsh), Philippa Boyens (screenplay), Peter Jackson (screenplay). *Starring*: Elijah Wood, Ian McKellen, Viggo Mortensen, Liv Tyler, Sean Astin, Cate Blanchett, John Rhys-Davies, Billy Boyd, Dominic Monaghan, Orlando Bloom, Christopher Lee, Hugo Weaving, Sean Bean.

Mad Max (1979). *Directed by* George Miller. *Writing Credits*: George Miller (story), Byron Kennedy (story), James McCausland (screenplay), George Miller (screenplay). *Starring*: Mel Gibson, Joanne Samuel, Hugh Keays-Byrne.

Maid in Manhattan (2002). *Directed by* Wayne Wang. *Writing Credits*: John Hughes (story), Kevin Wade (screenplay). *Starring*: Jennifer Lopez, Ralph Fiennes, Natasha Richardson, Stanley Tucci.

Malcolm X (1992). *Directed by* Spike Lee. *Writing Credits*: Alex Haley (book *The Autobiography of Malcom X*), Malcolm X (book *The Autobiography of Malcom X*), Arnold Perl (screenplay), Spike Lee (screenplay). *Starring*: Denzel Washington, Angela Bassett, Albert Hall, Al Freeman Jr., Delroy Lindo, Spike Lee, Theresa Randle.

The Maltese Falcon (1941). *Directed by* John Huston. *Writing Credits*: Dashiell Hammett (novel), John Huston (screenplay). *Starring*: Humphrey Bogart, Mary Astor, Gladys George, Peter Lorre.

Manhattan (1979). *Directed by* Woody Allen. *Writing Credits*: Woody Allen, Marshall Brickman. *Starring*: Woody Allen, Diane Keaton, Michael Murphy, Mariel Hemingway, Meryl Streep, Anne Byrne Hoffman, Karen Ludwig.

Metropolis (1927). *Directed by* Fritz Lang. *Writing Credits*: Fritz Lang, Thea von Harbou (also novel). *Starring*: Alfred Abel, Gustav Fröhlich, Brigitte Helm.

Minority Report (2002). *Directed by* Steven Spielberg. *Writing Credits*: Philip K. Dick (short story), Scott Frank (screenplay), Jon Cohen (screenplay). *Starring*: Tom Cruise, Colin Farrell, Steve Harris, Max von Sydow, Samantha Morton, Kathryn Morris.

Mr. Mom (1983). *Directed by* Stan Dragoti. *Writing Credits*: John Hughes. *Starring*: Michael Keaton, Teri Garr, Frederick Koehler.

Moby Dick (1956). *Directed by* John Huston. *Writing Credits*: Herman Melville (novel *Moby-Dick; or, The Whale*), Ray Bradbury, John Huston. *Starring*: Gregory Peck, Richard Basehart, Leo Genn, James Robertson Justice.

Modern Times (1936). *Directed by* Charles Chaplin. *Writing Credits*: Charles Chaplin. *Starring*: Charles Chaplin, Paulette Goddard, Henry Bergman.

Mrs. Doubtfire (1993). *Directed by* Chris Columbus. *Writing Credits*: Anne Fine (novel *Alias Madame Doubtfire*), Randi Mayem Singer (screenplay), Leslie Dixon (screenplay). *Starring*: Robin Williams, Sally Field, Pierce Brosnan, Harvey Fierstein.

Mulan (1998). *Directed by* Tony Bancroft and Barry Cook. *Writing Credits*: Robert D. San Souci (story) & Rita Hsiao. *Starring*: Ming-Na (voice) (as Ming-Na Wen), B. D. Wong (voice), Soon-Tek Oh (voice).

The Mummy (1932). *Directed by* Karl Freund. *Writing Credits*: Nina Wilcox Putnam (story), Richard Schayer (story), John L. Balderston. *Starring*: Boris Karloff, Zita Johann, David Manners.

The Mummy (1999). *Directed by* Stephen Sommers. *Writing Credits*: Stephen Sommers (screen story), Lloyd Fonvielle (screen story), Kevin Jarre (screen story), Stephen Sommers (screenplay). *Starring*: Brendan Fraser, Rachel Weisz, John Hannah, Arnold Vosloo.

My Darling Clementine (1946). *Directed by* John Ford. *Writing Credits*: Samuel G. Engel, Sam Hellman (story), Stuart N. Lake (book *Wyatt Earp, Frontier Marshal*), Winston Miller. *Starring*: Henry Fonda, Linda Darnell, Victor Mature, Cathy Downs, Walter Brennan.

New York Stories (1989). *Directed by* Woody Allen, Francis Ford Coppola, Martin Scorsese. *Writing Credits*: Richard Price, Woody Allen, Francis Ford Coppola, Sofia Coppola. *Starring*: Woody Allen, Marvin Chatinover, Mae Questel, Mia Farrow, Molly Regan.

1941 (1979). *Directed by* Steven Spielberg. *Writing Credits*: Robert Zemeckis (story), Bob Gale (story), John Milius (story). *Starring*: Dan Aykroyd, Ned Beatty, John Belushi.

Nosferatu (1922). *Directed by* F. W. Murnau. *Writing Credits*: Henrik Galeen. *Starring*: Max Schreck, Alexander Granach, Gustav von Wangenheim.

Of Human Hearts (1938). *Directed by* Clarence Brown. *Writing Credits*: Honore Morrow (story), Bradbury Foote (screenplay). *Starring*: Walter Huston, James Stewart.

Office Space (1999). *Directed by* Mike Judge. *Writing Credits*: Mike Judge (Milton animated shorts), Mike Judge (screenplay). *Starring*: Ron Livingston, Jennifer Aniston, Ajay Naidu, David Herman, Gary Cole, Stephen Root.

The Omen (1976). *Directed by* Richard Donner. *Writing Credits*: David Seltzer. *Starring*: Gregory Peck, Lee Remick, David Warner.

One Flew Over the Cuckoo's Nest (1975). *Directed by* Milos Forman. *Writing Credits*: Bo Goldman, Lawrence Hauben, Ken Kesey (novel). *Starring*: Jack Nicholson, Louise Fletcher, William Redfield. *Academy Awards*: Jack Nicholson (Best Actor in a Leading Role), Louise Fletcher (Best Actress in a Leading Role), Milos Forman (Best Director), Lawrence Hauben and Bo Goldman (Best Writing, Screenplay Adapted From Other Material).

100 Heroes and Villains (2003). *Directed by* Gary Smith. *Writing Credits*: Bob Gazzale (written by). *Starring*: various actress and actors.

Ordinary People (1980). *Directed by* Robert Redford. *Writing Credits*: Judith Guest (novel), Alvin Sargent. *Starring*: Donald Sutherland, Mary Tyler Moore, Judd Hirsch, Timothy Hutton, M. Emmet Walsh, Elizabeth McGovern. *Academy Awards*: Timothy Hutton (Best Actor in a Supporting Role), Robert Redford (Best Director), Ronald L. Schwary (Best Picture), Alvin Sargent (Best Writing, Screenplay Based on Material from Another Medium).

The Outlaw Josey Wales (1976). *Directed by* Clint Eastwood. *Writing Credits*: Forrest Carter (novel *Gone to Texas*), Sonia Chernus, Philip Kaufman (as Phil Kaufman). *Starring*: Clint Eastwood, Chief Dan George, Sondra Locke.

The Ox-Bow Incident (1943). *Directed by* William A. Wellman. *Writing Credits*: Walter Van Tilburg Clark (novel) & Lamar Trotti. *Starring*: Henry Fonda, Dana Andrews, Mary Beth Hughes, Anthony Quinn.

Pale Rider (1985). *Directed by* Clint Eastwood. *Writing Credits*: Michael Butler, Dennis Shryack. *Starring*: Clint Eastwood, Michael Moriarty, Carrie Snodgress, Chris Penn.

The Patriot (2000). *Directed by* Roland Emmerich. *Writing Credits*: Robert Rodat (written by). *Starring*: Mel Gibson, Heath Ledger, Joely Richardson, Jason Isaacs, Chris Cooper.

Payback (1999). *Directed by* Brian Helgeland. *Writing Credits*: Donald E. Westlake (novel *The Hunter*) (as Richard Stark), Brian Helgeland (screenplay), Terry Hayes (screenplay). *Starring*: Mel Gibson, Gregg Henry, Maria Bello, David Paymer.

The Penalty (1920). *Directed by* Wallace Worsley. *Writing Credits*: Charles Kenyon, Philip Lonergan, Gouverneur Morris (story). *Starring*: Lon Chaney, Ethel Grey Terry, Charles Clary.

Pinocchio (1940). *Directed by* Hamilton Luske and Ben Sharpsteen. *Writing Credits*: Aurelius Battaglia (story), Carlo Collodi (novel). *Starring*: Mel Blanc (voice), Don Brodie (voice).

Pocahontas (1995). *Directed by* Mike Gabriel and Eric Goldberg. *Writing Credits*: Carl Binder, Susannah Grant (screenplay), Philip LaZebnik. *Starring*: Irene Bedard, Judy Kuhn, Mel Gibson, Linda Hunt, John Kassir.

Poltergeist (1982). *Directed by* Tobe Hooper and Steven Spielberg. *Writing Credits*: Steven Spielberg (story), Steven Spielberg (screenplay), Michael Grais (screenplay), Mark Victor (screenplay). *Starring*: JoBeth Williams, Craig T. Nelson, Beatrice Straight.

Pretty Woman (1990). *Directed by* Garry Marshall. *Writing Credits*: J. F. Lawton (written by). *Starring*: Richard Gere, Julia Roberts, Ralph Bellamy, Jason Alexander, Laura San Giacomo, Hector Elizondo.

The Princess Diaries (2001). *Directed by* Garry Marshall. *Writing Credits*: Meg Cabot (novel), Gina Wendkos (screenplay). *Starring*: Julie Andrews, Anne Hathaway, Hector Elizondo, Heather Matarazzo, Mandy Moore, Caroline Goodall.

Psycho (1960). *Directed by* Alfred Hitchcock. *Writing Credits*: Robert Bloch (novel), Joseph Stefano (screenplay). *Starring*: Anthony Perkins, Vera Miles, John Gavin, Martin Balsam.

Ransom (1996). *Directed by* Ron Howard. *Writing Credits*: Cyril Hume (story), Richard Maibaum (story), Richard Price (screenplay), Alexander Ignon (screenplay). *Starring*: Mel Gibson, Rene Russo, Brawley Nolte, Gary Sinise, Delroy Lindo, Lili Taylor, Liev Schreiber, Donnie Wahlberg.

Red River (1948). *Directed by* Howard Hawks and Arthur Rosson. *Writing Credits*: Borden Chase (screenplay), Borden Chase (story "The Chisholm Trail"), Charles Schnee (screenplay). *Starring*: John Wayne, Montgomery Clift, Joanne Dru, Walter Brennan.

Rio Grande (1950). *Directed by* John Ford. *Writing Credits*: James Warner Bellah (story), James Kevin McGuinness. *Starring*: John Wayne, Maureen O'Hara, Ben Johnson.

The Robe (1953). *Directed by* Henry Koster. *Writing Credits*: Lloyd C. Douglas (novel), Gina Kaus (adaptation). *Starring*: Richard Burton, Jean Simmons, Victor Mature.

Rocky (1976). *Directed by* John G. Avildsen. *Writing Credits*: Sylvester Stallone. *Starring*: Sylvester Stallone, Talia Shire, Burt Young, Carl Weathers. *Academy Awards*: John G. Avildsen (Best Director).

The Royal Tennenbaums (2001). *Directed by* Wes Anderson. *Writing Credits*: Wes Anderson (written by), Owen Wilson (written by). *Starring*: Gene Hackman, Anjelica Huston, Gwyneth Paltrow, Ben Stiller, Luke Wilson, Owen Wilson, Danny Glover, Bill Murray, Alec Baldwin, Seymour Cassel.

Rushmore (1998). *Directed by* Wes Anderson. *Writing Credits*: Wes Anderson (written by), Owen Wilson (written by). *Starring*: Jason Schwartzman, Bill Murray, Olivia Williams, Seymour Cassel, Brian Cox.

Saving Private Ryan (1998). *Directed by* Steven Spielberg. *Writing Credits*: Robert Rodat (written by). *Starring*: Tom Hanks, Edward Burns, Tom Sizemore, Matt Damon, Jeremy Davies, Adam Goldberg, Barry Pepper, Giovanni Ribisi, Vin Diesel, Ted Danson, Max Martini, Dylan Bruno. *Academy Awards*: Steven Spielberg (Best Director).

Scarface (1983). *Directed by* Brian De Palma. *Writing Credits*: Oliver Stone. *Starring*: Al Pacino, Steven Bauer, Michelle Pfeiffer, Mary Elizabeth Mastrantonio, Robert Loggia, Miriam Colon, F. Murray Abraham.

Schindler's List (1993). *Directed by* Steven Spielberg. *Writing Credits*: Thomas Keneally (book), Steven Zaillian (screenplay). *Starring*: Liam Neeson, Ben Kingsley, Ralph Fiennes, Caroline Goodall, Jonathan Sagall, Embeth Davidtz. *Academy Awards*: Steven Spielberg (Best Director), Steven Zaillian (Best Writing, Screenplay Based on Material from Another Medium).

The Searchers (1956). *Directed by* John Ford. *Writing Credits*: Alan Le May (novel), Frank S. Nugent (screenplay). *Starring*: John Wayne, Jeffrey Hunter, Vera Miles.

Shane (1953). *Directed by* George Stevens. *Writing Credits*: Jack Schaefer (story), A. B. Guthrie. *Starring*: Alan Ladd, Jean Arthur, Van Heflin, Jack Palance, Ben Johnson. *Academy Awards*: Loyal Griggs (Best Cinematography, Color).

She Wore a Yellow Ribbon (1949). *Directed by* John Ford. *Writing Credits*: James Warner Bellah (stories "War Party" and "The Big Hunt"), Frank S. Nugent (as Frank Nugent), Laurence Stallings. *Starring*: John Wayne, Joanne Dru, John Agar, Ben Johnson.

The Silence of the Lambs (1991). *Directed by* Jonathan Demme. *Writing Credits*: Thomas Harris (novel), Ted Tally (screenplay). *Starring*: Jodie Foster, Anthony Hopkins, Scott Glenn, Anthony Heald, Ted Levine. *Academy Awards*: Anthony Hopkins (Best Actor in a Leading Role), Jodie Foster (Best Actress in a Leading Role), Jonathan Demme (Best Director).

Silverado (1985). *Directed by* Lawrence Kasdan. *Writing Credits*: Lawrence Kasdan, Mark Kasdan. *Starring*: Kevin Kline, Scott Glenn, Kevin Costner, Danny Glover.

Simple Twist of Fate, A (1994). *Directed by* Gillies MacKinnon. *Writing Credits*: George Eliot (novel), Steve Martin (written by). *Starring*: Steve Martin, Gabriel Byrne, Laura Linney, Catherine O'Hara.

Sleeping Beauty (1959). *Writing Credits*: Milt Banta, Winston Hibler. *Starring*: Mary Costa (voice), Bill Shirley (voice), Eleanor Audley (voice).

The Snake Pit (1948). *Directed by* Anatole Litvak. *Writing Credits*: Millen Brand, Frank Partos. *Starring*: Olivia de Havilland, Mark Stevens, Leo Genn. Academy Awards: Best Sound, Recording.

Snow White and the Seven Dwarfs (1937). *Writing Credits*: Ted Sears (story) and Richard Creedon (story). *Starring*: Roy Atwell (voice), Stuart Buchanan (voice), Adriana Caselotti (voice). Academy Awards: (Honorary Award) Walt Disney.

The Sons of Katie Elder (1965). *Directed by* Henry Hathaway. *Writing Credits*: Talbot Jennings (story), William H. Right (screenplay). *Starring*: John Wayne, Dean Martin, George Kennedy, James Gregory.

Spartacus (1960). *Directed by* Stanley Kubrick. *Writing Credits*: Howard Fast (novel), Dalton Trumbo. *Starring*: Kirk Douglas, Laurence Olivier, Jean Simmons, Charles Laughton, Peter Ustinov, John Gavin. *Academy Awards*: Peter Ustinov (Best Actor in a Supporting Role).

Spellbound (1945). *Directed by* Alfred Hitchcock. *Writing Credits*: Angus MacPhail (adaptation), Ben Hecht (screenplay). *Starring*: Ingrid Bergman, Gregory Peck, Michael Chekhov. *Academy Awards*: Miklós Rózsa (Best Music, Scoring of a Dramatic or Comedy Picture).

Stagecoach (1939). *Directed by* John Ford. *Writing Credits*: Ernest Haycox (story), Dudley Nichols. *Starring*: Claire Trevor, John Wayne, Andy Devine. *Academy Awards*: Thomas Mitchell (Best Actor in a Supporting Role).

Star Wars (1977). *Directed by* George Lucas. *Writing Credits*: George Lucas. *Starring*: Mark Hamill, Harrison Ford, Carrie Fisher, Peter Cushing, Alec Guinness.

Star Wars: Episode I — The Phantom Menace (1999). *Directed by* George Lucas. *Writing Credits*: George Lucas. *Starring*: Liam Neeson, Ewan McGregor, Natalie Portman, Jake Lloyd.

Star Wars: Episode II — Attack of the Clones (2002). *Directed by* George Lucas. *Writing Credits*: George Lucas (story), (screenplay). *Starring*: Ewan McGregor, Natalie Portman, Hayden Christensen, Christopher Lee, Samuel L. Jackson.

Star Wars: Episode III (2005). *Directed by* George Lucas. *Writing Credits*: George Lucas. *Starring*: Ewan McGregor, Natalie Portman, Hayden Christensen, Christopher Lee, Samuel L. Jackson, Frank Oz, Ian McDiarmid, Jimmy Smits.

Star Wars: Episode V — The Empire Strikes Back (1980). *Directed by* Irvin Kershner. *Writing Credits*: George Lucas (story), Leigh Brackett, Lawrence Kasdan. *Starring*: Mark Hamill, Harrison Ford, Carrie Fisher, Billy Dee Williams.

Star Wars: Episode VI — Return of the Jedi (1983). *Directed by* Richard Marquand. *Writing Credits*: George Lucas (story), Lawrence Kasdan. *Starring*: Mark Hamill, Harrison Ford, Carrie Fisher, Billy Dee Williams.

The Sunshine Boys (1975). *Directed by* Herbert Ross. *Writing Credits*: Neil Simon (also play). *Starring*: Walter Matthau, George Burns, Richard Benjamin. *Academy Awards*: George Burns (Best Actor in a Supporting Role).

The Sweet Smell of Success (1957). *Directed by* Alexander Mackendrick. *Writing Credits*: Ernest Lehman (novel), Clifford Odets. *Starring*: Burt Lancaster, Tony Curtis, Susan Harrison.

The Talented Mr. Ripley (1999). *Directed by* Anthony Minghella. *Writing Credits*:

Patricia Highsmith (novel), Anthony Minghella (screenplay). *Starring*: Matt Damon, Gwyneth Paltrow, Jude Law, Cate Blanchett, Philip Seymour Hoffman, Jack Davenport.

The Ten Commandments (1956). *Directed by* Cecil B. DeMille. *Writing Credits*: J. H. Ingraham (novel *Pillar of Fire* as Rev. J. H. Ingraham), A. E. Southon (novel *On Eagle's Wing* as Rev. A. E. Southon), Dorothy Clarke Wilson (novel *Prince of Egypt*), Æneas MacKenzie, Jesse Lasky Jr. (as Jesse L. Lasky Jr.), Jack Gariss, Fredric M. Frank. *Starring*: Charlton Heston, Yul Brynner, Anne Baxter, Edward G. Robinson, Yvonne De Carlo.

The Terminator (1984). *Directed by* James Cameron. *Writing Credits*: James Cameron, Gale Anne Hurd. *Starring*: Arnold Schwarzenegger, Michael Biehn, Linda Hamilton, Paul Winfield, Lance Henriksen.

Terminator 2 (1991). *Directed by* James Cameron. *Writing Credits*: James Cameron (written by), William Wisher Jr. (written by). *Starring*: Arnold Schwarzenegger, Linda Hamilton, Edward Furlong, Robert Patrick.

Terminator 3 (2003). *Directed by* Jonathan Mostow. *Writing Credits*: James Cameron (characters), Gale Anne Hurd (characters). *Starring*: Arnold Schwarzenegger, Nick Stahl, Claire Danes.

Three Godfathers (1936). *Directed by* Richard Boleslawski. *Writing Credits*: Peter B. Kyne (novel *The Three Godfathers*), Edward E. Paramore Jr., Manuel Seff. *Starring*: Chester Morris, Lewis Stone, Walter Brennan.

The Tin Star (1957). *Directed by* Anthony Mann. *Writing Credits*: Joel Kane (story), Dudley Nichols, Barney Slater (story). *Starring*: Henry Fonda, Anthony Perkins, Betsy Palmer.

To Kill a Mockingbird (1962). *Directed by* Robert Mulligan. *Writing Credits*: Harper Lee (novel), Horton Foote. *Starring*: Mary Badham, Gregory Peck, Phillip Alford, Robert Duvall. *Academy Awards*: Gregory Peck (Best Actor in a Leading Role), Alexander Golitzen, Henry Bumstead and Oliver Emert (Best Art Direction-Set Decoration, Black-and-White), Horton Foote (Best Writing, Screenplay Based on Material from Another Medium).

Treasure Island (1950). *Directed by* Byron Haskin. *Writing Credits*: Robert Louis Stevenson (novel), Lawrence Edward Watkin. *Starring*: Bobby Driscoll, Robert Newton, Basil Sydney, Walter Fitzgerald.

The Treasure of the Sierra Madre (1948). *Directed by* John Huston. *Writing Credits*: B. Traven (novel), John Huston. *Starring*: Humphrey Bogart, Walter Huston, Tim Holt, Bruce Bennett. *Academy Awards*: Walter Huston (Best Actor in a Supporting Role), John Huston (Best Director), John Huston (Best Writing, Screenplay).

The Unknown (1927). *Directed by* Tod Browning. *Writing Credits*: Tod Browning (story), Waldemar Young (scenario). *Starring*: Lon Chaney, Norman Kerry, Joan Crawford.

Vanilla Sky (2001). *Directed by* Cameron Crowe. *Writing Credits*: Alejandro Amenábar (film *Abre Los Ojos*), Mateo Gil (film *Abre Los Ojos*) (as Mateo Gil Rodríguez), Cameron Crowe (screenplay). *Starring*: Tom Cruise, Penélope Cruz, Cameron Diaz, Kurt Russell, Jason Lee.

Victory (1981). *Directed by* John Huston. *Writing Credits*: Evan Jones, Jeff Maguire (story), Djordje Milicevic (story), Yabo Yablonsky (screenplay), Yabo Yablonsky (story). *Starring*: Michael Caine, Sylvester Stallone, Max von Sydow.

Village of the Damned (1960). *Directed by* Wolf Rilla. *Writing Credits*: Stirling

Silliphant, Wolf Rilla, Ronald Kinnoch (as George Barclay). *Starring*: George Sanders, Barbara Shelley, Michael Gwynn.

The Westerner (1940). *Directed by* William Wyler. *Writing Credits*: Niven Busch, Stuart N. Lake (story). *Starring*: Gary Cooper, Walter Brennan, Doris Davenport. *Academy Awards*: Walter Brennan (Best Actor in a Supporting Role).

What a Girl Wants (2003). *Directed by* Dennie Gordon. *Writing Credits*: William Douglas-Home (play *The Reluctant Debutante*), William Douglas-Home (1958 screenplay), Jenny Bicks (screenplay), Elizabeth Chandler (screenplay). *Starring*: Amanda Bynes, Colin Firth, Kelly Preston.

What About Bob? (1991). *Directed by* Frank Oz. *Writing Credits*: Alvin Sargent (story), Laura Ziskin (story), Tom Schulman (screenplay). *Starring*: Bill Murray, Richard Dreyfuss, Julie Hagerty.

What Lies Beneath (2002). *Directed by* Robert Zemeckis. *Writing Credits*: Sarah Kernochan (story), Clark Gregg (story), Clark Gregg (screenplay). *Starring*: Harrison Ford, Michelle Pfeiffer, Diana Scarwid, Joe Morton, James Remar, Miranda Otto, Amber Valletta, Katharine Towne.

Whatever Happened to Baby Jane? (1962). *Directed by* Robert Aldrich. *Writing Credits*: Henry Farrell (novel), Lukas Heller. *Starring*: Bette Davis, Joan Crawford, Victor Buono.

Who Shot Liberty Valance (1962). *Directed by* John Ford. *Writing Credits*: James Warner Bellah, Willis Goldbeck, Dorothy M. Johnson (story). *Starring*: John Wayne, James Stewart, Vera Miles, Lee Marvin, Edmond O'Brien.

The Wizard of Oz (1939). *Directed by* Victor Fleming, Richard Thorpe. *Writing Credits:* L. Frank Baum (novel), Noel Langley. *Starring*: Judy Garland, Frank Morgan, Billie Burke. *Academy Awards*: Herbert Stothart (Best Music, Original Score); Harold Arlen (music), E. Y. Harburg (lyrics) Best Music, Song for the song "Over the Rainbow".

The Wolf Man (1941). *Directed by* George Waggner. *Writing Credits*: Curt Siodmak. *Starring*: Claude Rains, Warren William, Ralph Bellamy.

Working Girl (1988). *Directed by* Mike Nichols. *Writing Credits*: Kevin Wade (written by). *Starring*: Harrison Ford, Sigourney Weaver, Melanie Griffith, Alec Baldwin, Joan Cusack.

Wyatt Earp (1994). *Directed by* Lawrence Kasdan. *Writing Credits*: Dan Gordon (written by), Lawrence Kasdan (written by). *Starring*: Kevin Costner, Dennis Quaid, Gene Hackman.

Yentl (1983). *Directed by* Barbra Streisand. *Writing Credits*: Jack Rosenthal, Isaac Bashevis Singer (story "Yentl, the Yeshiva Boy"), Barbra Streisand. *Starring*: Barbra Streisand, Mandy Patinkin, Amy Irving.

Zelig (1983). *Directed by* Woody Allen. *Writing Credits*: Woody Allen. *Starring*: Woody Allen, Mia Farrow, John Buckwalter.

Bibliography

Adler, Alfred. 1927. *The Practice and Theory of Individual Psychology*. New York: Harcourt, Brace and World.

_____. 1931. *What Life Could Mean to You*. Boston: Little, Brown.

_____. 1939. *Social Interest*. New York: Putnam.

_____. 1954. *Understanding Human Nature*. New York: Fawcett.

Bettelheim, Bruno. 1982. *Freud and Man's Soul*. New York: Knopf.

Bowlby, John. 1969. *Attachment and Loss*. New York: Basic Books.

Bulfinch, Thomas. 1947. *Bulfinch's Mythology*. New York: T. Y. Crowell.

Campbell, Joseph. 1949. *The Hero with a Thousand Faces*. Princeton, N.J.: Princeton University Press.

_____, ed. 1970. *Myths, Dreams and Religion*. New York: E. P. Dutton.

_____. 1974. *The Mythic Image*. Princeton, NJ: Princeton University Press.

_____. 1982. *The Hero's Journey: Joseph Campbell on his Life and Work*. Phil Cousineau, (Ed.). New York: Harper & Row.

_____. 1986. *The Inner Reaches of Outer Space: Metaphor as Myth and as Religion*. Toronto: St. James Press.

_____. 1988. *An Open Life*. New York: Larson Publications.

_____. 1988. *The Power of Myth*. New York: Doubleday.

_____. 1990. *Transformation of Myth Through Time*. New York: Harper & Row.

Erikson, Erik. 1963. *Childhood and Society*. New York: Norton.

_____. 1968. *Identity, Youth and Crisis*. New York: Norton.

_____. 1974. *Dimensions of a New Identity*. New York: Norton.

_____. 1982, 1997. *The Life Cycle Completed: A Review*. New York: Norton.

Freud, Anna. 1946. *The Ego and the Mechanisms of Defense*. New York: International Universities Press.

_____. 1965. *The Writing of Anna Freud*. New York: International Universities Press.

Freud, Sigmund. 1900. *The Interpretation of Dreams*. (In *The Complete Psychological Works: Standard Edition*, Volumes 4 & 5).

_____. 1901. *The Psychopathology of Everyday Life*. (In *The Complete Psychological Works: Standard Edition*, Volume 6).

_____. 1905. *Three Essays on Sexuality*. (In *The Complete Psychological Works: Standard Edition*, Volume 7).

_____. 1910. *Five Lectures on Psychoanalysis*. (In *The Complete Psychological Works: Standard Edition*, Volume 11).

_____. 1917. *Introductory Lectures on Psychoanalysis*. (In *The Complete Psychological Works: Standard Edition*, Volumes 15 & 16).

_____. 1923. *The Ego and the Id.* (In *The Complete Psychological Works: Standard Edition*, Volume 19).

_____. 1938. *The Basic Writings of Sigmund Freud.* A. Brill, Trans. & Ed. New York: Random House.

_____. 1940. *An Outline of Psychoanalysis.* (In *The Complete Psychological Works: Standard Edition*, Volume 23).

_____. 1956. *The Complete Psychological Works: Standard Edition* (24 volumes). J. Strachey, Ed. London: Hogarth Press.

Herzberg, Max J. 1984. *Myths and their Meaning.* Boston: Allyn and Bacon, Inc.

Izod, John. 2001. *Myth, Mind and the Screen: Understanding the Heroes of Our Time.* Cambridge, England: Cambridge University Press.

Jung, Carl G. 1936. *Archetypes and the Collective Unconscious.* (In *Collected Works*, Vol. 9).

_____. 1936. *Synchronicity: An Acausal Connecting Principle.* (In *Collected Works*, Vol. 8).

_____. 1939. *The Integration of the Personality.* (In *Collected Works*, Vol. 11).

_____. 1951. *Two Essays on Analytical Psychology.* (In *Collected Works*, Vol. 7).

_____. 1953. *Collected Works.* H. Read, M. Fordham & G. Adler, eds. Princeton, N.J.: Princeton University Press.

_____. 1960. *Psychological Aspects of the Mother Archetype.* (In *Collected Works*, Vol. 9).

_____. 1961. *Memories, Dreams and Reflections.* New York: Random House.

_____. 1964. *Man and His Symbols.* New York: Doubleday.

May, Rollo. 1953. *Man's Search for Himself.* New York: Norton.

_____. 1969. *Love and Will.* New York: Norton.

_____. 1971. *The Portable Jung.* Joseph Campbell, ed. New York: Viking Penguin, Inc.

_____. 1975. *The Courage to Create.* New York: Norton.

_____. 1977. *The Meaning of Anxiety.* New York: Norton.

_____. 1983. *The Discovery of Being.* New York: Norton.

_____. 1991. *The Cry for Myth.* New York: Norton.

Rank, Otto. 1914/1959. *The Myth of the Birth of the Hero.* New York: Random

_____. 1941. *Beyond Psychology.* New York: Dover Publications.

_____. 1950. *Will Therapy and Truth and Reality.* New York: Alfred A. Knopf.

Segal, Robert. 1987. *Joseph Campbell: An Introduction.* New York: Garland.

Skal, David J. 1993. *The Monster Show: A Cultural History of Horror.* New York: Penguin Books.

_____. 1998. *Screams of Reason: Mad Science and Modern Culture.* New York: Norton.

Vogler, Christopher. 1998. *The Writer's Journey.* Los Angeles: Michael Wiese Productions.

Index